Walk Away

Political Theory for Today

Series Editor: Richard Avramenko, University of Wisconsin, Madison

Political Theory for Today seeks to bring the history of political thought out of the jargon-filled world of the academy into the everyday world of social and political life. The series brings the wisdom of texts and the tradition of political philosophy to bear on salient issues of our time, especially issues pertaining to human freedom and responsibility, the relationship between individuals and the state, the moral implications of public policy, health and human flourishing, public and private virtues, and more. Great thinkers of the past have thought deeply about the human condition and their situations—books in Political Theory for Today build on that insight.

Titles Published

Tradition v. Rationalism: Voegelin, Oakeshott, Hayek, and Others, edited by Gene Callahan and Lee Trepanier

Democracy and Its Enemies: The American Struggle for the Enlightenment, by Paul N. Goldstene

Plato's Mythoi: The Political Soul's Drama Beyond, by Donald H. Roy

Eric Voegelin Today: Voegelin's Political Thought in the 21st Century, edited by Scott Robinson, Lee Trepanier, and David Whitney

Walk Away: When the Political Left Turns Right, edited by Lee Trepanier and Grant Havers

Walk Away

When the Political Left Turns Right

Edited by
Lee Trepanier
Grant Havers

LEXINGTON BOOKS
Lanham • Boulder • New York • London

Published by Lexington Books
An imprint of The Rowman & Littlefield Publishing Group, Inc.
4501 Forbes Boulevard, Suite 200, Lanham, Maryland 20706
www.rowman.com

6 Tinworth Street, London SE11 5AL

Copyright © 2019 by The Rowman & Littlefield Publishing Group, Inc.

All rights reserved. No part of this book may be reproduced in any form or by any electronic or mechanical means, including information storage and retrieval systems, without written permission from the publisher, except by a reviewer who may quote passages in a review.

British Library Cataloguing in Publication Information Available

Library of Congress Cataloging-in-Publication Data Available

ISBN 9781498595193 (hardback : alk. paper) | 9781498595209 (electronic)
ISBN 9781498595216 (pbk: alk. paper)

♾️™ The paper used in this publication meets the minimum requirements of American National Standard for Information Sciences Permanence of Paper for Printed Library Materials, ANSI/NISO Z39.48-1992.

Contents

Introduction   vii
    Grant Havers

1   James Burnham: From Left to Right   1
    Paul Gottfried

2   Pondering the People: Willmoore Kendall's Intellectual Path from Progressive to Conservative Populism   15
    Christopher H. Owen

3   "Mugged by Reality": The Neoconservative Turn   35
    Lee Trepanier

4   George Grant and Charles Taylor: Canadian Owls   67
    Ron Dart

5   Alasdair MacIntyre's Revolutionary Peripateticism   81
    Kelvin Knight

6   Benedict Ashley's Reappraisal of Marxism   101
    Christopher S. Morrissey

7   Christopher Lasch: A Reconsideration   121
    Jeremy Beer

8   The Failure of Marxism through the Frankfurt School and Jürgen Habermas   139
    Pedro Blas González

9   Analytical Marxism and the Meaning of Historicism: Reflections on Kai Nielsen and G. A. Cohen   151
    Grant Havers

Index 175

About the Editors and Contributors 183

Introduction

Grant Havers

Winston Churchill, in "Consistency in Politics" (1932), astutely notes how the lack of consistency in politics is, ironically, a consistent pattern in the lives of famous politicians:

> Apart from action in the march of events, there is an inconsistency arising from a change of mood or heart. "*Le coeur a ses raisons que la raison ne connait pas.*" Few men avoid such changes in their lives and few public men have been able to conceal them. Usually youth is for freedom and reform, maturity for judicious compromise, and old age for stability and repose. The normal progression is from Left to Right and often from extreme Left to extreme Right.[1]

As Churchill well understood, the freedom to undertake this great ideological transition from youthful idealism to elderly wisdom is possible only in particular regimes. The statesmen to whom he refers in this essay were all sincere defenders of constitutional rule, a regime that encourages "judicious compromise." "A Statesman should always try to do what he believes is best in the long view for his country, and he should not be dissuaded from so acting by having to divorce himself from a great body of doctrine to which he formerly sincerely adhered."[2] This rule applies to political philosophers as well. One has a moral duty to modify or abandon ideas that fail to advance the well-being of one's nation or civilization.

The essays within this volume discuss a very diverse collection of political thinkers who, to varying degrees, undertook a walk away from the Left to the Right. Some of these figures made a partial transition rightward that did not lead them to jettison all of their leftist ideas. Others embraced a more dramatic transformation from extreme Left to extreme Right, to recall Churchill. Although it is imprudent to offer sweeping generalizations about the motives that inspired each of these figures to walk away from the Left, it is safe to claim that all of them relinquished ideas that, in their view, no longer seemed relevant to the task of maintaining a decent political order.

The most important reason that explains why most of these gentlemen moved from Left to Right lay in the abysmal failure of the Soviet Union to create a free, prosperous, and humane political order. Under the iron rule of Stalin, the USSR had become the first totalitarian regime in history, committing murder and terror on a mass scale while brutally controlling every single aspect of life within Soviet society. To be sure, there were always communist sympathizers outside the USSR who dismissed reports of this oppression as merely capitalist propaganda intended to undermine this fledging socialist regime. The seductive appeal of Marxist-Leninism, with its promise to build a world dedicated to justice and equality, undoubtedly encouraged many communist (and left-liberal) intellectuals to deny or play down the bloodthirsty behavior of Stalin and his successors.[3] This appeal was so powerful that it often took something akin to a religious conversion to shake it. Whittaker Chambers, who is justly famous for having undertaken the dramatic walk away from the role of communist spy to anti-communist informer, poignantly described this spiritual transformation:

> One thing most ex-Communists could agree upon: they broke because they wanted to be free. They do not all mean the same thing by "free." Freedom is a need of the soul, and nothing else. It is in striving toward God that the soul strives continually after a condition of freedom. . . . Hence every sincere break with Communism is a religious experience, though the Communist fail to identify its true nature, though he fail to go to the end of the experience. His break is the political expression of the perpetual need of the soul whose first faint stirring he has felt within him, years, months or days before he breaks. A Communist breaks because he must choose at last between irreconcilable opposites—God or Man, Soul or Mind, Freedom or Communism.[4]

Although not all of the figures discussed in this volume understood their walk away from the Left in these starkly theological terms, it will become evident that the partial or total abandonment of their radicalism was inspired by a common desire to be free of oppressive or deterministic dogmas.

Besides Chambers, some of the fiercest anti-communists in history had already experienced communism up close, explaining in part their determination to defeat this ideology. John Diggins, in his *Up from Communism: Conservative Odysseys in American Intellectual History* (1975) did not exaggerate when he noted that "About half of the *National Review*'s editorial board was, after all, Stalin's gift to the American Right."[5] The lives and careers of James Burnham and Willmoore Kendall certainly verify this observation.[6] As Paul Gottfried shows in his essay "James Burnham: From Left to Right," his subject's walk away from the Left to Right was particularly arresting. Burnham's move from communism to anti-communism paralleled a walk away from his patrician roots in New York high society all the way to communist activism during the Great Depression. Burnham was a prominent leader of the Socialist Workers Party from 1935 to 1939. He was also a close friend and associate of Leon Trotsky. Although Burnham admired Trotsky's attacks on Stalin, he eventually broke with his comrade over the latter's failure to recognize the overall brutality of the Soviet regime. The Nazi-Soviet pact of 1939 and the resultant Soviet occupation of Poland and the Baltic States "provided the final straw" for Burnham and many other communists in the West. At this tipping point in history, Burnham began his move to the Right. Although he agreed with Marxists that capitalism was a dying force (and never abandoned the Marxian view that economic determinism explained historical change), he did not agree that socialism would inherit the world. Instead, a new regime based on bureaucratic collectivism would dominate the old bourgeois democracies of the West. The rise of this administrative state did not particularly trouble the coolly pragmatic Burnham, who accepted the welfare state as a necessary part of an advanced industrial society. He was also unconventional in his admiration of Machiavelli, who endorsed the use of myths as an indispensable means to control and inspire the masses even as he defended an empirical analysis of politics. What did alarm Burnham were the aggressive and expansionist tendencies of the USSR during the Cold War, a pattern of behavior that, he believed, the United States must counter by force if necessary. Burnham had grave doubts that the liberal establishment was up to the job in resisting Soviet imperialism. As a senior editor at *National Review*, Burnham consistently warned that the West was failing to counter communism, due to the "suicidal" ideology of liberalism whose acolytes appeased and even facilitated the advance of communism around the world. In his Machiavellian view, every resource, including myth or propaganda, had to be mobilized to defeat communism. As Gottfried soberly notes, "Burnham in the end was thrown back on the noble lie as he sought to arouse America's intelligentsia to the communist danger."

Like his friend and colleague on the Right, Willmoore Kendall undertook a transformative journey from young idealistic Trotskyite to fierce anti-communist conservative. Long before he joined Burnham as a senior contributor and editor at *National Review* in the mid-1950s, this native of the Oklahoma heartland turned to communism while studying at Oxford during the Great Depression. Yet, as Christopher H. Owen explains in his "Pondering the People: Willmoore Kendall's Intellectual Path from Progressive to Conservative Populism," the leftist views that Kendall held at this time were not always consistent or deeply felt. Owen writes: "Kendall interspersed these views with countervailing political tendencies, including self-identification as a southerner who claimed to idolize the Lost Cause." As a result, he "was mostly a dabbler in communism" or fellow traveler "rather than being a committed believer." Outrage over communist brutality (which he personally witnessed as a journalist in 1930s Spain) undoubtedly motivated his move to the Right by the early 1940s. What remained constant in this journey, which included careers in journalism and the CIA before teaching political philosophy, was his populist goal of "empowering the [American] people to rule democratically and thereby to uphold a functional, morally just, tranquil, and socially cohesive polity." This faith in the self-governing capacity of the American people has made it difficult to classify Kendall within conventional left-right dichotomies. Although Kendall was as vigorously opposed to communist aggression during the Cold War as his colleagues at *National Review*, his iconoclastic sympathies with Rousseauian political philosophy, majority-rule democracy, and the moral necessity of suppressing dissenters (e.g., Socrates) often put him at odds with the rest of the conservative movement. Considering the resurgence of right-wing populism in Donald Trump's America, Kendall may turn out to be the most prophetic figure on the post–World War II Right.

No discussion of the "walk away" phenomenon would be complete without attention to the neoconservatives. This movement initially consisted of Trotskyites who opposed Soviet communism. Yet this family resemblance with Burnham and Kendall does not outweigh the vast differences between them and the neoconservatives. Unlike Burnham and Kendall, most neoconservatives originally heralded from a Jewish background. As Lee Trepanier reveals in his "'Mugged by Reality': The Neoconservative Turn," their walk away from Trotskyism or Marxism to the Right was also more gradual. Before Irving Kristol, Daniel Bell, Nathan Glazer, and others found a new home on the other side of the political spectrum, they first made a stop in what Arthur Schlesinger Jr. called "the vital center" of American politics, namely, New Deal liberalism. (In contrast, Burnham never paused here as he moved to the Right.)[7] In their view, as Trepanier shows, the New Deal offered a politics that was "one of middle-ground compromise about the welfare state and mixed economy." Yet the rise of the New Left, the expansion of the administrative state through the Great Society programs, race riots in American cities, and the anti-Vietnam protests in the 1960s all combined to shatter this vital center. Kristol and his fellow New Deal liberals became increasingly appalled at the failure of the Democratic Party to stem the radical tide that these movements had spawned. The New Left's denunciation of Israel also rankled these ex-communists who had already witnessed the rise of anti-Semitism on the Right during the 1930s. Feeling "mugged by reality," these defenders of the New Deal abandoned the Democratic Party for the Republicans by the early 1980s, sensing that the GOP was more determined to stand up to Soviet aggression. After the collapse of the USSR in the early 1990s, a younger generation of neoconservatives came to the fore, demanding a more assertive and expansionist foreign policy that would spread

America's democratic ideals on a global scale. Unlike Burnham or Kendall, these neoconservatives adhered to the faith that human beings all over the world desire American democracy, a dream that was shattered in the face of failed regime change in Iraq and Afghanistan during the Bush II era. By the dawn of the Trump era, neoconservatism had lost much of its previous allure, although its defenders still enjoyed considerable support among globalists in both major parties.

In retrospect, the walk-aways of Burnham, Kendall, and the neoconservatives were the least theological in tone or message, despite their shared belief that religion is a stabilizing force in politics. To recall Chambers, none of these gentlemen underwent a "religious experience." Although the Canadian political philosopher George Parkin Grant performed a walk away from Left to Right that is almost as dramatic as that of Burnham or Kendall, no reader can ignore the religiosity at play in Grant's journey. Grant, the preeminent defender of High Tory conservatism in the Canadian tradition, was raised in a liberal Protestant tradition that strongly identified with English progressivism. Like his fellow Canadian philosopher Charles Taylor, the young Grant strongly sympathized with Hegelian philosophy. The decisive difference between Grant and Taylor, however, as Ron Dart shows in his comparative essay "George Grant and Charles Taylor: Two Canadian Owls," lies in Grant's more radical departure from his ancestral and philosophical heritage. In his mature writings, Grant identified Hegel as the quintessential philosopher of liberal modernity, including its American incarnation. Taylor, by contrast, never truly moved beyond his early embrace of Hegel. Grant, a conservative Anglican, and Taylor, a liberal Catholic, clearly parted ways on the implications of progressivism. The universalism or globalism within Hegelian philosophy, as Grant came to understand it, provided a rationale for the extinction of the Canadian nation-state. For this reason, Grant philosophically turned toward "a form of Platonic Anglicanism" around the same time that he turned toward the nationalist wing of the Progressive Conservative Party. Dart writes: "Such a turn highlighted Grant's High Tory nationalism that did not square well with various stages of the Hegelian tradition in both Canada and the United States." In the process, Grant became a fierce critic of American foreign policy and the Western capitalist order, particularly during the Vietnam War, as emblematic of the most imperialist dimensions within liberal modernity. These anti-imperialist and anti-capitalist stances led many on the Canadian Left to mistake him for being a leftist or "Red Tory" (a label that Grant never truly welcomed). As a result, many of these admirers were confused when Grant defended conservative positions opposed to the dubious "right" to abortion and euthanasia in the 1970s and 1980s. Yet, in Grant's mind, there was no confusion. His conservative Christian respect for the sanctity of life made him equally opposed to democratic capitalist imperialism and rights-based liberalism during the Cold War.

Religious conversions do not necessarily eradicate long-held misgivings over the destabilizing and corrosive effects of capitalism. The persistence of these doubts explains why some ex-leftists do not perform a complete walk away from Marxism. The famous Scottish philosopher Alasdair MacIntyre began his political education when he joined Britain's Communist Party in his twenties. Although he left the party long before he converted to Catholicism, he did not leave Marxism behind in toto. As Kelvin Knight explains in his essay "Alasdair MacIntyre's Revolutionary Peripateticism," MacIntyre's main objection to Marxism lay in the fact that it had failed to provide a practical program that could effectively transform and replace the capitalist order. The defenders of this ideology also failed to develop an adequate theory of morality, oscillating between crude utilitarianism and Kantianism. Knight writes: "What was most obviously wrong with Marxism was that it lacked a moral theory of its own." Like Burnham, MacIntyre was also disillusioned by the fact that communism in practice had created a new tyranny based on bureaucratic or managerial control. Marxism as a whole was preoccupied only with "institutionalized social relations and not with individuals' goods and desires." In MacIntyre's mind, Aristotle (as understood by Aquinas) had to replace Marx as the philosopher best suited to help moderns address the moral abyss at the heart of the Enlightenment. Instead of recovering Kantianism or utilitarianism, he advocated a return to the Stagirite's focus on the cultivation of virtue through "shared practice." MacIntyre's reading of Aristotle, which jettisoned his cosmology, reinvented him as a defender of communitarian ethics. This modernized Aristotle encouraged human beings to pursue their goals or purposes in cooperation with each other, independent of bureaucratic control. If these ideas "had any political implication it was conservative: since rational action is grounded in customary rules, custom should be conserved." These practices are not the same as institutions, which are usually controlled by managers who are more preoccupied with money or power than with virtue. Knight contends that MacIntyre's unconventional politics makes it hard "to locate his type of political reasoning anywhere along liberal democracy's political spectrum, left, right, or center," precisely because MacIntyre was trying to develop a synthesis of Aristotelianism (informed by Thomism) and Marxism. MacIntyre repudiated the Scylla of leftist statism and the Charybdis of right-wing capitalism. This false choice conflicts "with this ethics of common goods and shared practices." In short, Aristotle provided the moral theory that had eluded Marxism.

The Dominican priest and philosopher Benedict Ashley also carried out one of the most theological walk-aways in the twentieth century, as Christopher Morrissey documents in his essay "Benedict Ashley's Reappraisal of Marxism." Although Ashley too made a dramatic transition from Trotskyite socialist during the Great Depression to anti-communist traditionalist in the Cold War era, his conversion to Catholicism in 1938 was the beginning of the end of his onetime adherence to dialectical materialism. His youthful attempt to reconcile Marxism with Catholic social teaching gave way to a categorical rejection of the teleological or deterministic metaphysics underlying orthodox Marxism. Like many of the ex-leftists discussed in this volume, Ashley never abandoned his radical misgivings over the exploitative nature of capitalism or his youthful passion for social justice. Yet the overriding atheism and materialism contained within Marxism ultimately convinced Ashley that an alternate metaphysics was necessary as a corrective to this crude modernism. Like MacIntyre, he found a more adequate teleology in Thomism, which, in his interpretation, explained the providential design of the universe without sacrificing modern scientific truth or humanitarian morality in the bargain. Still, Ashley never relinquished his original view "that Marxist theory needed to be clarified" through Aristotelian philosophy. Morrissey writes: "For Ashley, the dialectic of social justice pointed beyond this material world to a transcendent providence, acting as the ultimate efficient cause in history." In brief, while Ashley's and MacIntyre's turn to Catholicism confirms Chambers's contention that it takes a traditional religion to shake off communist dogmas, their conversions did not amount to an absolute rejection of their youthful leftism.

With the collapse of Soviet communism in the early 1990s, the Right finally seemed to have defeated its adversaries on the Left. Francis Fukuyama and others famously declared the final victory of liberal democracy over its communist and fascistic enemies.[8] Yet a victory dance was premature. The Right's preoccupation with communism had left it unprepared to deal with a post-Marxist radicalism that had already emerged during the Cold War era and has gained tremendous strength since the fall of the USSR. Paul Gottfried writes:

> The American Right, which still focused on a communist enemy, only glimpsed darkly what was then taking place at home. The foreign enemy on which they set their sights differed from the cultural forces that would occupy our public sector, media, and educational institutions. And that internal foe would be dangerous because of the relentless crusade it would wage against Western civilization and its defining social and moral institutions.[9]

This transformation of the Left helps to explain why some leftists who had once embraced Marxism made some tentative moves toward the old Right, even as this traditionalism was vanishing as a political force.

Not everyone on the Left has been comfortable with the post-Marxist leftist attack on tradition. The last three essays in this volume discuss leftists who embraced certain aspects of tradition without the need of a full throttle religious conversion in the process. As Jeremy Beer contends in his "Christopher Lasch: A Reconsideration," this self-styled "cultural conservative" retained leftist populist leanings that his parents had inculcated in him at an early age. As a young professor of history, Lasch came to embrace a synthesis of liberalism, Frankfurt School Marxism, and Freudianism. These various antecedents largely explain why he never supported capitalism even late in life. Ronald Reagan's celebration of "traditional values" was impossible to square with his support of endless economic growth. To quote Beer, "unlike Irving Kristol, he [Lasch] was not prepared to muster even one cheer for capitalism." By the 1960s, however, he was starting his own walk away from the Left. Taking aim at a new generation of elitist radical intellectuals on the Left, Lasch was outraged by their attack on traditional institutions such as the bourgeois family, which was already being weakened by the forces of statism and corporate capitalism. The traditional populism of the old Left had given way to the New Left, which was unwittingly complicit with these forces of cultural fragmentation. Despite their anti-capitalist rhetoric, these leftists encouraged a "narcissism" in the new "psychological man" that "had been effectively liberated from the allegedly repressive, authoritarian bourgeois order only to find himself enslaved by his own seeming ethereality and the paternalistic state." The "therapeutic ideology" that both consumerism and statism promoted in the late twentieth century threatened to destroy traditional mores that had bound together bourgeois society. What Lasch desired was a cultural conservatism that retained the old left-populist "tradition and its preference for a rooted life centered on family, neighborhood, and church." This version of conservatism also had to be taken "back from the capitalists." Late in life, Lasch's "increasing, if tentative, attraction to the Christian intellectual tradition" as a necessary corrective to the narcissism that he diagnosed as a product of mass culture also revealed how far he had walked away from the atheistic Left.

Jürgen Habermas, the famous Frankfurt School Marxist and communication theorist, also turned to Christian theology to counter the defects of modern thought, including Marxism.[10] However, this walk away from Marxian contempt for religion does not manifest an abandonment of Marxism altogether. In his essay "The Failure of Marxism through the Frankfurt School and Jürgen Habermas," Pedro Blas González notes that the "secular messianism of the Frankfurt School declared war on God, truth, and other values that were now re-packaged and vilified as being the tools of capitalism." Despite this atheistic program, Marxism remains a "secular religion." In this vein, González interprets Habermas's "return" to metaphysics as a desperate attempt to breathe life into a discredited ideology, which reduced human existence and history to economic motivations alone. For this reason, he analyzes Habermas's dialogue on the "dialectics of secularization" with Pope Benedict XVI in 2006. In this dialogue, however, Habermas revealed that his knowledge of metaphysics does not include sufficient awareness of Catholic philosophy. Instead, his notion of communicative rationality still rests on the Enlightenment tradition. Habermas's idea of perfect or undistorted communication does not escape the old Marxist reductionism or "radical empiricism" which is atheistic to the core. González writes: "The suggestion is that while God has failed man, science, technology and the state will assuage man's existential inquietude." Ironically, then, Habermas's limited walk away from traditional Marxism only reveals how his own theory of communication is stuck within its categories.

The analytical Marxists Kai Nielsen and Gerald Allen Cohen are also famous for attempting to walk away from the most discredited tenets of orthodox Marxism, including those that are hostile to traditional practices such as nationalism or religion. Unlike MacIntyre and Ashley, however, they do not seek a return to metaphysics. Instead, they employ the tools of analytical philosophy to provide a thoroughly empirical basis to Marxism, stripped of the teleology that once promised the inevitable triumph of communism in history. Even if they do not succeed in saving Marxism, they manage to salvage a philosophically defensible version of historicism that has surprisingly conservative implications. As Grant Havers explains in his "Analytical Marxism and the Meaning of Historicism: Reflections on Kai Nielsen and G. A. Cohen," the historicism that they defend has two merits. First, their version of historicism counters the charge (made most famously by Leo Strauss) that this focus on history as the standard by which to judge the truth of political ideas leads to fatalism and relativism. Their historicism stresses that we human beings are capable of creating history as well as critically and rationally evaluating the ideas of our time. Second, this new historicism is not wedded to the old Marxian preoccupation with class identity as the sole basis of human history and existence. Instead, it broadens our appreciation of history and tradition. For this reason, Cohen eventually acknowledged the importance of Christianity as the indispensable historical tradition at the heart of justice and equality (without actually converting to the faith, as other leftists did). Unlike Taylor or Grant, Cohen also interprets Hegel as a defender of Christian tradition. Although Nielsen, as an atheist, is resolutely opposed to any reliance on religion as a foundation for politics or morality, he demonstrates his own walk away from Marxism by turning to the nation-state as a desirable political entity that rightly protects the identity and traditions of its citizens. This conversion to nationalism also puts Nielsen to the right of Habermas, who dreams of a "transnational world society" free of nation-states.[11] Like Lasch, Nielsen and Cohen are opposed to thoughtless assaults on tradition, whether they be capitalist or leftist. Havers writes: "this conservative historicism reminds us of the necessity to save what is most valuable within the history of humanity. We cannot escape history precisely because we are responsible for creating and preserving history with thought and resolve. This is one saving tale that is worth preserving."

While it is risky to issue grand generalizations about the diverse collections of intellectuals discussed in this anthology, two conclusions are reasonably safe. First, the ease with which these figures moved from Left to Right depended on how leftist they were in the first place. It is likely that Burnham, Kendall, and Grant, who moved farthest to the Right during the Cold War era, had originally been leftists of the "head," not of the "heart."[12] A leftist of the heart would be truly convinced that human beings are equal, despite social or natural differences between them. By contrast, a leftist of the head would be mainly impressed with the empirical power of Marxism, as opposed to its utopian promise. The fact that Burnham retained a certain sympathy for Marxist economic determinism made him a leftist of the head, not a radical who dreams of a utopian regime that "would help produce altruistic human beings."[13] While Kendall retained a Rousseauvian trust in the virtue of the "people," he never held egalitarian views about all human beings (notwithstanding his celebration of his fellow Americans). Although Grant certainly embraced the idea of moral equality in the Christian sense, he never bought into the leftist idea that all hierarchical social arrangements were bad practices that the state had to reform or eliminate.

The neoconservatives only turned to the Right, by contrast, after a long sojourn in the fields of New Deal liberalism. This reluctance to take on conservative positions may explain why they were far less interested in fighting the culture wars than the old Right was. (As Irving Kristol observed in 1992, "I regret to inform Pat Buchanan that those wars are over, and the Left has won.")[14] The neoconservative desire to bring democracy to the world also reveals a latent egalitarian leftism of the heart. The rather qualified walk-aways from the Left that characterize the journeys of MacIntyre, Ashley, Lasch, Habermas, Nielsen, and Cohen similarly reveal their reluctance to abandon their fundamental belief in human equality. All of these gentlemen had been leftists of the heart and head at one time, an attitude that also explains why they never completely abandoned their shared animus toward the capitalist system.

My second conclusion is analogous to a prediction. The fact that these thinkers broke away from the Left because of disillusionment with orthodox communism suggests that their distinct versions of the walk away will probably not be repeated in our own time. Those who are tempted to move from the Left to the Right today may well find it far less urgent or appealing to make this journey than those in the past who desired to dissociate themselves from Stalinism or Maoism. The reason for this reluctance lies in the fact that the differences between Left and Right are not nearly as sharp or pronounced as they were during the Cold War. In our post-Marxist era, Republicans and Democrats (as well as political parties throughout the Western world) at the establishment level "have become united by a shared adoration for global democracy, human rights, and, with few exceptions, a global consumer culture."[15] Although there are still some major policy differences between the Left and Right on particular issues (e.g., the environment, progressive taxation), what was once called the "vital center" now consists of an unprecedented Left-Right consensus on the virtues of democratic social engineering at home and abroad. While the recent rise of the populist Right potentially presents a fatal challenge to this consensus, the prospect of prominent leftist intellectuals walking away from their ideological home towards this side of the political spectrum is unlikely. Instead, an undramatic move to a more conventional Right, which already endorses the values of the Left to some extent, seems more probable.

NOTES

1. Winston S. Churchill, "Consistency in Politics," in *Thoughts and Adventures* (New York: W. W. Norton and Co., 1990), 26.
2. Ibid., 29.
3. See Paul Hollander, *Political Pilgrims: Western Intellectuals in Search of the Good Society* (New York: Routledge, 2017).
4. Whittaker Chambers, *Witness* (New York: Random House, 1952), 16.
5. John P. Diggins, *Up from Communism: Conservative Odysseys in American Intellectual History* (New York: Harper and Row, 1975), 3.
6. Besides Burnham and Kendall, Frank S. Meyer (1909–1972) was an important presence at *National Review* who engaged in his own dramatic walk away from communism. Famous for developing the conservative-libertarian philosophy of fusionism during the Cold War era, Meyer had been an active member of the American Communist Party from the 1930s until the end of World War II.
7. See Diggins, *Up from Communism*, 14.
8. Francis Fukuyama, *The End of History and the Last Man* (New York: Simon & Schuster, 1992).
9. Paul E. Gottfried, *Encounters: My Life with Nixon, Marcuse, and Other Friends and Teachers* (Wilmington, DE: ISI Books, 2009), 184–85.
10. Jürgen Habermas, "Israel or Athens, or to Whom Does Anamnestic Reason Belong?" in *The Frankfurt School on Religion: Key Writings by the Major Thinkers*, Eduardo Mendieta, ed. (New York: Routledge, 2005), 293–301.
11. See Jürgen Habermas, *The Lure of Technocracy* (New York: Polity Press, 2015). For an illuminating conservative critique of Habermas's opposition to the nation-state, see Daniel J. Mahoney, *The Idol of Our Age: How the Religion of Humanity Subverts Christianity* (New York: Encounter Books, 2018), 115–19; see also Yoram Hazony, *The Virtue of Nationalism* (New York: Basic Books, 2018).
12. Diggins refers to "Marxists of the heart" with this point in mind. See *Up from Communism*, 2.
13. Gottfried, *Encounters*, 75.
14. Quoted in Patrick J. Buchanan, *The Death of the West: How Dying Populations and Immigrant Invasions Imperil Our Country and Civilization* (New York: Thomas Dunne Books, 2001), 255.
15. Gottfried, *Encounters*, 94.

BIBLIOGRAPHY

Buchanan, Patrick J. 2010. *The Death of the West: How Dying Populations and Immigrant Invasions Imperil Our Country and Civilization*. New York: Thomas Dunne Books.

Chambers, Whittaker. 1952. *Witness*. New York: Random House.

Churchill, Winston S. 1991. "Consistency in Politics." In Winston S. Churchill, *Thoughts and Adventures*. New York: W. W. Norton and Co. 23–30.

Diggins, John P. 1975. *Up from Communism: Conservative Odysseys in American Intellectual History*. New York: Harper and Row.

Fukuyama, Francis. 1992. *The End of History and the Last Man*. New York: Simon & Schuster.

Gottfried, Paul E. 2009. *Encounters: My Life with Nixon, Marcuse, and Other Friends and Teachers*. Wilmington, DE: ISI Books.

Habermas, Jürgen. 2005. "Israel or Athens, or to Whom Does Anamnestic Reason Belong?" In *The Frankfurt School on Religion: Key Writings by the Major Thinkers*, Eduardo Mendieta, ed. New York: Routledge. 293–301.

Habermas, Jürgen. 2015. *The Lure of Technocracy*. New York: Polity Press.

Hazony, Yoram. 2018. *The Virtue of Nationalism*. New York: Basic Books.

Hollander, Paul. 2017. *Political Pilgrims: Western Intellectuals in Search of the Good Society*. New York: Routledge.

Mahoney, Daniel J. 2018. *The Idol of Our Age: How the Religion of Humanity Subverts Christianity*. New York: Encounter Books.

Chapter One

James Burnham

From Left to Right

Paul Gottfried

Of all the figures associated with the conservative movement that took shape around William F. Buckley and *National Review* in the mid-1950s, James Burnham (1905–1987) may be the hardest to categorize. While other *National Review* editors and contributors rallied to presidential candidate Barry Goldwater in 1964, Burnham leaned toward that quintessential East Coast Republican Nelson Rockefeller. This was not because Burnham was ever a "liberal Republican." Anyone familiar with such works of his as *The Machiavellians* (1944) and *Suicide of the West* (1964) will grasp the terrifyingly sober quality of his mind. In the 1960s Burnham was convinced that the Republicans would wage the struggle against "world communism" more doggedly than their Democratic rivals. If an American government would be able to deal adequately with the communist enemy, then a Republican presidential candidate would have to win. Given the direction of American politics at the time, Burnham supported the Republican candidate whom he thought had the best chance of prevailing.

Someone who showed a single-minded concern with defeating communism, already in his tracts *The Struggle for the World* (1947) and *Containment or Liberation* (1952), Burnham argued against those who merely hoped to contain Soviet advances made during and after World War II.[1] He believed the US should assert world leadership and, if necessary, create a vast empire in order to dismantle Soviet tyranny. At the same time, Burnham held no brief for the progressive side of liberal Republican politics. His critical views of the unfolding civil rights revolution and Rockefeller's liberal internationalism come through clearly in *Suicide of the West*, which focuses on the liberal mind and its ideological affinity to communism. But Burnham was so preoccupied with what he regarded as the main issue, which was fighting communism, that he buried his scruples when he supported Rockefeller, as the most electable Republican candidate for the presidency in 1964.[2]

This came long after his engagement as a leader of the Trotskyist Socialist Workers Party (SWP) from 1935 until 1939. The author of a voluminous biography of Burnham, Daniel Kelly dutifully or ploddingly traces the steps by which Burnham went from being perhaps the brightest advocate of Trotskyist political policy in the US (and an intimate of the exiled, former Soviet leader) to a hardened anti-communist.[3] Superficially observed, Burnham followed the course of other Trotskyists, who joined the SWP and who, like Burnham, eventually grew disillusioned with Trotsky's cause for being insufficiently critical of Stalin's regime. Like Max Schachtman, Sidney Hook, and other disillusioned admirers of Trotsky, Burnham became irritated with their hero's insufficient recognition of Soviet crimes. Although Lenin's one-time heir apparent had been driven from Soviet Russia by his successful rival and knew about Stalin's mass murders (which on August 28, 1941 would include Trotsky himself then living in Mexico City), he persisted in soft-pedaling Soviet tyranny. For Trotsky, Stalin's Russia represented merely a "derailed form of socialism," and it remained incumbent on all revolutionary socialists, even Stalin's socialist enemies, to protect the Soviet experiment against Western "imperialism." But the Soviet-Nazi Pact of 1939 and Stalin's subsequent invasion of Poland and the Baltic States provided the final straw for wavering members of the Trotskyist SWP. Along with others, Burnham broke irreversibly with communism in any form in 1940.

Like other former Trotskyists, Burnham spent a number of eventful years on what came to be called "the democratic Left." After the Second World War, he joined members of this Left in forming the Congress for Cultural Freedom (CCF), which was an anti-communist front made up of celebrated progressive intellectuals such as Ignazio Silone, Andre Gide, Arthur Koestler, and Louis Fischer. Much has been made of the fact that the CIA gave funding to this group and also subsidized a magazine *Encounter*, which drew on contributors who belonged to the CCF. But the CIA typically funded groups and personalities on the anti-communist Left, on the sound assumption that these beneficiaries would be more useful than the anti-communist Right in changing pro-communist opinion among the American intelligentsia. These subsidies may well have followed Burnham into his collaboration with *National Review* in 1955, a fortnightly that stood well to the right of publications that the CIA would have likely funded.

In some respects, however, Burnham was markedly different from other recovering communists, and particularly the followers of Leon Trotsky. Most other leftists of his acquaintance were Eastern European Jews, whose parents had left a shtetl culture when they came to the US and settled in New York City. Although Burnham moved in their society, especially after he began teaching philosophy at NYU in 1929, he himself sprang from a very different background. His mother was English Catholic and his father English Protestant; and Burnham grew up in an affluent family in Chicago. He attended what was then still a white Anglo-Saxon Protestant (WASP) patrician citadel, Princeton University (and graduated from there with high honors). He thereafter studied at Balliol College at Oxford, when he came under the influence of such English Catholic professors as J. R. R. Tolkien and Martin D'Arcy. Although a free thinker on religious matters for most of his life, Burnham in his last days (after several debilitating strokes) returned to the Catholic faith of his youth.

One might wonder whether his beautiful elegant wife Marcia (née Lightner) whom he married in 1934 (and whom it was the pleasure of this author to know) would have fitted into the rough and tumble world of New York radical circles in the 1930s. Needless to say this question is rhetorical. Burnham-biographer Samuel T. Francis used to recount how annoyed his subject became when he stayed too long at the offices of *National Review* in mid-Manhattan.[4] The noisy argumentativeness of Frank S. Meyer and other former communists would clash with Burnham's delicate nerves and fastidious manners. At a certain point he would look desperately for an excuse to flee these verbal exchanges and get back to his home in Kent, Connecticut.

Although Burnham already by the end of 1939 had condemned the Soviet Union as an imperialistic regime that had betrayed true socialism, in February 1940, he produced *Science and Style: A Reply to Comrade Trotsky*, a critical examination of the Marxist-Leninist concept of dialectical materialism. In this investigation Burnham undertook to demonstrate why Marxism was based on thoroughly obsolete ideas.[5] This study, which was intended as a response to Trotsky's appeal to Marxism's "scientific materialism," is striking, in light of other events, such as the Soviet-Nazi Pact, events that erstwhile American Trotskyists were responding to by jumping ship. Why would Burnham bother to justify his break by telling us that Marx's materialist understanding of History no longer made scientific sense? Burnham cited among other sources for his argument the mathematics of Bertrand Russell and A. N. Whitehead and various logicians, some of whom he had studied with. Marxism, according to Burnham, ignored the complexities of human interactions and assumed necessary causal relations that simply could not be proven. Burnham also questioned whether "socialism is the only alternative to capitalism," and here one could read elements of his classic *The Managerial Revolution*, which was published little more than a year later, back into his *Reply to Comrade Trotsky*. Whatever the motives of others may have been, we may conclude that Burnham joined the SWP because he was convinced at least for a time that Marxism was true.[6]

In this respect he again differed from other New York radicals with whom he was interacting. Burnham was a teacher of logic who was never carried away by humanitarian sentiment. Nor was he an alienated Jewish intellectual for whom Marxist-Leninism offered an escape from a gentile world that he viewed as hostile to his group. Neither social marginalization nor a passion for the downtrodden seems to have fueled his decision to join the radical Left. And he quit that side once he convinced himself that their social and historical theories were false. In the 1930s he considered capitalism to be in crisis throughout the Western world; and he thought Marxism could explain what was happening and offer a way out of the prolonged economic depression and social unrest that he saw all around him. Equally significant might have been the milieu into which he was thrust after he came to New York City and began frequenting the company of articulate radicals. New York in all probability furnished a much more interesting environment than the staid academic one that Burnham experienced at Princeton and Oxford. He may therefore have allowed himself to be enticed by the ideas that held purchase in his new milieu.[7]

It is also apparent that some of the views that Burnham held as a Marxist found their way in a recognizable form into *The Managerial Revolution: What Is Happening in the World*. Several of the work's key assumptions, that capitalism was in a state of crisis, that it would soon be replaced by an alternative form of production, and that politics were subordinate to the dominant form of production and the economic ruling class, came straight out of Marxism. The stress on managerialism as the wave of the future was certainly not an idea that Burnham invented. It was already present in other thinkers, among them Marxists expressing second thoughts, like Bruno Rizzi, and the French Trotskyist Yvan Craipeau. Ideas about bureaucratic collectivism were already circulating on the radical Left, and in the US the New Deal theorist Adolph Berle had begun to write about this phenomenon, on the whole quite positively. And, of course, one cannot help noticing the links between Burnham's classic and Trotsky's analysis of the Soviet experiment as a noble undertaking that had been bureaucratically derailed.

But what made Burnham's formulation of bureaucratic collectivism and its consequences different from other treatments on the Left is that there is nothing truly leftist about its tone. While his former comrades in the SWP complained that Burnham had cribbed his work from the intellectually more erratic Italian Marxist Rizzi and from Rizzi's 1939 disquisition *La Bureaucratisation du Monde*, they may have missed the most striking point about Burnham's classic.[8] Burnham treats ideas about social equality with undisguised contempt as pie in the sky. He is not merely disappointed by revolutionary socialism. He looks at it with utter contempt.

The ideology of democratic capitalism, like all ideologies in Burnham's work, is the "verbal cement" holding together the fabric of American capitalist society. "Among the elements entering into the ideologies typical of capitalist society there must be prominently included, though it is not so easy to define what we mean by it, is individualism."⁹ Like Marxists, Burnham relegates "ideology" to the superstructure of capitalist societies, seeing in them the mere "cement" that serves the interests of dominant classes and which "can influence and win the acceptance of the great masses of people."¹⁰ Significantly, however, these evocative phrases and ideals will continue to be deployed even after the revolutionary movement, from a capitalist to a bureaucratized society, has taken place. As the last chapter in *The Managerial Revolution* underscores, ideologies become particularly critical in creating group solidarity in a contest for world dominance. A "struggle for the world" is fated, and it will involve three rival managerial powers, the Soviet state, Nazi Germany, and New Deal America.

Burnham viewed World War I, from a modified Leninist perspective, as a war for world dominance undertaken by competing capitalist empires. "The beginning of the Second World War was the formative stage of managerial society," and the US, though "unprepared to fill the role which opened up for her in the new historical era" had been drawn into the European conflict, even before formal war was declared. But the US as "the nucleus of one of the great super-states of the future" was in an ideal position "to make a bid for maximum world power as against the super-states to be based on the other two central areas." Unlike Germany, the US had most of its "strategic base included within its boundaries. Consolidation therefore reduces itself primarily to internal measures, to strengthening 'internal unity,' and coordinated efficiency."¹¹

Moreover, the US had successfully used both international agreements and military force to bring most of the Western Hemisphere under its control. This would result in a more benevolent form of what "Hitler aims at in Europe: the de facto elimination of independent sovereignty in all nations and colonies" in its sphere of influence. Burnham did not deny that Nazi Germany had pursued its geopolitical ends more brutally than the US, but because of its geographical and demographic advantage, the latter could afford to be less unpleasant in working toward global hegemony. Finally, the US, "in a development that would extend many decades," was becoming "the receiver for the disintegrating British Empire." The US would succeed in its "attempt to swing the orientation of the Empire from its historical dependence on Europe to dependence on and subordination to the American central area."¹²

All of these developments would occur while building and expanding a global managerial order, in which the US was destined to become the dominant player. But, this for Burnham was the precondition for American world dominance, the US must turn fully into a "managerial society," which had not yet been fully accomplished. We are told repeatedly in different ways that "the capitalist structure cannot hold its own in these scheduled conflicts."¹³ Regional conflicts over American economic interests, the building of armaments, and the raising of national morale in the face of impending war could no longer be addressed, according to Burnham, by the private sector. Indeed "modern total war is not profitable for capitalism and consequently capitalism can no longer fight it."[14] Nor can "economic world conflicts" any longer be "won along capitalist lines." Once the fateful turn toward the bureaucratization has been taken, "even if a return were institutionally possible, neither the managers nor the masses would permit it." The managers were by now intent on maintaining their power; and "however harsh the lot of the masses, they would choose to solve their problem by further advance along the managerial road, not by a return."[15]

Antiquated elements abound in Burnham's picture of the coming to power of managerial society. The specter of breadlines occasioned by the Depression creating distaste for capitalism among the masses and the growing entanglement of the US in a raging European war are now obsolete reference points. Still, the emergence of the US as a hegemonic power in the wake of the disintegration of the Soviet Empire bears some resemblance to the course of American Empire traced by Burnham. The call for the expansion of this empire becomes explicit in Burnham's post–World War II writings urging American world dominance for the purpose of defeating world communism. The identification of managerial rule with a struggle for world dominance is also a Burnhamite theme that resonated well beyond 1941. The concluding chapter of *The Managerial Revolution* provided material for George Orwell's dystopian novel *Nineteen Eighty-Four*. Orwell borrowed his picture of perpetual struggle among contending sections of the globe from Burnham's predictions. Although an idealistic socialist who found Burnham's disdain for egalitarian ideals and perhaps overly detached view of Nazi tyranny to be off putting,[16] Orwell was fascinated by his vision of continuing world conflict among three central regions.

Equally relevant in *The Managerial Revolution* is the detailed treatment of the ideological masks assumed by elites in order to keep the masses behind them. By 1943 Burnham had poured his thoughts on this matter into *The Machiavellians: Defenders of Freedom*, a work that celebrates the ideas of tough-minded analysts of the irrational sources of political behavior. In this book Burnham stresses that only by looking at his subjects, Niccolò Machiavelli, Gaetano Mosca, Georges Sorel, Robert Michels, and Vilfredo Pareto, could we understand the true nature of politics.[17] Through a study of such figures we would come to grasp the necessary laws and regularities of the political realm and avoided being entrapped by beguiling ideologies. In an interview in 1972, Burnham spoke of the "process of re-education" that he was undergoing while writing his book. Explaining his experience from a distance of many years, he observes: "Through the Machiavellians I began to understand more thoroughly what I had long felt: that only by renouncing all ideology can we begin to see the world and man."[18]

But it is hard to examine Burnham's focus on the pervasive nonrational character of political affairs and believe that he is teaching us to renounce "all ideology." Whether we are dealing with Sorel's notion of redemptive myths, Pareto's subconscious drives toward political actions, the cliquish, undemocratic nature of parliamentary politics in the writings of Michels and Mosca, or Machiavelli's recommendations of flattery and deceit in the pursuit of power, it is doubtful that Burnham is leading us away from ideology in *The Machiavellians*. This observation is not intended to belittle either him or the provocative thinkers explored in his book. It is only to point out the quandary that Burnham encountered after becoming an engaged anti-communist. He searched for ideological alternatives that would counter the utopian appeal of his Marxist-Leninist enemy. And he came up mostly empty-handed, as his now famous lament in *The Suicide of the West* strongly suggests. There Burnham observes with obvious sarcasm: "Except for mercenaries, saints and neurotics, no one is willing to sacrifice and die in the abstract, for the United Nations, or a 10 percent rise in social security payments."[19]

This problem was made even more acute for Burnham by the predominance in the West of "liberalism," a gateway drug that aided world communism because liberals were already "infected" with the leftist bacillus. For the liberal there was no enemy to the Left but only reactionaries who stood in the way of the achievement of social justice and racial equality. Burnham's subjects combined a sense of moral superiority with a nagging sense of guilt: "The real and motivating problem, for the liberals, is not to cure the poverty or injustice or what not in the objective world but to appease the guilt in their own breasts and what that requires is *some* program, some solution, some activity."[20] Given the prevalence of this type of personality among American and Western European cultural and political elites, Burnham worried about the absence of a counterdoctrine for resisting the suicidal liberal mindset. This mindset seemed all the more dangerous because of the presence of a communist adversary occupying large parts of the world's land mass.

Perhaps as important in this work for Burnham as the failure of the West to meet the communist challenge effectively is the evidence of Western decline. Since 1914, according to Burnham, the part of the world that was under Western control had contracted "like a film winding in reverse, with the West thrust backward reel by reel toward the original base from which it started its world expansion."[21] The West for Burnham seemed to have lost its will to survive, and the reasons that he gave include among others "the decay of religion and an excess of material luxury" and "just getting tired, worn-out, as all things temporal do." Again and again Burnham also returns to the liberal mindset which he assures his reader has nothing to do with a "consciously understood set of beliefs. These cultural and political subversives are motivated by a bundle of unexamined prejudices and conjoined sentiments."[22]

In the struggle against communism, Burnham preferred clearheaded actors like General Franco to leftist anti-communists, who presumably shared many of the same critical assumptions as the side they claimed to be fighting. In 1975, Burnham began an obituary for the then recently deceased Spanish head of state with these words: "Francisco Franco was our century's most successful ruler." What made this ruler stand out in a positive way were his "patient stubbornness, flawless prudence and unshakable faith in his mission." These qualities were evident in the General's struggle against communism, from the Spanish Civil War on. Yet even Franco, as depicted by Burnham, was driven by a sense of something beyond his own ruthless realism. He had stood before an altar where the Blessed Sacrament was performed, where he became "conscious of my responsibility before God and history." Franco viewed himself as a Catholic crusader who was combatting the legions of the Antichrist; and presumably this made him a fiercer warrior against what Burnham regarded as the greatest political evil of his lifetime. Presumably Burnham preferred these traditionalist sentiments in the present crisis to the ideological delusions of the liberal imagination that he spent entire books unmasking.

A debate has continued to rage over the years about where exactly we should place Burnham among those who abandoned communism and who thereafter gravitated toward the Right. A location that libertarians and establishment conservatives have both assigned to Burnham is in the antechamber of neoconservatism. Although Burnham renounced the Trotskyist form of communism, he spent years on the Democratic Left and was associated with such enterprises as the Congress for Cultural Freedom and *Partisan Review*. Even as late as the 1960s Burnham remained something of a centrist in American politics and like the neoconservatives, never viewed the growth of an American welfare state as a misfortune. In a famous essay for *Ramparts* in 1968, anarcho-libertarian Murray Rothbard identified Burnham with the liberal establishment that he and other members of the interwar Right were combatting: "Red-baiting and anti-communist witch hunting was originally launched by liberals; and even after McCarthy the liberals were the most effective at this game."[23]

Although a frequently made association that Daniel Kelly categorically affirms in his biography, the underlying assumption about Burnham as a precursor of the neoconservatives is for the most part wrong. The differences between Burnham and the neoconservatives are just too striking to be ignored. Unlike the latter, Burnham never believed in America's moral mission to spread democratic equality throughout the world; he was generally critical of the civil rights revolution; and his heroes were mostly figures of the traditional Right. It is also hard to find anything that Burnham said that indicated sympathy for the Jewish state of Israel. And if he accepted the existence of a welfare state, it was not because he viewed it as an instrument for improving the democratic quality of a society. He regarded the modern administrative state as historically inevitable, the consequence of the managerial revolution that was characteristic of the present age.[24]

It is also questionable whether Burnham's anti-communism, or for that matter that of William F. Buckley or Frank S. Meyer, had much in common with the anti-communist leftists whom Murray Rothbard considered the fons et origo of the post–World War II anti-communist crusade. Although Burnham wrote for the leftist anti-communist publication *Partisan Review*, one could easily distinguish his anti-communism from that of other leftist anti-communists. It also bore little resemblance to the anti-communism of the neoconservatives, who began as leftist anti-communists and who kept much of their original mindset into their later lives.[25] In the 1970s Burnham pointedly criticized the religious sociologist and longtime fixture at *Commentary*, Peter Berger, for advocating a "conservative international." Burnham sniffed neoconservative liberal internationalism in Berger's project, which he ascribed to its author's leftist disposition.[26] Already in the 1940s Burnham was evolving into a right-wing anti-communist, who viewed the communists as a more brutal version of the liberals he was fighting at home. Whether or not this was true, Burnham believed that there was such a connection and referred to it repeatedly in *Suicide of the West*.

It is certainly possible to treat Burnham as a possible forerunner of the alt-right, particularly since one of its founders, Samuel T. Francis, wrote extensively on Burnham, whom he clearly idolized.[27] As a fierce critic of egalitarianism, a fan of early twentieth-century Latin and German analysts of the irrational sources of political behavior and the permanent circulation of elites, and himself the author of voluminous works on managerialism, Francis provides an unmistakable bridge from Burnham to what is now pejoratively called the "extreme Right." (Dark Right may be a more appropriate term.) But certain qualifications are necessarily in order here. Like the neoconservatives, Burnham was an anti-communist American empire-builder. Although he did not take this position for neoconservative reasons, because of a commitment to democratic missionizing and a preoccupation with Israel, he sometimes reminds the reader of neoconservatives in his call for an American Empire.[28] Let us also not forget that Burnham sojourned on the anti-communist Left in the 1940s, like future neoconservatives.[29]

It may also be necessary to place Burnham's attacks on guilt-ridden humanitarians into the context of his longtime mission as an anti-communist. No one is claiming that Burnham did not hold traditional rightist views on a wide variety of subjects. Rather it is hard to look at those stands in a comprehensive way without taking into account Burnham's concern about the "protracted struggle" against the Soviets and world communism. We should therefore consider how Burnham saw "liberal" attitudes impacting on that struggle and on the possible outcome of the battle between the US as the premier Western power and the Soviet-led bloc. What diverted American efforts from this pressing matter, in Burnham's opinion, had to be deferred until that struggle was won.[30] Clearly Burnham held no brief for liberal positions and attitudes, but their conceivably negative effect on the Cold War rendered him even less comfortable with what in any case he might have rejected. Without that struggle, his censuring of liberal views and sentiments might not have been quite as vehement.

This last point should not be read as a dismissal of the rightist character of Burnham's worldview. That definable worldview was already evident in Burnham's writing while he was still formally on the Left. But the struggle against communism in which Burnham saw himself and the entire West engulfed also sharpened certain aspects of his thinking. Not all anti-communists, not even all of those identified with the conservative movement, went in the same direction. For example, the founding father of West Coast Straussianism Harry Jaffa linked fervent support for the war against racism to the struggle against communism.[31] Leftist anti-communists meanwhile argued that it was necessary for the US to carry out a civil rights revolution at home in order to deal more effectively with the Soviets. The US, according to this opinion, had to present itself as a credible defender of democratic equality in order to weaken Soviet charges that the West was being hypocritical when it claimed to stand for equality while tolerating racial discrimination. In fact, this position became characteristic of such political leaders as Lyndon B. Johnson, Hubert Humphrey, and Henry "Scoop" Jackson. Not insignificantly, it also became a dominant view of the conservative movement after the neoconservative ascendancy in the 1980s.

This was never the position of Burnham, however, even if he felt forced sometimes to make concessions toward the "liberal" side. Still it is hard to imagine that Burnham's heart was ever in compromising with what he regarded as a distasteful political necessity. Of all the onetime Far Leftists who ended up in the conservative movement, Burnham may have been the one who moved furthest to the right. This, however, should not surprise us. His statements as a leftist often prefigured his later right-wing worldview; and this connection was made abundantly clear by the time that he broke with Trotsky and his American followers and began working on *The Managerial Revolution*.

What was rightist about his thinking however was unrelated to what is now touted as "conservative," and which often looks like last year's progressivism. Rather Burnham viewed human beings as fickle and irrational and in need of traditional social and political authorities. Inequality was basic to human relation; and any attempt to appeal to the ideal of universal equality was bound to create instability and nurture dangerous illusions. In *Up from Communism*, John P. Diggins points out that Burnham was often stuck on the horns of a dilemma, having to appeal to a "crusade" against communism in works like *Containment or Liberation?* but also as an analyst of the "geopolitics of power," recognizing the inconsistency of his position. In his call for an accelerated struggle against the Soviet empire, "Burnham tries to accommodate both views, but ultimately the prudence of political realism yields to the pride of Wilsonian idealism, the mind surrenders to the will."[32] But Diggins also observes that Burnham's invocation of universal ideals is always "Sorel-like," a not entirely forthright effort to appeal to "myths" because humans act collectively on the basis of the irrational.[33]

One might also note a similar pattern in Burnham's lifetime devotee Samuel T. Francis, who tried to invoke Sorelian visions in appealing to "Middle American Radicals."[34] Like Burnham, Francis sought to awaken his contemporaries to what he perceived as the grave challenge of the present age, cultural and social radicalization. He undertook this task by appealing to what he considered evocative, historically relevant myths and symbols. But Francis, who appealed to these myths, remained himself a Machiavellian. He also exhibited another trait that Diggins observed in Burnham, a tendency to revert to Marxist-like, structuralist arguments in trying to explain socioeconomic and political phenomena.[35] This limits even more what the historical actor can be expected to achieve in a world in which natural leaders are required to invent myths in order to pursue higher ends.

Burnham underscored this "dilemma" in *The Machiavellians*: "The political life of the masses and the cohesion of society demand the acceptance of myths. A scientific attitude toward society does not permit the belief in the truth of the myths. But the leader must profess, indeed foster, belief in the myths or the fabric of society will be cracked and they will be overthrown. In short, the leaders, if they themselves are scientific, must lie."[36] Burnham in the end was thrown back on the noble lie as he sought to arouse America's intelligentsia to the communist danger. Not surprisingly, his disciple Francis advocated a similar course twenty years later as he looked for ways to battle the cultural Left.

We are therefore driven to the conclusion that neither figure of the intellectual Right found a way to reconcile real moral beliefs (perhaps his own) with strategies for influencing large masses of people, and so we may scoff at the cynical or tragic position into which each was driven by the logic of his ideas. But there was something honest as well as cold-blooded in how these genuine thinkers of the Right viewed their times and circumstances. Unmistakably absent from both were the noisy partisanship and happy talk that characterized a later generation of conservative activists.

NOTES

1. See *The Struggle for the World* (New York: John Day Co., 1947) and *Containment or Liberation: An Inquiry into the Aims of United States Foreign Policy* (New York: John Day Co., 1952).

2. Joseph R. Stromberg in a review of Daniel Kelly's biography of Burnham tries to explain Burnham's strong attachment to Rockefeller as a presidential candidate. "James Burnham and the Struggle for the World: A Life by Daniel Kelly." *Independent Review* 8/1 (Summer 2003), 141–45.

3. See Daniel Kelly, *James Burnham and the Struggle for the World* (Wilmington, DE: ISI Books, 2002).

4. In conversation with the author, September 6, 1986.

5. Burnham's "Science and Style" is reprinted in Leon Trotsky's *In Defense of Marxism*, (New York: Merit Publishers, 1965), 187–206.

6. An essay by Roger Kimball in *New Criterion* (September 2002) "The Power of James Burnham" captures the mindset of the young Burnham remarkably well. Available at https://www.newcriterion.com/issues/2002/9/the-power-of-james-burnham.

7. See Daniel Kelly, *James Burnham and the Struggle for the World*, 63–89.

8. For an informative assessment of Rizzi's place as a social theorist, see Ernest E. Haberkern's "Burno Rizzi, 'The Bureaucratization of the World,'" *World* in *Telos* 66 (1985–1986): 162–67.

9. James Burnham, *The Managerial Revolution* (Bloomington: University of Indiana Press, 1962), 25–26.

10. Ibid., 27–28.

11. Ibid., 262.

12. Ibid., 263, 264.

13. Ibid., 265.

14. Ibid.

15. Ibid., 271.

16. George Orwell, "Second Thoughts on James Burnham," *Polemic* (1946), available at http://orwell.ru/library/reviews/burnham/english/e_burnh.html. Orwell unloads on Burnham as a warmonger who favored brutal dictators.

17. James Burnham, *The Machiavellians: Defenders of Freedom* (Chicago: Gateway, 1963).

18. Interview held with George H. Nash on February 4, 1972, and quoted in the *Conservative Intellectual Movement in America*, second edition (Wilmington, DE: ISI Books, 1996), 81.

19. James Burnham, *Suicide of the West: An Essay on the Meaning and Destiny of Liberalism* (New Rochelle, NY: Arlington House, 1964), 334.

20. Ibid., 196–97.

21. Ibid., 14–17.

22. Ibid., 132.

23. Mises Institute, Mises Library, available at https://mises.org/library/confessions-right-wing-liberal; the original polemic appeared in *Ramparts* VI/4 (June 1968).

24. Clearly on this point I am breaking from the interpretation offered by a close friend of many years, David Gordon, who describes Burnham as reveling in managerial rule. Rather I see Gordon's target as accepting the hand dealt by Fate. David Gordon, "The Making of a Warmonger," *LewRockwell.com*, available at https://www.lewrockwell.com/1970/01/david-gordon/the-dark-heart-of-conservatism/.

25. For a discussion of these distinctions, see Gary Dorrien, *The Neoconservative Mind: Politics, Culture and the War of Ideology* (Philadelphia: Temple University Press, 1993), 19–67.

26. Samuel T. Francis provides a detailed discussion of Burnham's arguments against Berger in "Burnham Agonistes," *Chronicles* (July 2002), in the course of discussing Daniel Kelly's biography. Available at https://www.chroniclesmagazine.org/burnham-agonistes/. See also Peter Berger's "Two Paradoxes," *National Review*, May 12, 1972, 507–11.

27. Samuel T. Francis, *Power and History: The Political Thought of James Burnham* (Lanham, MD: University Press of America, 1984).

28. Adam Fuller reminds us of this connection in *Taking the Fight to the Enemy: Neoconservatism and the Age of Ideology* (Lanham: Lexington Books, 2011), 166–71.
29. Kelly, *James Burnham and the Struggle for the World*, 208–17.
30. Ibid., 297–306.
31. Harry Jaffa, "Equality as a Conservative Principle," in *How to Think about the American Resolution* (Durham: Carolina Academic Press, 1978), 39–43; Jaffa, "Theory and Practice in American Politics," in *Equality and Liberty* (Claremont: Claremont Institute, 1999), 137.
32. John P. Diggins, *Up from Communism: Conservative Odysseys in American Intellectual History* (New York: Harper and Row, 1975), 337.
33. Ibid., 336; passim, 304–10.
34. Samuel T. Francis and Jerry Woodruff, *Revolution from the Middle* (Raleigh: Middle American Press, 1997).
35. Samuel T. Francis's *Leviathan and Its Enemies* (Arlington: Washington Summit Publishers, 2016) includes posthumously published texts on managerialism and its effects that clearly reflect Burnham's pervasive influence on Francis. See also the foreword, introduction and afterword by Fran Griffin, Jerry Woodruff, and Paul E. Gottfried.
36. Burham, *The Machiavellians*, 304.

BIBLIOGRAPHY

Berger, Peter. 1972. "Two Paradoxes." *National Review*. May. 507–11.
Burnham, James. 1947. *The Struggle for the World*. New York: John Day Co.
———. 1952. *Containment or Liberation: An Inquiry into the Aims of United States Foreign Policy*. New York: John Day Co.
———. 1962. *The Managerial Revolution*. Bloomington: University of Indiana Press.
———. 1963. *The Machiavellians: Defenders of Freedom*. Chicago: Gateway.
———. 1964. *Suicide of the West: An Essay on the Meaning and Destiny of Liberalism*. New Rochelle: Arlington House.
———. 1965. "Science and Style." In *In Defense of Marxism*, Leon Trotsky, ed. New York: Merit Publishers. 187–206.
Diggins, John P. 1975. *Up From Communism: Conservative Odysseys in American Intellectual History*. New York: Harper and Rowe.
Dorrien, Gary. 1993. *The Neoconservative Mind: Politics, Culture and the War of Ideology*. Philadelphia: Temple University Press.
Francis, Samuel T. 1984. *Power and History: The Political Thought of James Burnham*. Lanham, MD: University Press of America.
———. 2002. "Burnham Agonistes." *Chronicles*. Available https://www.chroniclesmagazine.org/burnham-agonistes/.
———. 2016. *Leviathan and its Enemies*. Arlington: Washington Summit Publishers.
Francis, Samuel T., and Jerry Woodruff. 1997. *Revolution from the Middle*. Raleigh: Middle American Press.
Fuller, Adam. 2011. *Taking the Fight to the Enemy: Neoconservatism and the Age of Ideology*. Lanham, MD: Lexington Books.
Gordon, David. n.d. "The Making of a Warmonger." *LewRockwell.com*. Available at https://www.lewrockwell.com/1970/01/david-gordon/the-dark-heart-of-conservatism/.
Gottfried, Paul. 1986. "Interview with James Burnham." September 6.
Haberkern, Ernest. 1985–1986. "Burno Rizzi, 'The Bureaucratization of the World." *Telos* 66: 62–67.
Jaffa, Harry. 1978. "Equality as a Conservative Principle." In *How to Think about the American Revolution*. Durham: Carolina Academic Press. 39–43.
———. 1999. "Theory and Practice in American Politics." In *Equality and Liberty*. Claremont: Claremont Institute.
Kelly, Daniel. 2002. *James Burnham and the Struggle for the World*. Wilmington: ISI Books.
Kimball, Roger. 2002. "The Power of James Burnham." *New Criterion*. September. Available at https://www.newcriterion.com/issues/2002/9/the-power-of-james-burnham.

Mises Institute. n.d. Mises Library. Available at https://mises.org/library/confessions-right-wing liberal.

Nash, George H. 1966. *Conservative Intellectual Movement in America*. Wilmington: ISI Books.

Orwell, George. 1946. "Second Thoughts on James Burnham." *Polemic*. Available at http://orwell.ru/library/reviews/burnham/english/e_burnh.html.

Stormberg, Joseph R. 2003. "*James Burnham and the Struggle for the World: A Life* by Daniel Kelly." *Independent Review* 8/1 (Summer 2003): 141–45.

Chapter Two

Pondering the People

Willmoore Kendall's Intellectual Path from Progressive to Conservative Populism

Christopher H. Owen

Sometime during World War II, Willmoore Kendall deserted Karl Marx and embraced James Madison. Yet, whether writing from a left-wing perspective during the Depression years or from a right-wing perspective afterward, Kendall always argued that the United States operated at its best—was its most authentic self—as a people's republic. As a young scholar in the interwar period, Kendall saw himself as a Marxist and advocated collectivist economic principles. Thereafter, Kendall proclaimed himself a conservative and for more than two decades actively promoted a ferocious brand of anti-communism. In both phases of his career, however, Kendall focused most of his intellectual energy on creating and clarifying a vision of how American democracy ought to work. He sought consistently to demonstrate that for democracy to be real—for it to exist as more than a word—then "we the people" must possess and retain the power to make the most important political decisions. Kendall always despised any individual or group which tried to undermine the standing of the American people as the rightful sovereigns of the United States. It is my contention here, therefore, that one may best understand Kendall's ideas as being populist in character and that his mid-twentieth-century rightward journey involved traveling from one variant of populism to another.

To be sure, other scholars have picked up on the populist tendencies in Kendall's thought, with some noting that Kendall did not himself embrace the term populist.[1] Nevertheless, viewing Kendall as a populist thinker has many analytical advantages. Populism is the best label to describe the overarching pattern of Kendall's thought in part because it catches continuities in his ideas—as he moved from left to right on the political spectrum—that one might otherwise overlook. Using the populist schematic also resolves many of the conundrums associated with labeling Kendall a conservative. Many commentators on his work have noticed how at odds some of his ideas are with the best-known strains of conservatism. Kendall was not a neocon, not a theocon, not a paleocon, not a country-club Republican, not a state's rights advocate, not a libertarian. Some commentators have regarded Kendall as a follower of Leo Strauss. Yet, Straussian historian Harry Jaffa denounced Kendall's work as Calhounite, even fascistic, in character. Other labels for Kendall's scholarship, have included McCarthyite, Catholic, Trotskyist, and Rousseauian. Libertarian thinker Murray Rothbard called Kendall "the philosopher of the lynch mob."[2] Yet, none of these labels really fit, and none do justice to the complexity of Kendall's thought.

Even for those who do not agree with him, reading Willmoore Kendall is often instructive *because* his ideas do not lend themselves to simplistic left-right dichotomy. Kendall's readers often think: "Hey, I never thought about it that way."[3] As a young man of the Left, he embraced socialism but expressed little sympathy for Soviet principles. As an established personality of the Right, he proudly called himself a conservative but rejected many attacks on big government and heaped praise on Lyndon Johnson. Thus, Kendall's chroniclers (who were often his friends and students) have called him a "maverick" or "iconoclast." Like St. Athanasius, they proclaim, Willmoore often stood alone, *contra Mundum* (against the world).[4] It is tempting, therefore, to view Kendall's ideas as unique to him, seeing him as a quirky and often quarrelsome conservative whose ideas fit into no particular school of thought and which are therefore of little lasting interest.

Such judgment, however, would be a serious mistake. In the first place, Kendall's ideas have always maintained something of a cult following among conservative intellectuals, a number of whom have regarded his political theory as of the highest caliber. Jeffrey Hart, distinguished political essayist, Nixon speech writer, and Dartmouth professor, claimed that he "revered" Kendall and called him the "most important political theorist . . . since the end of World War II." United States Senator and political scientist John P. East regarded Kendall as "the most original, innovative, and challenging [political] interpreter of any period." According to the prominent contemporary conservative journalist Daniel McCarthy, Kendall "is one of the most overlooked founding fathers of the conservative movement and also one of the most interesting." He was "the top Americanist of the postwar conservative movement."[5]

Seeing Kendall primarily as a populist thinker—who (in his early years) was simultaneously a progressive and who (in his mature years) was simultaneously a conservative—makes much of his apparent quirkiness disappear.

Viewed through this lens, Kendall's political theory demonstrates more coherence and greater consistency over time than most scholars have realized. When one looks at Kendall's evolution as a thinker, movement to the Right is obvious. If one carefully observes Kendall making this journey, however, it also becomes clear that his thought always retained important features from his days as a leftist. Indeed, Kendall's *goal*—empowering the people to rule democratically and thereby to uphold a functional, morally just, tranquil, and socially cohesive polity—remained the same throughout his career. However, his ideas about the proper *means* by which to achieve this goal changed greatly.

Several scholars have previously proposed labeling Kendall's political theory as populist, but none has really pursued the implications of what such a characterization might mean. Historian George H. Nash, for example, dropped the theme of Kendall's populism because of various "tricky" ambiguities in the term.[6] Indeed, to many scholars, populism has appeared to be a "thin" ideology.[7] This claim arises chiefly because in practice populism often fails to coincide with traditional liberal-conservative divisions; in other words, there are both right-wing and left-wing populists. All sorts of groups, with wildly conflicting political programs, have claimed the populist mantle. One anthology on American populism from the 1970s, for example, included excerpts from both George Wallace and George McGovern as well as contributions from both Joseph McCarthy and Saul Alinsky.[8]

As a young man, Kendall himself recognized a similar tendency whereby political theorists often praised the principle of rule by popular majority in the abstract but felt little "obligation to formulate the ideas it represents or to seek out the arguments that might be urged in its favor."[9] Kendall made it his mission in life to correct this deficiency. For decades he used his formidable intellectual powers to formulate ways to strengthen the people's ability to rule themselves democratically. If one may define populism as "a political philosophy supporting the rights and power of the people in their struggle against the privileged elite,"[10] then Willmoore Kendall was already a populist in 1939 (when he published his first serious work in political theory), and he remained a populist until his death in 1967. Recent scholarship suggesting an "ideational" model for defining populism (and also includes reference to the Rousseauian notions of general will), applies even more clearly to Kendall. That Kendall did not label himself a populist in either phase of his intellectual life also fits here, for, as politics scholars Cas Mudde and Cristóbal Kaltwasser have suggested, the term often has negative connotations and is seldom self-proclaimed. Furthermore, as a "thin" ideology, populism "almost always appears attached to other ideological elements," which again fits Kendall's case.[11] Intellectually, Kendall's meticulously constructed political theory surely constituted—to borrow language from his friend Cleanth Brooks—a well-wrought urn. Therefore, to show that Kendall's views were populistic actually serves to "thicken" the concept of populism itself.

In his day Kendall was not only a thinker. He exercised public influence in three broad areas—as an intelligence officer; as a popular writer, teacher, and lecturer; and as a political theorist. He was an important formative figure of the CIA, composed some of the earliest treatises on psychological warfare, and crafted effective propaganda during the Korean War. In 1955 he co-founded *National Review*, where he served as a columnist and senior editor for nearly a decade. Kendall also exercised important public influence as a teacher. At Yale, most famously, Kendall propelled William F. Buckley, Jr. and L. Brent Bozell, Jr., into long careers of conservative political activism—helping to inspire (and to edit) the conservative classics—*God and Man at Yale* (1950) and *McCarthy and His Enemies* (1954). Kendall shined in debate, thriving in slashing but erudite showdowns with such left-leaning academics as Mulford Q. Sibley and James MacGregor Burns. Yet today Kendall is best known for his distinctive and original political theory. In the 1950s and 1960s, Kendall published a series of carefully constructed scholarly articles which extolled the deliberation function of Congress, promoted notions of popular political orthodoxy, and attacked the undemocratic nature of judicial review.

Unfortunately for his reputation as a thinker, Willmoore's tumultuous personal life often overshadowed his work as a public intellectual. A native of Oklahoma born in 1909, he was a child prodigy whose father pushed him relentlessly to excel. Family pressure facilitated his academic success—a BA from the University of Oklahoma at age eighteen, an MA from Northwestern at nineteen, then a Rhodes Scholarship to Oxford's Pembroke College in 1932. Kendall's later personal life was messy—two broken marriages, alcoholism, chain-smoking, testy relations with friends and colleagues. Personal issues pushed Kendall into a nomadic life—teaching at numerous (mostly first-rank) universities—and also drove him into an early grave when he suffered a fatal heart attack at age fifty-eight. Upon hearing of his mentor's death, William F. Buckley declaimed in *National Review* that Kendall "was indisputably among the two or three most brilliant political scientists in the United States, recognized as such by friends (they were few) and foes (they were numerous as the stars above) alike."[12] Only now—after Kendall has lain in his Oklahoma coffin for fifty years—has it become fairly easy for interlocutors to ignore his rough-edged personality. Because today the world chiefly remembers Kendall, insofar as it remembers him at all, as a political theorist, it is on that part of his rightward journey that this essay will focus.

One mostly thinks of him as a conservative, not just because that is where his politics ended up but also (and chiefly) because his intellectual views matured—and became significantly more profound—as he repositioned rightward. But Kendall, like *National Review* colleagues Frank Meyer and

James Burnham, began his professional career on the Left. His time as a radical progressive lasted some twelve years—from the time he went to study in Oxford in 1932 until about 1944 (two years after he had entered wartime service for the US government).[13] At Oxford Kendall studied with R. G. Collingwood, the great English historian and philosopher. There the young Oklahoman declared himself a communist and, egged on by his father, attempted to become a famous journalist, the next Walter Lippmann. During school breaks, Kendall, fluent in Spanish, traveled to Madrid where he became a United Press International (UPI) reporter, writing stories about the political unraveling of that country. He returned to the United States in 1936 shortly before the actual outbreak of the Spanish Civil War.

Kendall's radicalism from this period, his self-declared Trotskyism, became semi-legendary among friends and foes. Though he remained a man of the Left after returning from Europe, Kendall later liked to tell people that his hatred of communism began in 1930s Madrid when the Spanish Left was not content to blow up rival newspapers but began to shoot paper boys. In letters to his father, the young Rhodes Scholar professed his commitment to communism and argued for nationalizing American railways and banks. He proclaimed that his "purpose in life was to become a great Socialist Publicist."[14] All the while, however, Kendall interspersed these views with countervailing political tendencies, including self-identification as a southerner who claimed to idolize the Lost Cause. The young scholar was mostly a dabbler in communism—a fellow traveler in the movement—rather than being a committed believer, let alone serving any significant role in party leadership. Looking backward in 1942, for example, Kendall noted in a letter to his longtime friend, the political scientist Charles S. Hyneman, that: "I was never a member of any radical organization although my name must have been on the name of every Fourth International mailing list at the time."[15] Relying on such testimony, then, one must agree with the assessment of political scientist M. Susan Power that Kendall, even in his radical years, was as much a left-wing southern Democrat as Trotskyist.[16]

Once he returned to the United States in 1936, Kendall, with two Oxford degrees in hand, pursued an academic, not an activist path. He began his PhD program in politics at the University of Illinois, then taught for two years as an Instructor of Political Science at Louisiana State University (LSU). His departure from LSU was unhappy but apparently not related to his left-wing politics. In 1941 he completed his doctorate at Illinois. Kendall then taught briefly at Hobart College in Geneva, New York (1941–1942) and at the University of Richmond in 1942. His resignations from these institutions appear to have stemmed at least partly from his leftist political leanings. At Hobart Kendall resigned in protest when J. Raymond Walsh, a communist sympathizer and radical labor activist, was forced out as director of the Hobart Citizenship Program. Afterward Kendall went on a speaking tour with Walsh. At the University of Richmond Kendall could not stomach being a cheerleader for World War II, American entry into which he had passionately opposed.[17]

Kendall's prewar publications reveal a distinctly radical, left-wing but populistic social vision. His first foray into the academic world of political theory consisted of two articles—"On the Preservation of Democracy for America" and "The Majority Principle and the Scientific Elite"—both of which appeared in the *Southern Review* in 1939.[18] In "Preservation," Kendall uses a progressive rubric to suggest that the American Constitution was a Machiavellian mechanism to thwart the people's ability to rule. Lauding the wisdom of the "common man," Kendall attacks judicial review, portrays freedom of the press as an illusion to protect the powerful few, and specifically repudiates "any attempt . . . to equate democracy with a particular set of 'natural rights.'" Similarly, Kendall criticizes the Bill of Rights, the Constitution's "fantastically difficult amending process," and "separation of powers" as devices to perpetuate elite power. Congress frequently helps thwart the popular will, he argues, while the presidency, except on foreign policy, remains more attuned popular desires. Teaching the people to view the Constitution as a *"symbol,"* and therefore as basically unchangeable, also helped to frustrate democracy.[19]

Meanwhile, Kendall maintained that real democracy worked best at the local level where there were "deeply felt group relations" and that political theorists of his day ought therefore to focus most of their attention there. In what would become a lifelong fascination, he analyzed Rousseau's ideas on democracy and defended their relevance to the modern political situation. Kendall pondered the question of how minorities could be brought to accept the will of the majority. He lamented the prevalence of "boss and machine rule" in American local government which, he said, served to promote "oligarchic political control." Ultimately such weakness and corruption in local government, he claimed, resulted from lack of voter interest due to the fact that most of the really important political decisions in the United States occurred at the state or federal level. Thus, where individual votes mattered most (at the local level), voters could enact only minor political changes.[20]

In "Majority Principle," Kendall argues for a fundamentalist version of majoritarianism, namely: "that in any decision-making group one half of the members, plus one, have a *right* to commit one half of the members, minus one, to any policy they see fit to support." He also denounces a system "in which ultimate power is entrusted to an unremovable judiciary." In "Majority Principle" Kendall maintains that political decisions are ethical in nature and so accessible to uneducated citizens. Politics, he says, involves value judgments—decisions about what ought to be—and does not require specialized, "scientific" knowledge. Yet, conflict between the "small minority of scientifically literate elites and the masses is inevitable because the former confuse their knowledge of means—*how* to achieve goals—with the political/ethical process of deciding *what* goals to pursue. Throwing down a populist gauntlet, Kendall proclaims "that between those who accept the majority principle as the differentia of democratic government, and those who repudiate it, a wider gulf is fixed than that which separates the latter from the defenders of Fascism."[21]

Especially when compared to Kendall's later scholarship, both *Southern Review* articles appear crude. In "Preservation," for instance, Kendall begins with a simplistic Beardian analysis of the Constitution, an approach which had become pretty standard academic fare by that time. In apparently pro forma fashion, he then throws in tributes to the progressive political scientists J. Allen Smith and Louis B. Boudin. Meanwhile, in "Majority Principle," Kendall makes "science" into a rhetorical strawman with whom he then proceeds to argue in favor of democracy. In the same article, Kendall simply asserts—without argument or evidence—that disagreements about ethical principles are "beyond all hope of rational reconciliation" but rather stem from "self-evident" beliefs. Both articles are disjointed. "Preservation," for example, starts out by discussing the Constitutional Convention of 1787 and ends up with an analysis of local government.[22]

When read closely, however, the early articles demonstrate greater intellectual heft than at first glance, especially when perused in the light of Kendall's later scholarship. Kendall's later work, that is, his postwar scholarship written from a conservative perspective, is clearly more sophisticated than his pieces from 1939. However, these early articles offer a window into how Kendall's viewpoints developed over time. In embryonic form, several ideas appear in these articles which Kendall developed more fully as a conservative. His tributes to Smith and Boudin, for example, are not merely pro forma. He absorbs and agrees with many of their ideas, but then goes on to chide them for neglecting local politics where Kendall (and Rousseau) always thought democracy flourished best. And, as a conservative, Kendall will continue to stress the centrality of local politics. Kendall's worries about the Supreme Court, natural rights, and the Bill of Rights, as dangers to democracy survived his transition from left to right. As a conservative, Kendall raised the same questions in 1939 but came up with different answers. He always remained a majoritarian but articulated a much more nuanced position as a conservative. On some issues—the role of Congress in a democracy and on how to appraise constitutional impediments to change—Kendall the conservative would perform a complete volte-face, but, even here, the issues he addressed remained largely the same issues.

In 1941 Kendall published the book which established his academic reputation, *John Locke and the Doctrine of Majority Rule*. Published by the University of Illinois Press, the book was an expository tour de force in which Kendall's genius as a scholar came to life. Kendall's purpose remained pretty much the same as in his *Southern Review* articles, to understand and to strengthen the intellectual foundations of democratic majoritarianism.[23] Part I contains an exhaustive survey of how political philosophers—from Plato through Pufendorf, Althusius, and Spinoza to Hobbes—had addressed the theme of majority rule. After this review, Kendall opines that "if Locke espoused the doctrine of majority rule, he was the earliest writer to deal with it on a scale sufficiently ambitious to merit our attention."[24]

Kendall then sets out to show that Locke, contrary to previous scholarly claims, was an advocate of political "collectivism" rather than an individualism based in natural rights. Meticulous reading of Locke, Kendall claims, necessitates "*reassessment* of Locke's position in the history of political philosophy," overthrowing him as "a *symbol* in the continuing struggle for power under the American constitution . . . [who] has been extremely useful to those who prefer government by judiciary to majority-rule."[25] Kendall then concludes the first part of the book, proclaiming that he means to do more than state facts, as a pettifogging historian might do, but rather to elucidate the "important question of whether or not that doctrine [majority-rule] can be defended on rational grounds."[26]

After this introductory material, one sees Kendall's analytical genius come into its own. Most importantly, Kendall focused on *reading* Locke rather than relying on standard authorities. Right from the get-go, for example, Kendall shows that Locke's analysis did *not* in fact begin with the "state of nature" (that was chapter 2 of *The Second Treatise of Government*) per what everyone else said, but rather that it commenced with a strong defense of the community's ability to exercise political power up to and including imposition of the death penalty (that was chapter 1 of the *Second Treatise*). Kendall shows that Locke knew full well that individual rights were "not inalienable," understood that individuals could not exist except as "*community members,*" and put forward the state of nature simply as an "expository device."[27] Thus Locke, for the most part, was in the camp of "*the majority rule democrats.*"[28]

Kendall then subjects Locke's theses about the law of nature to blistering criticism, exposing serious contradictions in the English philosopher's work. Most basically, Kendall shows that Locke's analysis of the relationship between liberty (individual freedom based in natural rights) and democracy (binding rules established by the community) was horribly confused.[29] On the one hand, Locke argued, as summarized by Kendall, that "[t]he individual owes to the commonwealth . . . a duty of obedience which is absolute and perpetual and *must* be absolute and perpetual because the alternative is the anarchy of the state of nature."[30] On the other hand, such a position, Kendall notes, was logically incompatible with defining the individual as obligated to preserve "his life, liberty, and estate."[31] The English thinker, he says, "was trying to have it more ways than one with his law of nature."[32]

Locke, continues Kendall, then went on to argue that the majority had the right to rule and that the minority had a corresponding duty to accept "political subjection." Then Locke, again as paraphrased by Kendall, stated that the majority "may if it chooses, act to prevent the exercise of power by future majorities." Such delegation might be permanent and could even include cession of political power to "a *hereditary* monarchy." This argument was a non-sequitur, thought Kendall, for Locke's previously stated principles had excluded "a duty of obedience to any decrees *save* those of the majority (or its indisputable agent)."[33] Should the majority be oppressed, its chief, or only, remedy was, as expressed by Locke, "an appeal to heaven"; that is, political revolution. This position seems absurd to Kendall. The "logical corollary of Locke's doctrine of majority-rule," he contends, demanded that "the people as a matter of course are invited, from time to time, to express (by majority vote) their preferences regarding future government policy and personnel."[34]

To resolve the chief inconsistency he found in *The Second Treatise*, that is, the logical incompatibility between absolute liberty and absolute democracy, Kendall suggests in his own book's conclusion that Locke's political theory must have contained a "latent premise." He argues that Locke certainly believed in moral principles and so could not also think to define as right whatever the majority willed. Instead, Kendall maintains that Locke could "argue both for individual rights and for a right of the majority to define individual rights" because he thought the people "rational and just" enough "never to withdraw a right which the individual ought to have."[35] Kendall ends his book with this clever argument, but readers may well surmise that the latent premise was his own rather than Locke's.

For the next twenty-five years, Willmoore Kendall would ponder the same problems as he had in the prewar period but in time would reach quite different conclusions. According to then wife Katherine Kendall, Willmoore, "sometime in the mid-forties" made "a 180 degree turn to the right and undertook, as a Messianiac mission, the conversion of all his friends and colleagues to his brand of conservatism."[36] Rather than follow Willmoore the man through the complexities of his professional and personal life, it would be more useful, for the purpose of analyzing Kendall's intellectual negotiation of the Left-Right divide, to concentrate on his postwar scholarship. Such scholarship was far more extensive than his prewar output and, on the whole, considerably more sophisticated. Indeed, Kendall's thought is notoriously difficult to summarize. His best scholarly work—with the exception of *John Locke and the Doctrine of Majority Rule*—appeared in book reviews (of which he was a master), book chapters, and journal articles. Kendall frequently reexamined and refined his ideas in light of insights he gained from his voracious reading. Kendall also developed many of his ideas outside the scholarly research nexus, especially in his *National Review* column, in his publications for intelligence agencies, and in his letters. For the space limitations of a single essay, however, it is more feasible to narrow our focus to three particular pieces of Kendall's postwar work.

For purposes of comparison, then, I have selected three articles—"The Two Majorities," "The Open Society and Its Fallacies," and "American Conservatism and the 'Prayer' Decisions."[37] These pieces, the first two published in 1960 and the latter one in 1964, roughly twenty years after his *Southern Review* articles and the *Locke* book. Having served his country in World War II and Korea, lived through McCarthyism and various controversies at Yale, and absorbed many ideas from political philosophers Leo Strauss and Eric Voegelin, Kendall was at the height of his intellectual powers. His thought had reached full maturity, and his transition to conservativism was complete. Kendall—who often co-authored his publications with other scholars—produced each of these articles alone, penning passages in each of them which today seem startling in their political relevancy. Close reading of these texts will also honor Kendall's own methods of analysis by paying careful attention to his arguments and words in some of his most important writings. These three particular pieces are also broadly representative of the political theorist's scholarly oeuvre, dealing in turn with: 1) the advantages of maintaining and strengthening the powers of Congress; 2) the necessity for society to regulate individual rights; and 3) the dangers that judicial sovereignty poses for democracy. Each article also demonstrates that Kendall, even after he had moved decisively to the right, continued to possess a populist understanding of American politics.

In the 1950s and 1960s, Kendall decisively broke with the political science mainstream to set out his vision of Congressional supremacy. In 1960, he forcefully advanced the idea of the "two majorities" in an article published in the *Midwest Journal of Politics*. Presidential campaigns of both parties, he argues, tend to promote change and to seek *"popular mandates"* based on "lofty and enlightened principle." They proclaim broad, vaguely defined plans in order to attract voters in a country with many different factions and interest groups. Presidential elections lead to a *"plebiscitary* political system."[38] On the other hand, Kendall holds that Congress is nationalistic, linked to actual interests in *"structured communities,"* whose representatives seek real material gains for their constituents through pork barrel projects, and so ground the body politic in a healthy way.[39]

Kendall believes that the Founders had designed Congress to make the most important national decisions, even when those decisions meant rejecting some principled presidential initiative.[40] Kendall argues that leaders of the political science profession, and especially his colleague Robert Dahl from Yale, had done a serious disservice to the American political system by creating a false dichotomy that: "either the majority rules through the presidential elections . . . , or it does not rule at all."[41] Thereby, such political scientists, effectively "deny legitimacy . . . to Congress as a formulator of policy" and therefore to Congressional elections.[42] Dahl and his ilk portray Congress—with its staggered elections, seniority system, filibuster, and so forth—not as a form of democracy but rather as a barrier to democracy, created because of the "anti-democratic, anti-majority-rule bias of the Framers."[43]

To question this professional consensus, admits Kendall, "may seem an act of perversity."[44] But academic perversity was Willmoore's stock-in-trade. He then argues, quite convincingly, that the Framers possessed a deep "*commitment* to the majority principle."[45] They wanted to facilitate popular control over the government, not prevent it. They feared inflamed majorities "bent on injustice" but not the people per se. As father of the Constitution, for example, Madison had no problem with "popular majorities (as such) having their way. He simply wanted . . . the majority to be articulated and counted in a certain way."[46] Congress, then, was not a barrier to democracy but rather one of "*two* popular majorities."[47]

Moreover, the Congressional majority involves selection by the people of uninstructed legislators who possess the time and temperament carefully to consider the national interest and the interests of their own communities. Localities vote not mainly on issues but rather on individuals, selecting those whom they consider to be "virtuous men," the natural aristocrats of their particular places.[48] Such individuals, with deep roots at home and well-connected with local business leaders and professionals, represent the "interests and values" of hierarchically structured local communities in ways no distant president ever could.[49] Political discourse at the Congressional level deals with concrete situations so that candidates can "talk about something" rather than in presidential elections in which, using "pleasant-sounding maxims" penned by professional intellectuals, candidates talk "about nothing."[50]

Both in his personal life and in his scholarship, Willmoore Kendall was a notorious contrarian. In September 1956, for example, he gave a speech to a conservative conference in Buck Hill Falls, Pennsylvania. It was if Daniel had volunteered to enter the lion's den, for Kendall suggested that the people of Athens were right to put Socrates to death. Russell Kirk and Murray Rothbard were both in the audience and were, respectively, amused and horrified[51] (not coincidentally, both of these thinkers abhorred Rousseau but for diametrically opposed reasons). A couple of years later Kendall published a version of this talk, which maintained that to survive every society must and every society does impose limits on freedom, including freedom of expression. Furthermore, Kendall went on to argue that not only was Athens correct to force Socrates to drink Hemlock but also showed that Socrates himself accepted the verdict, and the principle of majority rule, by refusing to flee.[52]

In 1960, covering much the same ground, but in less shocking fashion, Kendall published an article in the flagship journal of his profession, *The American Political Science Review*, attacking the open society as championed by John Stuart Mill in the nineteenth century and in the twentieth by Karl Popper. To be published in this journal, Kendall had to overcome considerable liberal pushback against his thesis but in this case the editor's recognition of the quality of Kendall's discourse prevailed over the profession's ideological distaste for Kendall's ideas. Had he not already used a similar title in his Socrates article of the year before, Kendall might well have chosen to call this article: "The Case of the People vs. John Stuart Mill." Here Kendall takes on the role of prosecuting attorney, cross-examining Mill even more relentlessly than he had Locke two decades before and seeking a harsher sentence (Karl Popper, who popularized the term "open society," merits far less attention).

First, Kendall sets out to show the import of Mill's ideas through close reading and analysis of Mill's *On Liberty*. He demonstrates that Mill (with a handful of exceptions), favored "absolute freedom of thought and speech," even, perhaps especially, when involving "immoral" or subversive subjects.[53] Mill, says Kendall, insists that freedom is the open society's first duty, demands that all questions be treated as open questions, and "denies the existence ... of any truth whatever."[54] Mill posits no "right" to free speech because that would demand the recognition of an objective order of rights and duties. "In full rebellion against both religion and philosophy," Mill utterly rejects previous treatments of his subject and regards himself as "standing not upon the shoulders of giants but of pygmies." Pulling no punches, Kendall calls his nineteenth-century defendant "a teacher of evil."[55]

In the rest of the article, Kendall shows why an open society cannot work. He argues that Mill treats society as if it were a "*debating club* devoted above all to the pursuit of truth," whereas real societies cherish many other goods. Most societies want to preserve those ideas and practices which their members regard as true and by which their members try to live.[56] Mill assumes that free speech can do no social hurt, but most people disagree with him on this point and fear social hurts resulting from what others may say, or write, or think. Therefore, Kendall argues, the only way to establish a completely open society, à la Mill and Popper, is to coerce ordinary people into accepting a kind of society which they do not really want, that is, to silence those who oppose unlimited freedom of speech.[57] Moreover, without belief in truth, "extremes of opinion will ... grow further and further apart so that ... their bearers can less and less tolerate even the thought of one another, still less one another's presence in society." Amid universal skepticism, noisy clashes of opinion will replace the pursuit for truth, substituting "phosphorous" for "philosophy."[58]

Instead of modeling society on a debating club, Kendall suggests that a more appropriate comparison would be to an academic discipline. Within such scholarly communities, discussion is valued, preparation for serious discourse required, and a certain disciplinary "orthodoxy" assumed. Anyone who wants to promote change in an academic discipline (or in society) must normally work within the system's parameters and then "persuade the community to accept his point of view." For the would-be change agent, the alternatives, if the academic discipline (or society) rejects his initiative, are "isolation within or banishment from the community."[59]

In his "Prayer Decisions" article of 1964, Kendall returned to a theme he had raised as a Depression-era leftist. Kendall starts by discussing a situation in North Brookfield, Massachusetts. There the local school board had voted to defy the Supreme Court decisions—*Engel v. Vitale* (1962) and *Abington School District v. Schempp* (1963)—which had prohibited officially sponsored prayer in public schools. After commending the school board for defying the court by voting to uphold the views of local people, Kendall attacks the court as anti-democratic. He acknowledges how hard it will be to dislodge the court's power—given long traditions of judicial review and strong arguments from Madison and Marshall favoring such review. Resistance, he notes, appears unseemly to Massachusetts citizens who fear looking like "Governor Wallace."[60] Unseemly or not, however, Kendall argues that American citizens must rein in the court's power. Citizens ought not "argue-bargue" about the extent of the court's legal authority—narrow or broad—but rather should reassert their own power, as citizens in a democracy, to make prudential decisions, especially local decisions, concerning the good of society.[61]

Conservatives, he argues, must prepare themselves intellectually for future liberal challenges in order to meet the onslaught of "liberal" elites determined to promote change and backed by federal authorities (and the court's prestige).[62] If not reined in, the court will soon ban "Christmas plays and public *crèches* and religious songs . . . invocations and benedictions at school graduation exercises."[63] The Supreme Court will impose such changes, even though the people oppose them, thus demonstrating that the judiciary is a danger to democracy. For Kendall nothing was more vital for American well-being than deliberation among citizens. On the national level, that meant that Congress, after due deliberation, ought to make the most important decisions. To protect the people's right to deliberate and decide at local and state levels, Kendall believed that Americans must "curb" the Supreme Court's power. One way was to repeal the Fourteenth Amendment; another was for Congress to restrict the Court's authority, under the Amendment, and so protect state laws from judicial overreach.[64] In any case, democracy depended on discovering the "deliberate sense" of the citizens through the give and take of elected assemblies. "Let the people of the local community work the matter out," says Kendall, "as part of their general problems of living together on their little portion of American real estate."[65]

Stepping back to compare Kendall's prewar and postwar scholarship, then, significant changes and significant continuities are apparent as he journeyed right. Kendall the conservative, for example, would continue to make excellent use of close reading and of the inquisitorial style which Kendall the progressive had pioneered in *Locke and the Doctrine of Majority Rule*. On the other hand, Kendall reversed parts of his conceptual framework to scholarship. For example, as a progressive, Kendall spoke negatively of political *symbols*. In 1939 he sees symbols as a sort of false consciousness preventing the people from pushing forward with needed changes. Even in 1964 he hints how symbols (the Supreme Court's prestige) may act as a barrier to prevent the restriction of judicial power. But the conservative Kendall, drawing on the work of Eric Voegelin, would mostly portray symbols positively. No longer, for example, would he think, as he did in 1939, that viewing the Constitution as a symbol was negative, for such symbolism, if understood correctly, provides the stability which American democracy needed to function well.[66]

On substantive issues related to the American political system, one also sees a mixture of change and continuity as Kendall moved right. In both phases of his career, following Rousseau, he would uphold the vital importance of local politics (though in more nuanced fashion as a conservative). Perhaps the most glaring change is in Kendall's political theory was his reversal on what rule by the people—majority rule—meant. The prewar Kendall viewed Congress as a problem, as an institution which too often blocked the democratic will of the people. In 1960 Kendall still acknowledged that Congress slowed down the pace of political change, but he now regarded this fact as beneficial. He thought the seniority system for committees, the filibuster, and so forth, helped maintain social and political stability and thereby to preserve, rather than to thwart, democracy. Through checking overly ambitious presidential agendas, Congress allowed consensus to develop before major changes could occur. Then, once these impediments to change were overcome, Congress after thorough deliberation, could pass legislation on the matter at hand. With such enactment, one might then presume that the American people had reached political consensus, thereby moving forward carefully rather than rashly.

To push through major changes with a mere numerical majority (50 percent plus one) could, he now thought, poison politics, producing an enduring and bitter backlash, a phenomenon which Kendall called irredentism. He feared such results could collapse American democracy. Indeed, Kendall argued that deliberative self-governance was the cornerstone of the US political tradition—not individual liberty not political equality—but deliberative self-governance. Successful and stable governance existed in the US because majorities in Congress generally exercised their power with restraint to serve their constituents and to conciliate potentially recalcitrant minorities. Thus, Kendall the conservative almost completely repudiated his extreme majoritarian position of 1939. For him, 50 percent plus one of voters in any particular election no longer equated to the vox populi, let alone the vox Dei. Having learned to see Congress as a menace to democracy from progressive political scientist J. Allen Smith,[67] Kendall changed his mind.

On the other hand, Kendall's views about the Supreme Court changed much less. In both phases of his career he portrayed the Court as a danger to democracy. In 1939 and in 1941, he attacked the Court for serving as one of the chief bastions protecting big business from socialistic reforms desired by the people. By 1964 he feared the Court's ever-growing intrusiveness upon democratic decision-making at the federal, state, and local levels. Reading only Kendall's postwar work, one is tempted to ascribe his distaste for the court's power to his uneasiness about demands of the civil rights movement. However, Kendall's concerns about judicial supremacy did not start with *Brown v. Board* but rather went back to *Lochner v. New York*. He explicated his concerns more fully and in a more sophisticated way as a conservative, but, having learned to see the Court as a menace to democracy from the communist political theorist Louis Boudin,[68] Kendall never really changed his mind.

At first glance, Kendall's attitude toward individual rights also appears to have changed only moderately. In both phases of his career, he argued that to treat personal liberties as sacrosanct was impractical and anti-democratic because, where a majority did not support such rights, then some force—a minority—must impose them upon the people. As a conservative, however, Kendall—influenced by Leo Strauss's view that one could derive ethical principles through reason—significantly extended and clarified his prewar stance. Perhaps, most importantly, he suggested that calls for unrestrained freedom, at least in modern times, were based in relativism and therefore not just impractical but evil. The conservative Kendall thought liberals of Mill's ilk avoided privileging any one philosophy because they thought nothing objectively true. If applied to society this liberal view would lead to a chaos of clashing opinions (none true and none false). In response, Kendall proposed that any society, to cohere, requires an "orthodoxy" grounded in truth (or at least in what the society's members take to be truth).

In conclusion, Willmoore Kendall altered several aspects of his political theory during his transformation from communist dilettante to conservative sage. His understanding of what constituted majority rule changed a great deal, as he abandoned the rather simple majoritarianism of his youth for the nuanced approach of the two majorities. As regards the role of the Supreme

Court and the role of individual liberties, on the other hand, Kendall deepened and expanded ideas which he had already held as a leftist. Meanwhile, he also matured as a thinker by adopting principles from Eric Voegelin and Leo Strauss and integrating their precepts about symbols and natural right with his own previous notions about how democracy should work. Throughout his career, however, Kendall relentlessly championed democracy, cogitating constantly on how a free people might best govern the American Republic to accomplish its will. Above all, Kendall thought that the American people needed to govern themselves well, or a dictator (or a court or an unelected bureaucracy) would. In some sense, Kendall's ideas were unique to him, but if one must attach a label beyond generic conservative to them, that label would be populist. Kendall's teaching was an intricate construction and understanding it can therefore deepen our understanding of populism. It would be far too grand to claim that such well-wrought populist ideas can *transcend* divisions of left and right, but, looking at Kendall's own intellectual journey, one might say that such ideas can *traverse* divisions of left and right.

NOTES

1. George H. Nash, "Willmoore Kendall: Conservative Iconoclast (II)," *Modern Age* 19 (Summer 1975): 245; Grant Havers, "Leo Strauss, Willmoore Kendall, and the Meaning of Conservatism," *Humanitas* XVIII/1 and 2 (2005): 16–17.

2. Havers, "Meaning," 17; David Gordon, ed., *Strictly Confidential: The Private Volker Fund Memos of Murray N. Rothbard* (Auburn, AL: Ludwig von Mises Institute, 2010), 44.

3. For an early example of this tendency, see the comments of R. B. McCallum. McCallum, future Inkling and future Master of Pembroke College, was Kendall's tutor at Oxford. Willmoore Kendall (hereafter WK) to Willmoore Kendall, Sr. (hereafter WKS), October 16, 1933 in *The Oxford Years: The Letters of Willmoore Kendall to His Father*, Yvona Kendall Mason, ed. (Bryn Mawr, PA: Intercollegiate Studies Institute, 1993), 282.

4. John A. Murley and John E. Alvis, eds., *Willmoore Kendall: Maverick of Conservatives* (Lanham, MD: Lexington Books, 2002); George H. Nash, "Willmoore Kendall: Conservative Iconoclast (I)," *Modern Age* 19 (Spring 1975): 127–35; Nellie Kendall, ed., *Willmoore Kendall Contra Mundum* (New Rochelle, NY: Arlington House, 1972).

5. Jeffrey Hart, "Willmoore Kendall: Philosopher of Consensus," *National Review*, September 1, 1978, 1084–85; John P. East, "The Political Thought of Willmoore Kendall," *The Political Science Reviewer* 3 (1973): 201–39; Daniel McCarthy, "The Constitution Versus Calhoun: Why Harry Jaffa Is Still Wrong about Willmoore Kendall," *American Conservative*, September 23, 2013, available at https://www.theamericanconservative.com/mccarthy/the-constitution-vs-calhoun-why-harry-jaffa-is-still-wrong-about-willmoore-kendall. See also Matthew Continetti, "'Genuine Civil War Potential:' Willmoore Kendall, Donald Trump, and American Conservatism," *Washington Free Beacon*, July 27, 2018, available at https://freebeacon.com/columns/genuine-civil-war-potential/.

6. Nash, "Iconoclast (II)," 245.

7. Cas Mudde and Cristóbal Rovira Kaltwasser, *Populism: A Very Short Introduction* (Oxford: Oxford University Press, 2017), 6.

8. George McKenna, *American Populism* (New York: G.P. Putnam's Sons, 1974).

9. WK, "The Majority Principle and the Scientific Elite, *Southern Review* (Winter 1939): 467.

10. *American Heritage Dictionary of the English Language*, Fifth Edition, Harcourt Publishing Company. Available at https://www.thefreedictionary.com/populism.
11. Mudde and Kaltwasser, *Willmoore Kendall*, 2–6.
12. William F. Buckley, "Willmoore Kendall, RIP," *National Review*, June 25, 1967.
13. WK to WKS, October 16, 1933, *Oxford Years*, 275–76.
14. WK to WKS, August 17, 1934 and January 8, 1935, *The Oxford Years*, 394–95, 458–59; WKS to Katherine Tuach Kendall, April 13, 1935, Box 4, Folder 2, Willmoore Kendall Papers, Hoover Institution, Stanford University.
15. WK to WKS, June 2, 1933, *Oxford Years*, 208–9; WK to Charles S. Hyneman, February 11, 1942, Box 7, Charles S. Hyneman Papers, Indiana University Archives.
16. M. Susan Power, "Willmoore Kendall: The Early Years," *Modern Age* 38 (Fall 1995): 82–87.
17. "Dr. Eddy Hints at Departure from Hobart," *Rochester Democrat and Chronicle*, February 26, 1941, 7; "Leader Backs One to Leave," *Rochester Democrat and Chronicle*, February 26, 1941, 30; WKS to WK (February 1941), Box 5, Folder 1, Kendall Papers; WK to Hyneman, February 11, 1942.
18. WK, "On the Preservation of Democracy for America," *Southern Review* (Summer 1939): 53–68; WK, "Majority Principle," 463–73.
19. WK, "Preservation," 53–58.
20. Ibid., 59–68.
21. WK, "Majority Principle," 463–73.
22. WK, "Preservation," *passim*; WK, "Majority Principle," 467–71.
23. WK, *John Locke and the Doctrine of Majority Rule* (Urbana: University of Illinois Press, 1941), 33, 37–38.
24. WK, *Locke*, ch. II, 52–53.
25. Ibid., 55, 57.
26. Ibid., 59.
27. Ibid., 69, 74–75.
28. Ibid., 66–67.
29. Ibid., ch. V.
30. Ibid., 103.
31. Ibid., 107.
32. Ibid.
33. Ibid., 122–24.
34. Ibid., 128–31.
35. Ibid., 134–36.
36. Katherine Kendall to John W. Fiser, January 21, 1982, Box 18, Katherine A. Kendall Papers, Social Welfare Archive, University of Minnesota Archives and Special Collections, Minneapolis, Minnesota.
37. WK, "The Two Majorities," *Midwest Journal of Politics* 4/4 (November 1960b): 317–45; WK, "The Open Society and Its Fallacies," *American Political Science Review* 54/4 (December 1960a): 972–79; WK, "American Conservatism and the 'Prayer' Decisions." *Modern Age* 8/3 (Summer 1964): 245–59.
38. WK, "Two Majorities," 319–22, 324.
39. Ibid., 319–21, 340.
40. Ibid., 321–25.
41. Ibid., 330.
42. Ibid.
43. Ibid., 330–31.
44. Ibid., 331.
45. Ibid., 332.
46. Ibid., 333–35.
47. Ibid., 336.
48. Ibid., 336–39.
49. Ibid., 340.
50. Ibid., 342–45.

51. Russell Kirk, Excerpt from *The Wanderer*, Box 23, Folder 2, Kendall Papers; Gordon, 35–50.
52. WK, "The People versus Socrates Revisited: The Perplexities of the Athenian Jury System Are Our Own Problem," *Modern Age* 3/1 (Winter 1958–1959): 98–111.
53. WK, "Fallacies," 972–74.
54. Ibid., 974–75.
55. Ibid., 976.
56. Ibid., 977.
57. Ibid., 977–78.
58. Ibid., 978–79.
59. Ibid., 979.
60. WK, "Prayer," 245–49.
61. Ibid., 251–52.
62. Ibid., 250–51, 255.
63. Ibid., 251.
64. Ibid., 254–55.
65. Ibid., 258.
66. Willmoore Kendall and George W. Carey, *The Basic Symbols of the American Political Tradition* (Baton Rouge: Louisiana State University Press, 1970).
67. J. Allen Smith, *Growth and Decadence of Constitutional Government* (New York: Henry Holt, 1930), 71–72.
68. Louis B. Boudin, *Government by Judiciary* (New York: William Godwin, 1932), I: vi–viii.

BIBLIOGRAPHY

Boudin, Louis B. 1932. *Government By Judiciary*. 2 vols. New York: William Godwin.
Buckley, William F. 1967. "Willmoore Kendall, RIP." *National Review*, June 25.
Continetti, Matthew. 2018. "'Genuine Civil War Potential:' Willmoore Kendall, Donald Trump, and American Conservatism." *Washington Free Beacon*, July 27. Available at https://freebeacon.com/columns/genuine-civil-war-potential/.
East, John P. 1973. "The Political Thought of Willmoore Kendall," *The Political Science Reviewer* 3: 201–39.
Gordon, David, ed. 2010. *Strictly Confidential: The Private Volker Fund Memos of Murray N. Rothbard*. Auburn, AL: Ludwig von Mises Institute.
Hart, Jeffrey. 1978. "Willmoore Kendall: Philosopher of Consensus." *National Review*, September 1, 1083–86.
Havers, Grant. 2005. "Leo Strauss, Willmoore Kendall, and the Meaning of Conservatism." *Humanitas* 18/1 and 2: 5–25.
Hyneman, Charles S. "Charles S. Hyneman Papers." Indiana University Archives, Archives Online at Indiana University.
Kendall, Katherine A. "Katherine A. Kendall Papers." Social Welfare Archive, University of Minnesota Archives and Special Collections, Minneapolis, Minnesota.
Kendall, Nellie, ed. 1972. *Willmoore Kendall Contra Mundum*. New Rochelle, NY: Arlington House.
Kendall, Willmoore. (n.d.). "Willmoore Kendall Papers." Hoover Institution. Palo Alto, CA: Stanford University.
Kendall, Willmoore. 1939. "The Majority Principle and the Scientific Elite." *Southern Review*: 463–73.
———. 1939. "On the Preservation of Democracy for America." *Southern Review*, Summer: 53–68.
———. 1941. *John Locke and the Doctrine of Majority Rule*. Urbana: University of Illinois Press.
———. 1958–1959. "The People versus Socrates Revisited: The Perplexities of the Athenian Jury System Are Our Own Problem." *Modern Age* 3/1: 98–111.

———. 1960a. "The Open Society and Its Fallacies." *American Political Science Review* 54/4: 972–79.

———. 1960b. "The Two Majorities." *Midwest Journal of Politics* 4/4: 317–45.

———. 1964. "American Conservatism and the 'Prayer' Decisions." *Modern Age* 8/3: 245–59.

Kendall, Willmoore, and George W. Carey. 1970. *The Basic Symbols of the American Political Tradition*. Baton Rouge: Louisiana State University Press.

Mason, Yvona Kendall, ed. 1993. *The Oxford Years: The Letters of Willmoore Kendall to His Father*. Bryn Mawr, PA: Intercollegiate Studies Institute.

McCarthy, Daniel. 2013. "The Constitution Versus Calhoun: Why Harry Jaffa Is Still Wrong about Willmoore Kendall." *American Conservative*, September 23. Available at https://www.theamericanconservative.com/mccarthy/the-constitution-vs-calhoun-why harry-jaffa-is-still-wrong-about-willmoore-kendall/.

McKenna, George, ed. 1974. *American Populism*. New York: G.P. Putnam's Sons.

Mudde, Cas, and Cristóbal Rovira Kaltwasser. 2017. *Populism: A Very Short Introduction*. Oxford: Oxford University Press.

Murley, John A., and John E. Alvis, eds. 2002. *Willmoore Kendall: Maverick of Conservatives*. Lanham, MD: Lexington Books.

Nash, George H. 1975. "Willmoore Kendall: Conservative Iconoclast (I)." *Modern Age* 19: 127–35.

———. 1975. "Willmoore Kendall: Conservative Iconoclast (II)." *Modern Age* 19: 236–48.

Power, M. Susan. 1995. "Willmoore Kendall: The Early Years." *Modern Age* 38: 82–87.

Smith, J. Allen. 1930. *Growth and Decadence of Constitutional Government*. New York: Henry Holt.

Chapter Three

"Mugged by Reality"

The Neoconservative Turn

Lee Trepanier

This chapter examines the neoconservative movement, liberal hawks who became increasingly disenchanted with the Democratic Party's foreign policy, Great Society Program, and the cultural values of the New Left.[1] Neoconservatives favored a vigorous anti-communist and activist foreign policy, a strong relationship with Israel, and believed that the United States should be the global hegemon to establish international order. Abandoning the Democratic Party in the late 1960s and early 1970s, neoconservatives eventually joined the Republican Party and served in Republican administrations. Although influential in the foreign policy of these administrations, neoconservatives' effectiveness was ultimately limited with the practitioners of realism emerging dominant in both the second terms of the Reagan and George W. Bush administrations. During periods when Republicans were not in the White House, neoconservatives promoted their ideas and policies through publications, think tanks, and the mainstream media. It remains to be seen what role, if any, neoconservatives will play in the Trump administration.

In spite of the evolution and diversity of their ideas and policies, neoconservatives have four fundamental principles in their ideology: 1) a distrust of social engineering projects, such as the Johnson administration's Great Society programs; 2) a defense of cultural and educational standards informed by Western civilization and traditional social values; 3) a skepticism of international law and institutions to achieve security and justice; and 4) a belief that the United States should be the hegemonic power in international politics. This last principle, American predominance in global politics, later included the promotion of liberal democracy by the second generation of neoconservatives and was realized in the 2003 Iraq Invasion. Even though there have been severe setbacks in Iraq, neoconservatives today still adhere to an activist foreign policy of promoting liberal democracy.

In reviewing the origins, history, and evolution of neoconservatism, we will show the relationships among neoconservatives, liberals, the New Left, and traditional conservatives, raising the question whether neoconservatives fundamentally belong to the history of liberal or conservative thought. We also will see how neoconservatives' views in foreign policy have changed from an activist anti-communist policy of containment to the promotion of liberal democracy. Finally, we will see the rise and fall of neoconservative's influence in Republican administrations and the relationship between the Republican Party and the neoconservative movement.

ORIGINS

In the mid- to late 1930s and early 1940s, a group of Jewish intellectuals at City College of New York would form the basis of the neoconservative movement of the late 1960s and early 1970s: Irving Kristol (1920–2009), Daniel Bell (1919–2011), Irving Howe (1920–1993), Seymour Martin Lipset (1922–2006), Philip Selznick (1919–2010), Nathan Glazer (1923–), and later the Catholic Daniel Patrick Moynihan.[2] This group was a combination of Trotskyites and others committed to left-wing politics who opposed Stalinist communism. The disillusionment over the brutality of a Stalinist communist regime, which had undermined communism's idealist goals, made this group anti-communist but not for the same reasons of traditional conservatives, who had rejected communism because it was atheistic, expansionist, and anti-free market.[3] By contrast, these Jewish intellectuals sympathized with the social and economic aims of communism but acknowledged that its implementation had yielded only violence rather than communism's stated intentions.

After the death of President Franklin Roosevelt in 1945 and the beginning of the Cold War in 1947, liberals were divided about how to preserve and continue the reforms of the New Deal: some were willing to form a coalition with communists to work for more domestic reform and an accommodation with the Soviet Union, while others supported President's Truman's anti-communist foreign policy.[4] The Americans for Democratic Action (ADA) was created in 1947 by Arthur Schlesinger Jr. (1917–2007), Reinhold Niebuhr (1892–1971), Humbert Humphrey (1911–1978), Eleanor Roosevelt (1884–1962), and others to support the Truman administration. Truman's victory in the 1948 presidential election secured the anti-communist faction's dominance among liberals and included the group that would later be known as neoconservatives.[5] This liberal consensus, or "vital center" as named by Schlesinger, opposed communism through deterrence, favored American global engagement through multilateral alliances, and promoted economic global integration to preserve peace, security, and prosperity.[6]

The liberal consensus also sought to preserve and expand the achievements of the New Deal's social welfare state and expand civil rights legislation with its coalition of unions, farmers, intellectuals, African Americans, and southern whites.[7] With socialism opposed and conservatism marginalized, New Deal liberalism was the only ideology that had mainstream intellectual and electoral support.[8] Among postwar liberal academics, a new political theory emerged where interest groups and expertise triumphed over ideology and politics.[9] This theory was articulated in Bell's *The End of Ideology* (1960) where the ideologies of the Enlightenment had been exhausted and discredited by the experience of Nazi and Soviet totalitarianism and the only politics remaining was one of middle-ground compromise about the welfare state and mixed economy.[10] Politics was dictated by bureaucratic expertise, interest groups demands, and global events like the Cold War.

THE NEW LEFT

The conservative movement in America began to rehabilitate itself with a body of serious thought by Russell Kirk (1919–1994), William F. Buckley (1925–2008), and a group of European emigres such as Friedrich von Hayek (1899–1992), Leo Strauss (1899–1973), and Eric Voegelin (1901–1985).[11] The various strands of conservative intellectual thought and political support cohered into "fusionism" where the traditional, libertarian, and anti-communist elements of the conservative movement came together.[12] Furthermore, the expansion of the New Deal into the Great Society social welfare programs, the expansion of civil rights legislation to African Americans, and a relaxing of law enforcement on crimes provided an opportunity for conservatives to tap into working-class white frustration against the federal government.[13] Although Barry Goldwater lost by a landslide in the 1964 presidential election, the groundwork for a conservative movement was established to bloom later.[14]

If the conservative movement failed to challenge the liberal consensus, then the New Left was successful. However, initially the New Left had little impact on politics and the Democratic Party. Less a set of political doctrines or policy positions, the New Left represented attitudes of feeling alienated from their social and cultural environment and impatient about the pace of gradual reform.[15] The *Port Huron Statement* (1962) was emblematic of early New Left with a call to awaken the social conscience of the average American and demand social welfare reforms that eventually would be realized in the Johnson administration's Great Society programs.[16] It was only in the mid-1960s when the New Left abandoned its commitments to nonviolence and rational persuasion for revolutionary violence, mass protest, and identity politics to protest the Vietnam War, racial discrimination, and the collaboration between universities and the military.[17] The liberal consensus, and the Democratic Party, collapsed into the factions of liberals, the New Left, and working-class whites.[18]

With the escalation of the Vietnam War abroad and race and student riots at home, neoconservatives were concerned about the loss of the authority of social and political institutions and the demands of the New Left, which no longer recognized the limits of pluralist democracy. As Jeane Kirkpatrick wrote "The counter-culture was much broader than the anti-war movement with which it was associated and, I believe, constituted a sweeping rejection of traditional American attitudes, values, and goals."[19] Jewish liberals also were concerned with the New Left's criticisms of Israel which they saw as thinly veiled anti-Semitism.[20] The result was, as Joshua Muravchik, explained, "The [New] Left drove neoconservatives out of the Democratic Party, stolen the 'liberal' label, and successfully affixed to us the name 'neoconservative.'"[21] By the late 1970s these New Deal liberals were being called "new conservatives" or "neoconservatives." The term was first used by the socialist Michael Harrington to define the ideologies of Daniel Bell, Irving Kristol, Daniel Patrick Moynihan, and others and later adopted by Irving Kristol in his 1979 article entitled, "Confessions of a True, Self-Confessed Neoconservative."[22]

Having abandoned its universal commitments in favor of identity politics, American liberalism under the New Left was no longer able to make decisions about serving the public interest and reflecting the country's common values.[23] Neoconservatives saw themselves as the heirs of a liberalism that was betrayed. As Tod Lindberg puts it, "what is being conserved is *our* liberalism"; or, as Irving Kristol characterized neoconservatism as "reformationist. It tries to 'reach beyond' contemporary liberalism . . . a return to the original sources of liberal vision and liberal energy so as to correct the warped version of liberalism that is today's orthodoxy."[24] For Kristol, neoconservatism sought to conserve society based on liberal ideals: "What is 'neo' ('new') about this conservatism is that it is resolutely free of nostalgia. It, too, claims the future."[25] The past presidentcies of Coolidge, Hoover, Eisenhower are overlooked for Theodore Roosevelt, Franklin Roosevelt, and Ronald Reagan.[26]

THE PUBLIC INTEREST

In addition to their antipathy to the New Left, neoconservatives reconsidered the social welfare reforms of the Kennedy and Johnson administrations. The social disorder and urban riots of the mid- and late 1960s led to a new appreciation of the role of traditional institutions and authority in society as well as questioning of the efficacy and efficiency of the government's adoption of unproven theories and social science methods to socially engineer reforms in society. These concerns were articulated in a journal founded in 1965 by Daniel Bell and Irving Kristol called *The Public Interest* (1965–2005).[27] Later, other publications like *Commentary* (1945–) under Norman Podhoretz (1930—with editorship 1960–1995) and *Policy Review* (1977–2013), would be academic and public venues for neoconservatives to express their ideas and policies.[28]

The Public Interest attracted academics and public intellectuals who adopted social science approaches to analyze the cause of societal problems and ills and reflected a skepticism of government intervention to solve them. James Q. Wilson (1931–2012), Glenn Loury (1948–), Charles Murray (1943–), Stephen (1934–) and Abigail (1936–) Thernstorm, Nathan Glazer (1923–2019), Daniel Patrick Moynihan (1927–2003), and others contributed to this journal, which laid down the intellectual foundation for neoconservative domestic policies in the 1980s and 1990s.[29] These contributors wrote how crime policy should focus on short-term symptoms rather than the underlying causes of poverty and racism (the "broken window" policy); the problems welfare policies created when they neglected the role of the family structure and social habits; and, perhaps most controversially, the negative effects of affirmative action because it stigmatized people and set up a perverse system of incentives for social advancement.

For example, Glazer's and Moynihan's 1963 study on ethnicity, *Beyond the Melting Pot*, was skeptical about the effectiveness of integrationist policies because racial prejudice was beyond the ability of the government to solve.[30] While both Glazer and Moynihan supported anti-discrimination laws, they also believed that discrimination was only one reason among many (e.g., family structure and values) that resulted in minority poverty. When the civil rights movement shifted from anti-discrimination to equality of results, neoconservatives revised their position from support to opposition.

The publication and reaction to Moynihan's *The Negro Family: A Case for National Action* captured this change among neoconservatives' views about the civil right movement.[31] The study was produced when Moynihan was Johnson's Assistant Secretary of Labor and argued that civil rights and voting legislation was necessary but not sufficient for African Americans to take advantage of these newly created opportunities. The structure and values of the black family, as caused by slavery, segregation, and discrimination, resulted in an absent father figure, teenage pregnancies, and juvenile delinquencies. No legislation or government program could remedy this situation.

The report antagonized the African American community, the civil rights movement, and the New Left because it appeared to blame African Americans for their own situation and bolstered racist stereotypes during a time of racial unrest.³² However, liberals, especially in the media and the universities, did not defend Moynihan from these accusations because they also feared being labeled racist and reactionary by the black militants, the civil rights movement, and the New Left. These groups had created an atmosphere of ideology rather than of thought at the universities, which James Q. Wilson describes at Harvard as

> the most serious threats to certain liberal values—the harassment of unpopular views, the use of force to prevent certain persons from speaking, the adoption of quota system either to reduce the admission of other kinds, and the politicization of the university to make it an arena for the exchange of manifestos rather than a forum for the discussion of ideas.³³

Neoconservatives were furious that liberals not only failed to defend Moynihan but that they had lost their nerve in defending their own liberal values, not seeing that what was being tolerated in the name of tolerance was actually undermining liberalism itself.³⁴

Neoconservatives believed that individual rights were being sacrificed for group rights. By exacerbating demands for group rights rather than individual ones, the Johnson administration's Great Society social welfare policies mobilized racial, ethnic, and social-economic groups against one another in the United States.³⁵ Although in the past they had supported the welfare state, neoconservatives now opposed its expansion because of its focus on groups rather than individuals as well as their costs and unlikely chance to succeed. Instead, neoconservatives wanted to improve existing programs by relocating administrative responsibility from the federal government to local authorities and the choice of individuals.³⁶ Neoconservatives believed that social problems could be ameliorated by government programs but these problems could never be solved. In this sense, neoconservatives accepted social and economic inequality in society and supported establishing true equality of opportunity for individuals to succeed or fail on their own.

THE DEMOCRATIC PARTY

In foreign policy neoconservatives were influenced by the writings of Reinhold Niebuhr and Arthur M. Schlesinger Jr., both of whom opposed communism and supported liberal democracy.³⁷ This consensus existed in the American foreign policy establishment from 1948 until the mid-1960s when some liberals sought to reduce American commitments overseas, particularly in the Vietnam War, for an international regime of economic interdependence and transnational law. Unlike the New Left, who opposed the Vietnam War because they believed it was a product of American imperialism, neoconservatives objected to the war because the United States made a geopolitical miscalculation about its national interest.[38] In other words, neoconservatives thought American involvement in the Vietnam War was a mistaken attempt by the United States to contain communism.

More broadly, the dispute about the Vietnam War between the New Left and neoconservatives was about the United States' values, culture, and institutions. From the neoconservatives' perspective, the New Left saw the United States as morally bankrupt with violence replacing civic participation and ideological purity substituting for rational discourse.[39] The failure of liberals was to understand that the dangers of the New Left would eventually lead to the collapse of American liberalism, institutions, and values. As Irving Kristol put it:

> One wonders: how can a bourgeois society survive in a cultural ambiance that derides every traditional bourgeois virtue and celebrates promiscuity, homosexuality, drugs, political terrorism—anything, in short, that is in bourgeoise eyes perverse.[40]

Confronted with the New Left's ideology, neoconservatives, as Norman Podhoretz recalled, began to appreciate

> the virtues of the American political system and of its economic and social underpinning. So profoundly affected were we by this new appreciation that we have been devoting ourselves ever since to defending America against the defamations of its enemies abroad and the denigrations of its critics at home. Almost every idea espoused by the neoconservatives relates back to this central impulse to defend America against the assaults of the left.[41]

Neoconservatives wanted to make sure that the United States did not suffer, as Theodore Draper characterized, the "specter of Weimar": the collapse of liberal society to extremist ideological movements.[42] Because they saw themselves as the true heirs of liberalism, neoconservatives struggled to maintain a role for themselves in the Democratic Party. In 1969 George McGovern and the New Left introduced new rules for the Democratic Party that gave women and ethnic and racial minorities more representation, something to which neoconservatives futilely objected because it was a form of positive discrimination against the white working class.[43] Furthermore, the neoconservatives' support for Senator Henry M. Jackson's (1912–1983) failed bids to gain the 1972 and 1976 Democratic presidential nomination and the diminishing influence of the Coalition for a Democratic Majority (CDM) in the Democratic Party illustrated neoconservatives' weakening power in the party.[44] By the early 1970s, neoconservatives began to abandon their liberal credentials and the Democratic Party.

COMMUNISM

Having been "mugged by reality," neoconservatives started a robust defense of American values, culture, and institutions and aligned themselves with the conservative movement and Republican Party.[45] In practical terms this translated into abandoning the nonpartisan attitude of *The Public Interest* for the political ideology of "American bourgeois populism": politics over economics, standards of excellence and virtue in culture and economics, a deference to ordinary citizens rather than intellectuals.[46] According to neoconservatives, the class of intellectuals and professionals sought social and cultural equality because they benefited from these industries and envied and despised the business class of the country. Neoconservatives consequently tried to persuade the business community of the importance of their ideas, and as a result received financial support. Organizations like the American Enterprise Institute, the Hoover Institution, and Institute for Educational Affairs were revitalized or created to promote neoconservative ideas.[47]

With the American defeat in the Vietnam War, neoconservatives became more interested in US foreign policy. They supported a projection of American values, culture, and institutions abroad and rejected the New Left's acceptance of "third-worldism" in the United Nations where the problems of the Third World were blamed on the West.[48] Neoconservatives criticized the Establishment of a New International Economic Order (1975), the Charter of Economics Rights and Duties of States (1975), and United Nation's Resolution 3379, which stated that Zionism was a form of racism and racial discrimination.[49] Moynihan, who was the US ambassador to the United Nations in 1975–1976, blamed the moral decay of the United Nations on liberals who accepted "third-worldism."[50] Later Kirkpatrick, who served as the US ambassador (1981–1985), argued that the United Nations could be useful if it served American interests, but it was now under Marxian "Third World Ideology" and therefore was fundamentally anti-American. Like the New Left in the Democratic Party, the United Nations betrayed the liberal principles on which it was founded.[51]

Besides opposing "third-worldism," neoconservatives also objected to the foreign policy doctrine of realism of Henry Kissinger (1923–) in the 1970s.[52] Realists believed that power is the most important value in international politics, that all nations struggle for it, and therefore liberal democracy is not inherently superior to nondemocratic societies and values. Realists were wary about crusading democratic idealism which they thought can be destabilizing to international politics. Kissinger, as the US National Security Advisor (1969–1975) and Secretary of State (1973–1977) pursued a policy of détente in seeking accommodation with the Soviet Union. This goal was realized in the Strategic Arms Limitation Talks Treaties (SALT) in 1972 and

1979, which limited the number and types of nuclear weapons between the United States and Soviet Union.

Neoconservatives criticized SALT for both strategic and moral reasons: the limitations of the number of nuclear weapons the United States could possess gave the Soviet Union a nuclear advantage which it would exploit and the treaties provided legitimacy to the Soviet Union, making it and the United States morally equivalent.[53] Neoconservatives also opposed détente because they believed the Soviet Union was an ideologically expansionist state rather than, as Kissinger thought, a typical state that was motivated by power.[54] Furthermore, neoconservatives feared that détente would weaken the United States' support of Israel and strengthen the Soviet Union's support for Israel's Arab enemies. The 1973 Arab-Israeli War appeared to confirm the neoconservatives' fears: the United States ultimately joined the Soviet Union in cosponsoring a United Nation's resolution for a cease-fire and threatened Israel to cut assistance if it did not agree to negotiations.[55]

Neoconservatives' criticism of American foreign policy continued under the Carter administration which continued the policy of détente. The CDM, the neoconservative faction in the Democratic Party, joined the hard-line anti-communist Republican organization, the Committee on the Present Danger, to revive the doctrine of containment to be at the core of the United States foreign policy.[56] After Carter was elected president, both organizations lobbied Carter to return to a doctrine of containment and presented it a list of sixty neoconservatives for appointment in the administration. Although many neoconservatives campaigned for him, Carter refused to appoint them in his administration because he wanted to continue détente and thereby further alienated neoconservatives from the Democratic Party.

While Carter later increased military spending, reinstated draft registration, and imposed trade sanctions on the Soviet Union, his administration's credibility had been damaged beyond repair with neoconservatives due to the Iranian Revolution and Soviet invasion of Afghanistan.[57] Neoconservatives supported Ronald Reagan's 1980 campaign for the presidency. Reagan promised to restore America's national confidence and sense of purpose by expanding government powers to fight communism overseas while, at the same time, deregulate markets, privatize state services, and reduce social welfare policies to simulate capitalism at home.[58] Those neoconservatives who did not campaign for Reagan nevertheless joined the Republican Party after his election, with over sixty members of the CDM appointed to the administration, including Kirkpatrick as ambassador to the United Nations, Elliott Abrams (1948–) as Assistant Secretary of State (1981–1985), and Richard Perle (1941–) as Assistant Secretary of Defense (1981–1987).[59]

With the election of a conservative president to the White House, the relationship between neoconservatives and traditional conservatives came to the fore.[60] Neoconservatives' relationship with traditional conservatives had been ambiguous, with some having benefited from neoconservatives' access to influential journals, newspapers, and think tanks to spread traditional ideas, values, and institutions. But other traditional conservatives resented the influence of neoconservatives as well as criticized neoconservatives' acceptance of the welfare state, activist foreign policy, and unconditional support of Israel. The conflation of these two strands of conservatism as one in the public mind also has created annoyance, if not outright antagonism, between these two groups.[61]

CULTURE AND CAPITALISM

Neoconservatives supported the Reagan administration's vigorous anti-communist and activist foreign policy, particularly in US support of "freedom fighters" in Nicaragua and Afghanistan as well as the introduction of the Strategic Defense Initiative (SDI) to defend the United States from Soviet nuclear missiles.[62] They also approved of Reagan's rhetoric calling the Soviet Union an "evil empire." According to their beliefs, neoconservatives' ideas and policies were responsible for the collapse of communism in Eastern Europe and the Soviet Union.

However, a closer examination of the Reagan administration foreign policy reveals that neoconservatives had influence in policy formulation and decision but it was limited.[63] Neoconservatives did not occupy any key foreign policy posts in the Reagan administration and they often disagreed among themselves. Furthermore, the realist camp in the Reagan administration ultimately emerged victorious with the ratification of 1987 the Intermediate-Range Nuclear Force Treaty and the start of talks for the 1991 Strategic Arms Reduction Treaty. In short, neoconservatives were influential but not dominant, especially in the second term, of the Reagan administration's foreign policy.

Neoconservatives also championed capitalism but, unlike their neoliberal counterparts, believed its success depended upon community and virtue rather than on individual entrepreneurial freedom, free markets, private property, and free trade.[64] In publications like *The Public Interest* and *The National Interest* (1985–) Irving Kristol played a crucial role in the publication of the works of thinkers like Jude Wanniski, George Gilder, and others who laid the foundation of what later became known as "Reaganomics."[65] The theory is that government revenue increases when tax rates are low because people will work harder when they are allowed to keep their money, and, since people make more money, there will be more for the government to tax. However, neoconservatives were worried that capitalist society without a virtuous culture would ultimately collapse because the values that sustain capitalism would be undermined by the commodification of values and the radical individualism of capitalism.[66]

Even with the United States' success in the Cold War, neoconservatives believed this victory would be pyrrhic unless "Victorian values" could reassert themselves in American culture and higher education.[67] Criticizing multiculturalism, philosophical relativism, and Marxist politics, neoconservatives in their publications, such as *The New Criterion* (1982–) and *First Things* (1990–), and organizations, like the National Association of Scholars (1987–), advocated for a return to educational standards and behavior based on the "great books" of Western civilization, traditional sexual propriety, and a deference to academic and familial authority.[68] Neoconservatives found allies with socially conservative Christian groups—the Moral Majority in the 1980s, the Christian Coalition in the 1990s—to push back against the cultural and educational values of the New Left.[69] However, their success was limited as the commanding heights of mainstream culture—entertainment, education, and media—remained a bastion for New Left values.[70]

THE NEXT GENERATION

The end of the Cold War led some neoconservatives to think it was "the end of history," as Francis Fukuyama (1952–) wrote initially in *The National Interest* in 1989 and later a book in 1992.[71] According to Fukuyama, there is a universal desire to live in a modern society with its technology, high standard of living, and access to the global world. Economic modernization tends to drive political participation in the creation of a middle class with its concern about education, protection of property, and individual rights. Over time, liberal democracy becomes a universal aspiration. However, this historical process is not inevitable, with chance, agency, and ideas playing a role in the outcome of a regime.[72] Nevertheless, history is conceived as ultimately progressive in a teleological sense with liberal democracy as the final goal, regardless of whether it is realized.

In this era of the "end of history," neoconservatives were divided among themselves, with the older generation like Irving Kristol, Jeane Kirkpatrick, and Nathan Glazer calling for a more limited interpretation of national interest, while the younger generation, such as William Kristol (1952–) and Robert Kagan (1958–), advocating an expansive, interventionalist foreign policy of promoting liberal democracy abroad.[73] Calling for a return to "national greatness," younger neoconservatives rejected the Clinton administration's wavering humanitarian intervention in Somalia, Rwanda, Haiti, and Balkans during the 1990s and criticized the administration for not articulating a national purpose in American foreign policy.[74] These neoconservatives established the think tank, Project for a New American Century (PNAC)

(1997–2009), which outlined the objectives of challenging regimes hostile to American interests and values, increasing the US defense budget, promoting economic and political freedom abroad, strengthening democratic alliances, and preserving America's hegemonic role in international politics.[75]

Strangely, this second generation of neoconservatives had little, if anything, to say about the formation of new international institutions that governed and regulated global trade and investment, like the General Agreement on Tariffs and Trades (GATT) and the World Trade Organization (WTO). One has to look at the first generation of neoconservatives for commentary on the international economic policy, which generally followed the positions of neoliberals.[76] But in terms of political and military foreign policy, this second generation of neoconservatives rejected liberal internationalism and supported the US promotion of democracy abroad, even if it required regime change in Iran, Iraq, North Korea, and China, a view articulated in publications like *Commentary* and *The Weekly Standard* (1995–2018).[77]

THE BUSH DOCTRINE

In spite of their interest and expertise in foreign affairs, neoconservatives missed the threat of 9/11 to the United States. According to neoconservatives, rouge states with weapons of mass destruction, China, Russia, and regional challenges to American hegemony should be the US' foreign policy priorities.[78] Terrorism was barely mentioned. But when 9/11 did occur, neoconservatives quickly interpreted the event in ideological and stark existential terms, viewing the threat of radical Islam as broadly characterizing the Islamic world rather than seeing that the ideology of radical Islam is held only by a minority of Muslims.[79] The fact that most Muslims disliked US foreign policy (e.g., support of Israel and the House of Saud) rather than the United States itself was ignored by neoconservatives.[80] Instead neoconservatives claimed that the failure of the United States to project its power overseas during the 1990s—Saddam Hussein remaining in power in Iraq; the withdrawal from Somalia after American soldiers were killed; and the attacks on the World Trade Center in 1993, American military bases in Saudi Arabia in 1996, American embassies in Africa in 1998, and the Navy's USS *Cole* in 2000—all encouraged the terrorists to attack the United States.[81]

The response of the George W. Bush administration to 9/11 was to create a new federal agency, the Department of Homeland Security; pass new legislation, the Patriot Act, to give domestic law enforcement greater power to prevent terrorism; and announce a new strategic doctrine of preventive war that would fight enemies abroad rather than rely upon containment and deterrence.[82] The result of this new strategic doctrine was the 2001 invasion of Afghanistan and the 2003 invasion of Iraq.[83] Neoconservatives supported all these actions but especially Bush's new strategic doctrine and the invasion of Iraq, shifting US focus from al-Qaeda to Saddam Hussein.[84] These policies were the realization of neoconservative ideas of regime change, benevolent hegemony, preemption, and American exceptionalism and ultimately became known as the Bush Doctrine.[85]

One of the intellectual influences on the formulation of the Bush Doctrine was Albert Wohlstetter (1913–1997) who was a teacher of Paul Wolfowitz (1943–), US Deputy Secretary of Defense (2001–2005); Richard Perle, Chairman of Defense Policy Board Advisory Committee (2001–2003), and Zalmay Khalilzad (1951–), US Ambassador to Afghanistan (2003–2005), Iraq (2005–2007), and the United Nations (2007–2009).[86] Wohlstetter was an influential and controversial nuclear strategist at the RAND Corporation and later the University of Chicago. Wohlstetter believed in nuclear deterrence—countries had to worry about their vulnerability to a nuclear strike—and was skeptical about the 1968 Nonproliferation Treaty, which allowed countries having only civilian nuclear power, and the 1972 and 1979 Strategic Arms Limitation Talks Treaties, which limited American and Soviet offensive nuclear weapons but did not address the Soviet counterforce capacities.

A second but less important influence was Leo Strauss (1899–1973) whose student, Allan Bloom (1930–1992) briefly taught Paul Wolfowitz.[87] Strauss was a political philosopher who spent most of his academic career at the University of Chicago where he taught students about natural rights, the relationship between reason and faith, and problems of philosophical relativism.[88] Strauss did not write directly about contemporary politics but his students politicized his writings by contending the United States was the apotheosis of the Western philosophical tradition and that the cultural values of this tradition were being undermined by philosophical relativism at American colleges and universities.[89] His students also emphasized the importance of the political regime and how the regime shaped the institutions and cultural values of a society which comported with the Bush Doctrine of regime change.[90]

After the American victory in Iraq, the Bush administration had unrealistic and optimistic assumptions about the post-Saddam country that ignored the reality that regime change was a slow and difficult process and not just a matter of removing the old regime.[91] Furthermore, the mismanagement of the American occupation of Iraq, including the torture of Iraqi prisoners, and the absence of weapons of mass destruction led some neoconservatives, such as Richard Perle and David Brooks, to distance themselves from the war and even some, like Francis Fukuyama and Michael Lind, to break ranks with the neoconservatives.[92] However, most neoconservatives continued to defend the Iraq War and its aftermath, with the 2004 reelection of George W. Bush to the presidency confirming their support.[93]

Like Ronald Reagan in his second term, George W. Bush favored the realists in his own foreign policy after his reelection with Condoleezza Rice serving as Secretary of State and neoconservatives Paul Wolfowitz and Douglas Feith leaving government.[94] The setbacks in a post-Saddam Iraq as well as the new assertiveness of Iran and North Korea forced the Bush administration to acknowledge a decline in American power and consequently adopt a different approach to foreign policy. Although neoconservatives still had influence in the Bush administration, such as the president's approval of increased troop strength in Iraq to restore security in order to create a space for political reconciliation, their mark in the second term of the Bush administration's foreign policy was severely diminished.[95]

THE AFTERMATH

There have been several analyses about the failure of the Bush doctrine with its neoconservative vision of regime change in Iraq. For example, Vaïsse attributes overconfidence and arrogance to neoconservatives after America's victory in the Cold War as well as the second generation's intellectual laziness in lacking regional expertise, properly understanding the nature of radical Islam, and a naïvete about the power of democracy to change a society's culture and institutions.[96] Drolet also agrees with Vaïsse's analysis that neoconservatives' lack of humility combined with a flawed understanding of politics—an ahistorical and acontextual account of politics with a fetishization of political culture—that led to neoconservatives' imperial delusions.[97] Cooper, who is more sympathetic to neoconservatives, nevertheless acknowledges that their ideology about the importance of regime—and regime change—was not adequately examined by neoconservatives to see whether this premise is correct.[98]

By contrast, Halper and Clarke favor the realist school of diplomacy to address the Iraqi crisis and believe that the Iraq War ultimately was a distraction from the US' global war on terrorism (i.e., Afghanistan), leading to a rise in global negative perception of the United States.[99] Fukuyama, who had left neoconservatism, believes it is the lack of competence in the Bush administration and neoconservatives, and more broadly the United States' foreign policy establishment, to govern global affairs and therefore should adopt a different foreign policy that is open to new, innovative, and transparent international organizations, rules, and laws.[100] But instead of reexamining their ideas and policies, most neoconservatives refused to admit their mistakes and instead focused on a "league of democracies" rather than regime change so that the world's democracies could promote and defend their values.[101]

Neoconservatives continued to have a strong national presence in the media and think tanks with the *Foreign Policy Initiative* (2009–2017) and *Global Governance Watch* (2003–2007, 2009–) that criticized the Obama administration's foreign policy.[102] During this period, neoconservatives' major concerns were Obama's overtures to Iran, China's military assertiveness, and fear of a decline of American power.[103] But not being in the Obama administration, neoconservatives had no influence or impact on American foreign policy.

With the 2016 election of Donald Trump to the presidency, neoconservatives have some influence with the appointment of John Bolton (1948–) as National Security Advisor (2018–) and supported the Trump administration's foreign policy of not certificating the Obama administration's Joint Comprehensive Plan of Action with Iran, relocating the American Embassy in Israel to Jerusalem, and increasing the US defense budget.[104] However, the relationship has been ambiguous, partially because Trump himself lacks clear ideological and policy positions and partially because neoconservatives disdain Trump's lack of policy expertise and personality.[105] It remains to be seen whether neoconservatives will ultimately endorse the Trump administration, selectively support it, or act as an alternative and even opposition voice.

The success of neoconservatives in American politics and policy has been effective but limited. While there has been a halt to the expansion of social welfare programs in the 1980s and 1990s, the George W. Bush administration passed the 2003 Medicare Modernization Act and the Obama administration passed the 2010 Patient Protection and Affordable Care Act. Furthermore, the 2015 *Obergefell v. Hodges* case, the entrenchment of multiculturalism in American universities, and the Left's control of mainstream media and entertainment are contrary to neoconservatives social and educational values. Finally, neoconservative's skepticism about international institutions and rules and a belief in American hegemony in international politics are dependent if a Republican, and one who agrees with their views, is president. In short, neoconservatives have created an idea and policy infrastructure that reflects their views but it is only one of many perspectives about American politics and foreign affairs that exist.

Although neoconservatives have changed their partisan affiliations, their roots stretch back to a New Deal liberalism and, at least for the first generation, saw themselves as the true heirs of this movement. Because of its origins, Vaïsse argues that a history of neoconservatism belongs to a history of liberalism *and* conservatism and that neoconservatism is both a new school of thought *and* a reaction to the New Left.[106] Drolet disagrees, stating that neoconservatism is "a reaction to liberal modernity and the cultural forces the latter generates."[107] Reviewing the evolution of neoconservatism, I believe both scholars are correct: the first generation of neoconservatives were both liberal and conservative, reactionary and innovative, while the second generation of neoconservatives belong to the conservative school of thought that is different from libertarianism and traditional conservatism. Over time we will see how neoconservatism will develop in the future–whether it will continue on a new path, return to its origins, or assimilates with other ideologies. In the meantime it will be interesting to see how neoconservatives preserve, adopt, and adjust their ideas and policies in the ever-changing world of politics.

NOTES

1. I would like to thank Richard Avramenko, the Center for the Study of Liberal Democracy at the University of Wisconsin-Madison, and Saginaw Valley State University for supporting my sabbatical which enabled me to write this chapter and co-edit this volume.

2. Norman Podhoretz, *Breaking Ranks: A Political Memoir* (New York: Harper and Row, 1979); Peter Steinfels, *The Neoconservatives: The Origins of a Movement* (New York: Simon & Schuster, 1979a); and *The Neoconservatives: The Men Who Are Changing America's Politics* (New York: Simon & Schuster, 1979b); Irving Kristol, *Reflections of a Neoconservative* (New York: Basic Books, 1983); *Neoconservatism: The Autobiography of an Idea* (New York: Free Press, 1995d); *Ex-Friends* (New York: Free Press, 1999); and "Neoconservatism: A Eulogy," in *The Norman Podhoretz Reader*, Thomas L. Jeffers, ed. (New York: Free Press, 2004), 269–84; Alexander Bloom, *Prodigal Sons: The New York Intellectuals and Their World* (Oxford: Oxford University Press, 1986); Alan M. Wald, *The New York Intellectuals: The Rise and Decline of the Anti-Stalinist Left from the 1930s to the 1980s* (Chapel Hill, NC: University of North Carolina Press, 1987); Gary Dorrien, *The Neoconservative Mind: Politics, Culture, and the War of Ideology* (Philadelphia: Temple University Press, 1993); Jacob Heilbrunn, *They Knew They Were Right: The Rise of the Neocons* (New York: Doubleday, 2008); Justin Vaïsse, *Neoconservatism: The Biography of a Movement* (Cambridge, MA: Belknap, 2010); Joseph Dorman, *Arguing the World: New York Intellectuals in Their Own Words* (Chicago: University of Chicago Press, 2001); Murray Friedman, *Jewish Intellectuals and the Shaping of Public Policy* (Cambridge: Cambridge University Press, 2004), 1–63; Alan Frachon and Daniel Vernet, *L'Amérique messianique* (Paris: Editions de Seuil, 2004); Adam L. Fuller, *Taking the Fight to the Enemy: Neoconservatism and the Age of Ideology* (Lanham, MD: Lexington Books, 2012).

3. Daniel Bell, "First Love and Early Sorrow," *Times Higher Education Supplement* (January 16, 1981), available at http://www.pbs.org/aruging/nyintellectuals_bell_2.html; and "Afterword, 1988: The End of Ideology Revisited" in *The End of Ideology: On the Exhaustion of Political Ideas in the Fifties* (Cambridge, MA: Harvard University Press, 1988a), 415; Irving Kristol, "Memoirs of a Trotskyist," in *Neoconservatism: The Autobiography of an Idea* (New York: Free Press, 1995a), 469–80; Seymour Martin Lipset, "Out of the Alcoves," *The Wilson Quarterly* 23/1 (1999): 37–48.

4. For more about the fighting among the American political Left, see John Ehrman, *The Rise of the Neoconservatism: Intellectuals and Foreign Affairs 1945–1994* (New Haven: Yale University Press, 1994), 1–32; John Diggins, *The Rise and Fall of the American Left* (New York: W.W. Norton, 1992), 145–210; Friedman, *The Neoconservative Revolution*, 62–79.

5. Kristol, *Reflections of a Neoconservative*, x–xi.

6. Arthur M. Schlesinger Jr. *The Vital Center: The Politics of Freedom* (Boston: Houghton Mifflin, 1949), 244; also see Thomas J. McCormick, *America's Half-Century: United States Foreign Policy in the Cold War and After* (Baltimore: John Hopkins University Press, 1995); and Robert Latham, *The Liberal Moment: Modernity, Security, and the Making of Postwar International Order* (New York: Columbia University Press, 1997).

7. Steve Fraser and Gary Gerstle, *The Rise and Fall of the New Deal Order, 1930–1980* (Princeton: Princeton University Press, 1990).

8. Lionel Trilling, *The Liberal Imagination* (New York: Anchor Books, 1950); Louis Hartz, *The Liberal Tradition in America* (New York: Harcourt Brace Jovanovich, 1955); George Nash, *The Conservative Intellectual Movement in America since 1945* (New York: Harper, 1976).

9. Kenneth Prewitt, "Political Ideas and a Political Science for Policy," *The Annals of the American Academy of Political and Social Science* 600/1 (2005): 14–29; Lee Trepanier, "The Relevance of Political Philosophy and Political Science" in *Why the Humanities Matter Today: In Defense of Liberal Education*. Lee Trepanier, ed. (Lanham, MD: Lexington Books, 2017): 127–44.

10. Daniel Bell, *The End of Ideology: On the Exhaustion of Political Ideas in the Fifties* (Cambridge, MA: Harvard University Press, 1988b); also see Chaim I. Waxman, ed., *The End of Ideology Debate* (New York: Funk and Wagnalls, 1968).

11. William F. Buckley, *God and Man at Yale* (Chicago: Regency, 1951); Eric Voegelin, *The New Science of Politics* (Chicago: University of Chicago Press, 1952); Russell Kirk, *The Conservative Mind* (Chicago: Regency, 1953); Leo Strauss, *Natural Right and History* (Chicago: University of Chicago Press, 1953); Friedrich von Hayek, *The Constitution of Liberty* (Chicago: University of Chicago Press, 1960).

12. Nash, *The Conservative Intellectual Movement*; Sara Diamond, *Roads to Dominion: Right-Wing Movements and Political Power in the United States* (New York: Guildford Press, 1995); also see Friedman, *The Neoconservative Revolution*, 80–99.

13. Kevin Phillips, *The Emerging Republican Majority* (New York: Anchor Books, 1970); Mary C. Brennan, *Turning Right in the Sixties: The Conservative Capture of the GOP* (Chapel Hill: University of North Carolina Press, 1995); John A. Andrew III, *The Other Side of the Sixties: Young Americans for Freedom and the Rise of Conservative Politics* (New Brunswick, NJ: Rutgers University Press, 1997).

14. Lee Edwards, *The Conservative Revolution* (New York: Free Press, 1999); Jonathan M. Schoenwald, *A Time for Choosing: The Rise of Modern American Conservatism* (Oxford: Oxford University Press, 2001).

15. William O'Neill, *The New Left: A History* (Wheeling, IL: Harlan Davidson, 2001); Van Goose, *Rethinking the New Left: An Interpretative History* (London: Palgrave Macmillan, 2006).

16. Students for a Democratic Society, *Port Huron Statement*, June 15, 1962, available at https://archive.org/details/PortHuronStatement/page/n0.

17. Goose, *Rethinking the New Left*; William O'Neill, *Coming Apart: An Informal History of America in the 1960s* (New York: Times Books, 1974).

18. Ibid.; also see Christopher Lasch, *The Agony of the American Left* (New York: Knopf, 1969).

19. Jeane Kirkpatrick, "Neoconservatism as a Response to the Counter-Culture," in *The Neocon Reader*, Irwin Stelzer, ed. (New York: Grove Press): 234–40.

20. Stephen H. Norwood, *Anti-Semitism and the American Far Left* (Cambridge: Cambridge University Press, 2013).

21. Joshua Muravchik, "Operational Comeback," *Foreign Policy* (October 16, 2009), available at https://foreignpolicy.com/2009/10/16/the-fp-memo-operation-comeback/.

22. Michael Harrington, "The Welfare State and Its Neoconservative Critics," *Dissent* (Fall 197), available at https://www.dissentmagazine.org/article/the-welfare-state-and-its-neoconservative-critics. Irving Kristol, "Confessions of a True, Self-Confessed Neoconservative," *Public Opinion* (October/November 1979).

23. William Kristol, "Will Obama Save Liberalism?" *New York Times*, January 26, 2009, available at https://www.nytimes.com/2009/01/26/opinion/26kristol.html; also see Friedman, *The Neoconservative Revolution*, 100–136.

24. Tod Lindberg, "Neoconservatism Liberal Legacy," *Policy Review*, October 1, 2004, available at https://www.hoover.org/research/neoconservatisms-liberal-legacy; Kristol, *Reflections of a Neoconservative*, 75; also see Hilton Kramer and Roger Kimball, eds., *The Betrayal*

of Liberalism: How the Disciples of Freedom and Equality Helped Foster the Illiberal Politics of Coercion and Control (New York: Ivan R. Dee, 1985).

25. Kristol, *Reflections of a Neoconservative*, xii.

26. Irving Kristol, "The Neoconservative Persuasion: What It Was and What It Is," *The Weekly Standard*, August 25, 2003, available at https://www.weeklystandard.com/irving-kristol/the-neoconservative-persuasion.

27. Daniel Bell and Irving Kristol, "What Is the Public Interest?" *The Public Interest* (1965): 3–6; also see Irving Kristol, "Skepticism, Meliorism and *The Public Interest*," *The Public Interest* (1985): 31–42; Seymour Martin Lipset, "The Wavering Polls," *The Public Interest* (1976): 70–90. Online access to *The Public Interest* archives are available at https://www.nationalaffairs.com/.

28. Nathan Abrams, *Norman Podhoretz and Commentary Magazine: The Rise and Fall of the Neocons* (London: Continuum, 2010). Online access to *Commentary* is available at https://www.commentarymagazine.com/; online access to *Policy Review* archives are available at https://www.hoover.org/publications/policy-review.

29. Some of the articles written in *The Public Interest* were expanded into published books, such as Daniel Patrick Moynihan, *Maximum Feasible Misunderstanding* (New York: Free Press, 1970); and *The Politics of Guaranteed Income* (New York: Vintage, 1973); Nathan Glazer, *Affirmative Discrimination* (New York: Basic Books, 1975); James Q. Wilson, *Thinking about Crime* (New York: Simon & Schuster, 1985); Charles Murray, *Losing Ground: American Social Policy: 1950–1980* (New York: Basic Books, 1984).

30. Nathan Glazer and Daniel Patrick Moynihan, *Beyond the Melting Pot: The Negroes, Puerto Ricans, Jews, and Irish of New York* (Cambridge, MA: MIT Press, 1963).

31. Daniel Patrick Moynihan, *The Negro Family: A Case for National Action* (Washington, DC: Office of Policy Planning and Research, US Department of Labor, 1965).

32. Lee Rainwater and William L. Yancey, *The Moynihan Report and the Politics of Controversy* (Cambridge, MA: MIT Press, 1967).

33. James Q. Wilson, "Liberalism versus Liberal Education," *Commentary* (June 1972): 50–55.

34. Irving Kristol, "Teaching In, Speaking Out: The Controversy over Vietnam," *Encounter* (August 1965): 65–70; Daniel Patrick Moynihan and Irving Kristol, eds., *Confrontation: The Student Rebellion and the Universities* (New York: Basic Books, 1968).

35. Irving Kristol, *Two Cheers for Capitalism* (New York: Basic Books, 1978b), 171; see Nathan Glazer, "The Limits of Social Policy," *Commentary* (September 1971): 51–59.

36. For example, Eveline M. Burns, "Where Welfare Falls Short," *The Public Interest* (Fall 1965): 82–95; Gilbert Y. Steiner, "Reform Follow Reality: The Growth of Welfare," *The Public Interest* (Winter 1974): 47–65; Marc F. Plattner, "The Welfare State vs. the Redistributive State," *The Public Interest* (Spring 1979): 28–48; Bradley R. Schiller, "Welfare: Reforming Our Expectations" *The Public Interest* (Winter 1981): 55–65; Nathan Glazer, "Towards a Self-Service Society?" *The Public Interest* (Winter 1983): 66–90; Charles Murray, *Losing Ground*; Michael Harrington, *The New American Poverty* (New York: Henry Holt Publishing, 1984); Steven Kelman, "'Public Choice' and Public Spirit," *The Public Interest* (Spring 1987): 80–94. School choice is a particular policy that neoconservatives have supported where responsibility falls to local authorities and individuals. See David K. Cohen and Eleanor Farrar, "Power to the Parents?—The Story of Education Vouchers," *The Public Interest* (Summer 1977): 72–97; Myron Lieberman, *Privatization and Education Choice* (New York: Palgrave Macmillan, 1989); and "School Choice Schism," *The Public Interest* (Spring 2002): 122–25; John E. Chubb and Terry M. Moe, *Politics, Markets, and American Schools* (Washington, DC: Brookings Institute, 1990); Christine Roch, Mark Schneider, Melissa Marschall, and Paul Teske, "School Choice Builds Community," *The Public Interest* (Fall 1997): 86–90; Brian Elliott and David MacLennan, "Education, Modernity, and Neo-Conservative School Reform in Canada, Britain, and the U.S." *British Journal of Sociology of Education* 15/2 (1994): 165–85.

37. George H. Quester, *American Foreign Policy: The Lost Consensus* (Santa Barbara, CA: Praeger, 1982); Arthur Schlesinger Jr., "Reinhold Niebuhr's Long Shadow," *New York Times* (June 22, 1992), available at https://www.nytimes.com/1992/06/22/opinion/reinhold-niebuhr-s-

long-shadow.html; also see Diggins, *The Rise and Fall of the American Left*, 145–210; Kristol, *Reflections of a Neoconservative*, x–xi.

38. Michael Gerson, *The Neoconservative Vision: From Cold War to Culture Wars* (Lanham, MD: Madison Books, 1997), 112–16; Irving Kristol, "Facing the Facts in Vietnam," *The New Leader* (September 30, 1963); and "We Can't Resign as Policeman of the World," *New York Times Magazine* (May 12, 1968); Nathan Glazer, "The New Left and Its Limits," *Commentary* (July 1968): 31–40.

39. Nathan Glazer, *Remembering the Answers: Essays on the American Student Revolt* (New York: Basic Books, 1972); Jeane Kirkpatrick, "The Revolt of the Masses," *Commentary* (February 1973): 58–62; and "Neoconservatism as a Response to the Counter-Culture"; also see O'Neill, *The New Left* and *Coming Apart*; Goose, *Rethinking the New Left*.

40. Irving Kristol, "Urban Civilization and Its Discontents," *Commentary* (July 1970a): 34–35.

41. Norman Podhoretz, "New Vistas for Neoconservatives," *Conservative Digest* 15 (1989): 56–57

42. Theodore Draper, "The Specter of Weimar," *Commentary* (December 1971): 43–50.

43. Theodore H. White, *The Making of the President 1972* (New York: Antheneum Publishers, 1973), 17–33, 283–87.

44. Seymour Martin Lipset, *American Exceptionalism: A Double-Edged Sword* (New York: W. W. Norton, 1996), 198. For about Senator Jackson's presidential bids, see Robert G. Kaufman, *Henry M. Jackson: A Life in Politics* (Seattle: University of Washington Press, 2000), 223–41, 301–40; For more about the CDM, see Justin Vaïsse, *Neoconservatism*, 86–100.

45. The reference "mugged by reality" is from Irving Kristol's quote, "[a neoconservative] is a liberal who has been mugged by reality. A neoliberal is a liberal who got mugged by reality but has not pressed charges." Douglas Murray, *Neoconservatism: Why We Need It* (San Francisco: Encounter, 2006), 89.

46. Kristol, *Reflections of a Neoconservative*, xii–xiv.

47. James A. Smith, *The Idea Brokers: Think Tanks and the Rise of the New Policy Elite* (New York: Free Press, 1991); Murray Friedman, *The Neoconservative Revolution: Jewish Intellectuals and the Shaping of Public Policy* (Cambridge: Cambridge University Press, 2005), 133; Paul Gottfried, *Conservatism in America: Making Sense of the American Right* (New York: Palgrave Macmillan, 2007), 59–68; Irving Kristol, *The Problem of Doing Good: Irving Kristol's Philanthropy* (Washington DC: Hudson Institute, 2010).

48. Norman Podhoretz, "The Culture of Appeasement," *Harper's* (October 1977), available at https://harpers.org/archive/1977/10/the-culture-of-appeasement/; Gerson, *The Neoconservative Vision*, 167–68.

49. P. T. Bauer, "Western Guilt and Third World Poverty," *Commentary* (January 1976): 31–39; Daniel Patrick Moynihan, *A Dangerous Place* (New York: Little, Brown, 1976), 158; Gerson, *The Neoconservative Vision*, 158.

50. Daniel Patrick Moynihan, "The United States in Opposition," *Commentary* (March 1975): 31–45.

51. Jeane Kirkpatrick, *The Reagan Phenomenon—and Other Speeches on Foreign Policy* (Washington DC: American Enterprise Institute Press, 1982), 111–12.

52. Henry Kissinger, *A World Restored: Europe after Napoleon* (Gloucester, MA: Peter Smith, 1973); *Diplomacy* (New York: Simon & Schuster, 1994); and "Between the Old Left and the New Right," *Foreign Affairs* 78/3 (1999): 99–116.

53. Commentary Symposium, "America Now: A Failure of Nerve?" *Commentary* (July 1975): 16–98; Norman Podhoretz, "Making the World Safe for Communism," *Commentary* (April 1976): 31–42; Dana H. Allin, *Cold War Illusions: America, Europe, and Soviet Power, 1969–1989* (New York: St. Martin's Press, 1976), 31–42.

54. Irving Kristol, "My Cold War," in *Neoconservatism: The Autobiography of an Idea* (New York: Free Press, 1995b), 481–86.

55. Walter Laqueur, "Kissinger and the Politics of Détente," *Commentary* (December 1973): 46–53; also see McCormick, *America's Half Century*, 179–80.

56. Lipset, *American Exceptionalism*, 194; Jerry Sanders, *Peddlers of Crisis: The Committee on the Present Dangers and the Politics of Containment* (Boston: South End Press, 1983); Vaïsse, *Neoconservatism*, 180–219.

57. Diamond, *Roads to Dominion*, 197–200.

58. Norman Podhoretz, "The Neo-Conservative Anguish over Reagan's Foreign Policy," *New York Times Magazine* (May 2, 1982): 30–31; Fred Halliday, *The Making of the Second Cold War* (London: Verso, 1986); William A. Niskanen, *Reaganomics: An Insider's Account of Policies and the People* (Oxford: Oxford University Press, 1988).

59. Sanders, *Peddlers*, 9; Friedman, *The Neoconservative Revolution*, 137–60; Vaïsse, *Neoconservatism*, 203–8.

60. Paul Gottfried, *Conservatism in America*, 43–76, 93–113; Friedman, *The Neoconservative Revolution*, 132–36.

61. The split between traditional and neoconservatives continued after the conclusion of the Cold War with the traditional conservatives opposing American intervention in the 1991 Gulf War and the 2003 Iraq Invasion as well as objecting the expansion of the federal government under George W. Bush administration (e.g., 2002 Homeland Security Act; 2003 Medicare Modernization Act). For more, see Ibid.

62. Friedman, *The Neoconservative Revolution*, 161–76; Jay Winik, *On the Brink: The Dramatic, Behind-the-Scenes Saga of the Reagan Era and the Men and Women Who Won the Cold War* (New York: Simon & Schuster, 1996); Frances FitzGerald, *Way Out There in the Blue: Reagan, Star Wars, and the End of the Cold War* (New York: Simon & Schuster, 2000); Jesus Velasco, *Neoconservatives in U.S. Foreign Policy under Ronald Reagan and George W. Bush: Voices behind the Throne* (Baltimore: John Hopkins University Press, 2010).

63. Vaïsse, *Neoconservatism*, 186–97.

64. Daniel Bell, *The Cultural Contradictions of Capitalism* (New York: Basic Books, 1978); Daniel Bell and Irving Kristol, eds., *Capitalism Today* (New York: Basic Books, 1972); and Commentary Symposium, "Capitalism, Socialism, and Nihilism," *Commentary* (April 1978a): 29–72; For more about the relationship between neoliberals and neoconservatives, see Jean-François Drolet, *American Neoconservatism: The Politics and Culture of a Reactionary Idealism* (London: Hurst and Company, 2011), 91–122.

65. June Wanniski, *The Way the World Works* (New York: Gateway Books, 1978a) and "Taxes, Revenues, and the 'Laffer Curve,'" *The Public Interest* (Winter 1978b): 3–16; Irving Kristol, "Ideology and Supply-Side Economics," *Commentary* (April 1981): 48–56; George Gilder, *Wealth and Poverty* (New York: Basic Books, 1981); and "A Supply-Side Economics of the Left," *The Public Interest* (Summer 1983): 29–43; also see Michael Novak, *The Spirit of Democratic Capitalism* (Lanham, MD: Madison Books, 1991); Friedman, *The Neoconservative Revolution*, 181–204; Gerson, *The Neoconservative Vision*, 204–6; Vaïsse, *Neoconservatism*, 203–6. The *National Interest* was founded by Irving Kristol in 1985 with a focus on foreign policy and international politics. Its archives are available at https://nationalinterest.org/.

66. Bell, *The Cultural Contradictions*; Irving Kristol, "When Virtue Loses All Her Loveliness—Some Reflections on Capitalism and 'The Free Society,'" *The Public Interest* (Fall 1970b): 3–12; *Two Cheers for Capitalism* and "Adam Smith and the Spirit of Capitalism," in *Neoconservatism*, 258–299.

67. Kristol, *Neoconservatism*, 486; Gertrude Himmelfarb, *The New History and the Old* (Cambridge, MA: Harvard University Press, 1987) and *The Demoralization of Society: From Victorian Virtues to Modern Values* (New York: Knopf, 1995).

68. Hilton Kramer, *The Revenge of the Philistines: Arts and Culture, 1972–1984* (New York: Free Press, 1985); Allan Bloom, *The Closing of the American Mind* (New York: Simon & Schuster, 1987); James Q. Wilson, *The Moral Sense* (New York: Free Press, 1993); and "Cultural Meltdown," *The Public Interest* (Fall 1999): 99–104; Diane Ravitch, *The Language Police: How Pressure Groups Restrict What Students Learn* (New York: Knopf, 2003).

69. Friedman, *The Neoconservative Revolution*, 205–23.

70. For example, see Time Groseclose, *Left Turn: How Liberal Media Bias Distorts the American Mind* (New York: St. Martin's Press, 2011); and Neil Gross, *Why Are Professors Liberal and Why Do Conservatives Care?* (Cambridge, MA: Harvard University Press, 2013). *First Things* and *The New Criterion* also features criticisms of American art, culture, and

entertainment as advocating New Left values. *First Things* is available at https://www.firstthings.com/; and *The New Criterion* is available at https://www.newcriterion.com/.

71. Francis Fukuyama, "The End of History," *The National Interest* (Summer 1989): 3–18 and *The End of History and the Last Man* (New York: Free Press, 1992).

72. For more about the debate about Fukuyama's thesis, see Fukuyama, *America at the Crossroads: Democracy, Power, and the Neoconservative Legacy* (New Haven: Yale University Press, 2006), 53–61.

73. Jeane Kirkpatrick, "A Normal Country in a Normal Time," *The National Interest* (Fall 1990): 40–43; Irving Kristol, "Defining Our National Interest," *The National Interest* (Fall 1990): 16–25; Nathan Glazer, "A Time for Modesty," in *America's Purpose: New Visions of US Foreign Policy*, Owen Harries, ed. (San Francisco: Institute of Contemporary Studies, 1991), 133–41; William Kristol and Robert Kagan, "Toward a Neo-Reaganite Foreign Policy," *Foreign Affairs* 75/4 (1996): 18–32; and *Present Dangers: Crisis and Opportunity in American Foreign and Defense Policy* (San Francisco: Encounter, 2000b); David Brooks, "A Return to National Greatness," *The Weekly Standard* (March 3, 1997), available at https://www.weeklystandard.com/david-brooks/a-return-to-national-greatness; Robert Kagan, "America's Crisis of Legitimacy," *Foreign Affairs* 83/2 (2004): 65–87; and "A Matter of Record," *Foreign Affairs* 84/1 (2005): 170–73; also see Robert W. Tucker and David C. Hendrickson, "The Sources of American Legitimacy," *Foreign Affairs* 83/6 (2004): 18–32.

74. Robert Kaplan, "The Coming Anarchy," *Atlantic Monthly* 273/2 (1994): 44–76; and *Paradise and Power: America and Europe in the New World Order* (London: Atlantic Books, 2003); Donald Kagan and Frederick W. Kagan, *While America Sleeps: Self-Delusions, Military Weakness, and the Threat to Peace Today* (New York: St. Martin's Press, 2000); Paul Wolfowitz, "Remembering the Future," *The National Interest* (Summer 2000): 67–73; Stefan Halper and Jonathan Clarke, *America Alone: The Neo-Conservatives and the Global Order* (Cambridge: Cambridge University Press, 2004), 74–111.

75. Project for the New American Century, "Statement of Principles," (June 1997), available at http://www.newamericancentury.org. PNAC would be succeeded by the think tank, *The Foreign Policy Initiative* (2009–2017). The archives are available at https://web.archive.org/web/20130609011554/http://newamericancentury.org/ and https://foreignpolicyi.org/.

76. Fukuyama, *America at the Crossroads*, 43–45.

77. The archives of *The Weekly Standard* are available at https://www.weeklystandard.com/.

78. Kagan and Kristol, *Present Dangers*; Commentary Symposium, "America Power–For What? A Symposium" (January 2000a), available at https://www.commentarymagazine.com/articles/american-power-for-what/.

79. Eliot Cohen, "World War IV: Let's Call the Conflict What It Is," *Wall Street Journal* (November 20, 2001), available at https://www.wsj.com/articles/SB1006219259392114120; Norman Podhoretz, "World War IV: How It Started, What It Means, and Why We Have to Win," *Commentary* (2004): 17–54; and *World War IV: The Long Struggle Against Islamofascism* (New York: Doubleday, 2007); Charles Krauthammer, "In Defense of Democratic Realism," *The National Interest* (Fall 2004), available at https://nationalinterest.org/article/in-defense-of-democratic-realism-699. For a contrary view, see Oliver Roy, *The Failure of Political Islam* (Cambridge, MA: Harvard University Press, 1996); and *Globalized Islam: The Search for a New Universal* (New York: Columbia University Press, 2004); also see The National Commission on Terrorist Attacks, *The 9/11 Commission Report: Final Report of the National Commission on Terrorist Attacks upon the United States* (New York: W. W. Norton, 2004).

80. United Nations Development Programme, *Arab Human Development Report 2002: Creating Opportunities for Future Generations* (New York: United Nations Publication, 2002); Max Boot, "Exploiting the Palestinians: Everyone's Doing It," *Weekly Standard*, January 28, 2003; Barry Rubin, "The Real Roots of Arab Anti-Americanism," *Foreign Affairs* 81/6 (2002): 73–85.

81. Donald Kagan and Frederick W. Kagan, *While America Sleeps*; Robert Kagan, *Of Paradise and Power*; Vaïsse, *Neoconservatism*, 232–39.

82. James Mann, *The Rise of the Vulcans: The History of the Bush's War Cabinet* (New York: Viking, 2004); Alexander Moens, *The Foreign Policy of George W. Bush: Values, Strategy, and Loyalty* (New York: Routledge, 2004); John T. Soma, Maury M. Nichols, Ste-

phen D. Rynerson, Lance A. Maish, and Jon David Rogers, "Balance of Privacy vs. Security: A Historical Perspective of the USA PATRIOT Act," *Rutgers Computer & Technology Law Journal* 31/2 (Winter 2005): 285–346; Amitai Etzioni, *How Patriotic Is the Patriot Act? Freedom versus Security in the Age of Terrorism* (New York: Routledge, 2005); Jack Goldsmith, *The Terror Presidency: Law and Judgment Inside the Bush Administration* (New York: W. W. Norton, 2007); George W. Bush, *Decision Points* (New York: Crown Publishing, 2010); Susan N. Herman, *Taking Liberties: The War on Terror and the Erosion of American Democracy* (Oxford: Oxford University Press, 2011); Christos Boukalas, *Homeland Security, Its Laws and Its State: A Design of Power for the 21st Century* (New York: Routledge, 2014).

83. Mary Buckley and Robert Singh, *The Bush Doctrine and the War on Terrorism: Global Responses, Global Consequences* (New York: Routledge, 2006); Stanley A. Renshon and Peter Suedfeld, eds., *Understanding the Bush Doctrine: Psychology and Strategy in an Age of Terrorism* (New York: Routledge, 2007); Terry H. Anderson, *Bush's Wars* (Oxford: Oxford University Press, 2011).

84. Ibid.; also see Fukuyama, *America at the Crossroads*; Robert G. Kaufman, *In Defense of the Bush Doctrine* (Lexington: University Press of Kentucky, 2007); Vaïsse, *Neoconservatism*, 239–79; François Drolet, *American Neoconservatism*, 147–59; Danny Cooper, *Neoconservatism and American Foreign Policy: A Critical Analysis* (New York: Routledge, 2011).

85. Mann, *The Rise of the Vulcans*, 234–358; Fukuyama, *America at the Crossroads*, 66–94; Halper, *America Alone*, 138–56; Vaïsse, *Neoconservatism*, 244–55; Drolet, *American Neoconservatism*, 147–59; Cooper, *Neoconservatism and American Foreign Policy*, 142–51; Buckley and Singh, *The Bush Doctrine and the War on Terrorism*, 12–31; Stanley A. Renshon, "The Bush Doctrine Reconsidered," in Renshon and Suedfeld, *Understanding the Bush Doctrine*, 1–38; Jacks S. Levy, "Preventive War and the Bush Doctrine," in Renshon and Suedfeld, *Understanding the Bush Doctrine*, 175–201; Jesus Velasco, *Neoconservatives in U.S. Foreign Policy*.

86. Albert Wohlsetter, Fred Hoffman, R. J. Lutz, and Henry S. Rowen, *Selection and Use of Strategic Air Bases* (Santa Monica, CA: Rand Corporation, R-266, 1954); Albert Wohlstetter, *Legends of the Strategic Arms Race* (Washington, DC: United States Strategic Institute, USSI Report 75-1, September 1974); Henry S. Rowen and Albert Wohlsetter, *US Non-Proliferation Strategy Reformulated* (Los Angeles, CA: PAN Heuristics, August 29, 1979); Albert Wohlsetter, Robert Wohlstetter, Gregory S. Jones, and Henry Rowen, *Towards a New Consensus on Nuclear Technology* (Los Angeles, CA: PAN Heuristics, 1979); Albert Wohlstetter, "Can We Afford SALT?," *The New York Times*, March 25, 1979, available at https://www.nytimes.com/1979/03/25/archives/foreign-affairs-can-we-afford-salt.html.

87. Gerhard Spörl, "The Leo-Conservatives," *The New York Times*, August 4, 2003, available at https://www.nytimes.com/2003/08/04/international/europe/the-leoconservatives.html. For misperceptions about Strauss's influence on neoconservatism, see Mark Lilla, "Leo Strauss: The European," *The New York Review of Books*, October 21, 2004, available at https://www.nybooks.com/articles/2004/10/21/leo-strauss-the-european/; "The Closing of the Straussian Mind," *The New York Review of Books*, November 4, 2004, available at https://www.nybooks.com/articles/2004/11/04/the-closing-of-the-straussian-mind/.

88. Leo Strauss, *Natural Rights and History*; also see Heinrich Meier, *Leo Strauss and the Theologico-Political Problem* (Cambridge: Cambridge University Press, 2006); and Thomas Pangle, *Leo Strauss: An Introduction to His Thought and Intellectual Legacy* (Baltimore: John Hopkins University Press, 2006); Paul Gottfried, *Leo Strauss and the Conservative Movement* (Cambridge: Cambridge University Press, 2011).

89. Harry V. Jaffa, *Crisis of the House Divided: An Interpretation of the Lincoln-Douglas Debates* (Seattle: University of Washington Press, 1959); *A New Birth of Freedom: Abraham Lincoln and the Coming Civil War* (Lanham, MD: Rowman & Littlefield, 2000); Bloom, *The Closing of the American Mind*.

90. Fukuyama, *America at the Crossroads*, 25–29; Drolet, *American Neoconservatism*, 53–90.

91. Halper, *America Alone*, 201–29; Vaïsse, *Neoconservatism*, 255–70; Drolet, *American Neoconservatism*, 147–59; Cooper, *Neoconservatism and American Foreign Policy*, 125–52.

92. David Brooks, "For Iraqis to Win, the U.S. Must Lose," *New York Times* (May 11, 2004), available at https://www.nytimes.com/2004/05/11/opinion/for-iraqis-to-win-the-us-must-lose.html; Richard Perle, "Ambushed on the Potomac," *The National Interest* (January–February 2009), available at https://nationalinterest.org/article/ambushed-on-the-potomac-2953; Michael Lind, "A Tragedy of Errors," *The Nation* (February 5, 2004); Available at https://www.thenation.com/article/tragedy-errors/; Francis Fukuyama, *America at the Crossroads*.

93. Robert Kagan and William Kristol, "The Right War for the Right Reasons," *Weekly Standard* (February 23, 2004), available at https://www.weeklystandard.com/robert-kagan-and-william-kristol/the-right-war-for-the-right-reasons; Krauthammer, "In Defense of Democratic Realism."

94. Halper, *America Alone*, 201–29; Vaïsse, *Neoconservatism*, 255–70; Drolet, *American Neoconservatism*, 147–59; Cooper, *Neoconservatism and American Foreign Policy*, 125–52.

95. Ibid.; Frederick W. Kagan, *Choosing Victory: A Plan for Success in Iraq* (Washington DC: American Enterprise Institute, January 5, 2007), available at http://www.aei.org/publication/choosing-victory-a-plan-for-success-in-iraq/.

96. Vaïsse, *Neoconservatism*, 260–66.

97. Drolet, *American Neoconservatism*, 151–59; also see Jason Blakely, "Nihilism as Right-wing Political Rhetoric," *Theory and Event* 22, no. 1, January 2019.

98. Cooper, *Neoconservatism and American Foreign Policy*, 10–12; 72–99.

99. Halper, *America Alone*, 227–31.

100. Fukuyama, *America at the Crossroads*, 111–13, 155–94.

101. Robert Kagan, "The Case for a League of Democracies," *Financial Times* (May 13, 2008), available at https://www.ft.com/content/f62a02ce-20eb-11dd-a0e6-000077b07658; also see Drolet, *American Neoconservatism*, 147–59; Vaïsse, *Neoconservatism*, 266–70.

102. *The Foreign Policy Initiative* is at https://foreignpolicyi.org/; the *Global Governance Watch* is at https://www.globalgovernancewatch.org/.

103. Douglas Murray, *Neoconservatism: Why We Need It*; Charles Krauthammer, "Hope and Change—But Not for Iran," *Jerusalem Post* (June 21, 2009a), available at https://www.jpost.com/Opinion/Op-Ed-Contributors/Hope-and-change-but-not-for-Iran; and "Decline Is a Choice" *Weekly Standard* (October 19, 2009b), available at https://www.weeklystandard.com/charles-krauthammer/decline-is-a-choice-270813; Robert Kagan, "Obama Siding with the Regime," *Washington Post* (June 17, 2009), available at http://carnegieendowment.org/2009/06/17/obama-siding-with-regime-pub-23285; Paul Wolfowitz, "Think Again Realism," *Foreign Policy* (August 27, 2009), available at https://foreignpolicy.com/2009/08/27/think-again-realism/; also see Cooper, *Neoconservatism and American Foreign Policy*, 153–65.

104. Curt Mills, "Are the Necons Finally with Trump?" *The National Interest* (October 17, 2017), available at https://nationalinterest.org/feature/after-the-neocons-finally-trump-22767; Julie Hirschfield Davis, "Jerusalem Embassy Is a Victory for Trump and a Complication for Middle East Peace," *New York Times* (May 14, 2018), available at https://www.nytimes.com/2018/05/14/us/politics/trump-jerusalem-embassy-middle-east-peace.html; Michael D. Shear and Jennifer Steinhauer, "Trump to Seek $54 Billion Increase in Military Spending," *New York Times* (February 27, 2017), available at https://www.nytimes.com/2017/02/27/us/politics/trump-budget-military.html. For Bolton's views, see John Bolton, *Surrender Is Not an Option: Defending America at the United Nations and Abroad* (New York: Simon & Schuster, 2008).

105. Max Boot, "There Is No Escape from Trump," *Commentary* (March 3, 2016), available at https://www.commentarymagazine.com/foreign-policy/donald-trump-foreign-policy-no-escape/; Jacob Heilbrunn, "The Neocons vs. Donald Trump," *New York Times* (March 10, 2016), available at https://www.nytimes.com/2016/03/13/opinion/sunday/the-neocons-vs-donald-trump.html; Sebastian Gorka, "Trump Is Not a Neoconservative and Never Will Be," *The Hill* (April 16, 2018), available at https://www.realclearpolitics.com/2018/04/16/trump_is_not_a_neoconservative_and_never_will_be_439862.html. For a contrary view about Trump's lack of ideological and policy consistency, see Marc Benjamin Sable and Angel Jaramillo Torres, *Trump and Political Philosophy: Patriotism, Cosmopolitanism, and Civic Virtue* (New York: Palgrave Macmillan, 2018).

106. Vaïsse, *Neoconservatism*, 276–79.

107. Drolet, *American Neoconservatism*, 8; also see 189–207.

BIBLIOGRAPHY

Abrams, Nathan. 2010. *Norman Podhoretz and Commentary Magazine: The Rise and Fall of the Neocons*. London: Continuum, 2010.
Allin, Dana H. 1976. *Cold War Illusions: America, Europe, and Soviet Power, 1969–1989*. New York: St. Martin's Press.
Anderson, Terry H. 2011. *Bush's Wars*. Oxford: Oxford University Press.
Andrew III, John A. 1997. *The Other Side of the Sixties: Young Americans for Freedom and the Rise of Conservative Politics*. New Brunswick, NJ: Rutgers University Press.
Bauer, P. T. 1976. "Western Guilt and Third World Poverty." *Commentary*, January: 31–39.
Bell, Daniel. 1978. *The Cultural Contradictions of Capitalism*. New York: Basic Books.
———. 1981. "First Love and Early Sorrow." *Times Higher Education Supplement*, January 16. Available at http://www.pbs.org/aruging/nyintellectuals_bell_2.html.
———. 1988a. "Afterword, 1988: The End of Ideology Revisited." In *The End of Ideology: On the Exhaustion of Political Ideas in the Fifties*. Cambridge, MA: Harvard University Press.
———. 1988b. *The End of Ideology: On the Exhaustion of Political Ideas in the Fifties* Cambridge, MA: Harvard University Press.
Bell, Daniel, and Irving Kristol. 1965. "What Is the Public Interest?" *The Public Interest*: 3–6.
———, eds. 1972. *Capitalism Today*. New York: Basic Books.
Blakely, Jason. 2019. "Nihilism as Rightwing Political Rhetoric." *Theory and Event* 22, no. 1 (January).
Bloom, Alexander. 1986. *Prodigal Sons: The New York Intellectuals and Their World*. Oxford: Oxford University Press.
Bloom, Allan. 1987. *The Closing of the American Mind*. New York: Simon & Schuster.
Bolton, John. 2008. *Surrender Is Not an Option: Defending America at the United Nations and Abroad*. New York: Simon & Schuster.
Boot, Max. 2003. "Exploiting the Palestinians: Everyone's Doing It." *Weekly Standard*, January 28.
———. 2016. "There Is No Escape from Trump." *Commentary*, March 3. Available at https://www.commentarymagazine.com/foreign-policy/donald-trump-foreign-policy-no-escape/.
Boukalas, Christos. 2014. *Homeland Security, Its Laws and Its State: A Design of Power for the 21st Century*. New York: Routledge.
Brennan, Mary C. 1995. *Turning Right in the Sixties: The Conservative Capture of the GOP* Chapel Hill: University of North Carolina Press.
Brooks, David. 1997. "A Return to National Greatness." *The Weekly Standard*. March 3. Available at https://www.weeklystandard.com/david-brooks/a-return-to-national-greatness.
———. 2004. "For Iraqis to Win, the U.S. Must Lose." *New York Times*, May 11. Available at https://www.nytimes.com/2004/05/11/opinion/for-iraqis-to-win-the-us-must-lose.html.
Buckley, Mary, and Robert Singh. 2006. *The Bush Doctrine and the War on Terrorism: Global Responses, Global Consequences*. New York: Routledge.
Buckley, William F. 1951. *God and Man at Yale*. Chicago: Regency.
Burns, Eveline M. 1965. "Where Welfare Falls Short." *The Public Interest* (Fall): 82–95.
Bush, George W. 2010. *Decision Points*. New York: Crown Publishing, 2010.
Chubb, John E., and Terry M. Moe. 1990. *Politics, Markets, and American Schools*. Washington, DC, Brookings Institute.
Cohen, David K., and Eleanor Farrar. 1977. "Power to the Parents?—The Story of Education Vouchers." *The Public Interest* (Summer): 72–97.
Cohen, Eliot. 2001. "World War IV: Let's Call the Conflict What It Is." *Wall Street Journal*, November 20. Available at https://www.wsj.com/articles/SB1006219259392114120.
Cooper, Danny. 2011. *Neoconservatism and American Foreign Policy: A Critical Analysis*. New York: Routledge.

Davis, Julie Hirschfield. 2018. "Jerusalem Embassy Is a Victory for Trump and a Complication for Middle East Peace." *New York Times*, May 14. Available at https://www.nytimes.com/2018/05/14/us/politics/trump-jerusalem-embassy-middle-east-peace.html.
Diamond, Sara. 1995. *Roads to Dominion: Right-Wing Movements and Political Power in the United States*. New York: Guildford Press.
Diggins, John. 1992. *The Rise and Fall of the American Left*. New York: W. W. Norton.
Dorman, Joseph. 2001. *Arguing the World: New York Intellectuals in Their Own Words*. Chicago: University of Chicago Press.
Dorrien, Gary. 1993. *The Neoconservative Mind: Politics, Culture, and the War of Ideology*. Philadelphia: Temple University Press.
Draper, Theodore. 1971. "The Specter of Weimar." *Commentary*, December: 43–50.
Drolet, Jean-François. 2011. *American Neoconservatism: The Politics and Culture of a Reactionary Idealism*. London: Hurst and Company.
Edwards, Lee. 1999. *The Conservative Revolution*. New York: Free Press.
Ehrman, John. 1994. *The Rise of the Neoconservatism: Intellectuals and Foreign Affairs 1945–1994*. New Haven: Yale University Press.
Elliott, Brian, and David MacLennan. 1994. "Education, Modernity, and Neo-Conservative School Reform in Canada, Britain, and the U.S." *British Journal of Sociology of Education* 15/2: 165–85.
Etzioni, Amitai. 2005. *How Patriotic Is the Patriot Act? Freedom versus Security in the Age of Terrorism*. New York: Routledge.
FitzGerald, Frances. 2000. *Way Out There in the Blue: Reagan, Star Wars, and the End of the Cold War*. New York: Simon & Schuster.
Frachon, Alan, and Daniel Vernet. 2004. *L'Amérique messianique*. Paris: Editions de Seuil.
Fraser, Steve, and Gary Gerstle. 1990. *The Rise and Fall of the New Deal Order, 1930–1980*. Princeton: Princeton University Press.
Friedman, Murray. 2004. *Jewish Intellectuals and the Shaping of Public Policy*. Cambridge: Cambridge University Press.
———. 2005. *The Neoconservative Revolution: Jewish Intellectuals and the Shaping of Public Policy*. Cambridge: Cambridge University Press.
Fukuyama, Francis. 1989. "The End of History." *The National Interest* (Summer): 3–18.
———. 1992. *The End of History and the Last Man*. New York: Free Press.
———. 2006. *America at the Crossroads: Democracy, Power, and the Neoconservative Legacy*. New Haven: Yale University Press.
Fuller, Adam L. 2012. *Taking the Fight to the Enemy: Neoconservatism and the Age of Ideology*. Lanham, MD: Lexington Books.
Gerson, Michael. 1997. *The Neoconservative Vision: From Cold War to Culture Wars*. Lanham, MD: Madison Books.
Glazer, Nathan. 1968. "The New Left and Its Limits." *Commentary*, July: 31–40.
———. 1971. "The Limits of Social Policy." *Commentary*, September: 51–59.
———. *Remembering the Answers: Essays on the American Student Revolt*. New York: Basic Books.
———. 1975. *Affirmative Discrimination*. New York: Basic Books.
———. 1983. "Towards a Self-Service Society?" *The Public Interest* (Winter): 66–90.
———. 1991. "A Time for Modesty." In *America's Purpose: New Visions of US Foreign Policy*, Owen Harries, ed. San Francisco: Institute of Contemporary Studies: 133–41.
Gilder, George. 1981. *Wealth and Poverty*. New York: Basic Books.
———. 1983. "A Supply-Side Economics of the Left." *The Public Interest* (Summer): 29–43.
Glazer, Nathan, and Daniel Patrick Moynihan. 1963. *Beyond the Melting Pot: The Negroes, Puerto Ricans, Jews, and Irish of New York*. Cambridge, MA: MIT Press.
Goldsmith, Jack. 2007. *The Terror Presidency: Law and Judgment Inside the Bush Administration*. New York: W. W. Norton.
Goose, Van. 2006. *Rethinking the New Left: An Interpretative History*. London: Palgrave Macmillan.

Gorka, Sebastian. 2018. "Trump Is Not a Neoconservative and Never Will Be." *The Hill*, April 16. Available at https://www.realclearpolitics.com/2018/04/16/trump_is_not_a_neoconservative_and_never_will_be_439862.html.
Gottfried, Paul. 2007. *Conservatism in America: Making Sense of the American Right*. New York: Palgrave Macmillan.
———. 2011. *Leo Strauss and the Conservative Movement*. Cambridge: Cambridge University Press.
Groseclose, Time. 2011. *Left Turn: How Liberal Media Bias Distorts the American Mind*. New York: St. Martin's Press.
Gross, Neil. 2013. *Why Are Professors Liberal and Why Do Conservatives Care?* Cambridge, MA: Harvard University Press.
Halliday, Fred. 1986. *The Making of the Second Cold War*. London: Verso.
Halper, Stefan, and Jonathan Clarke. 2004. *America Alone: The Neo-Conservatives and the Global Order*. Cambridge: Cambridge University Press.
Harrington, Michael. 1973. "The Welfare State and Its Neoconservative Critics." *Dissent*, Fall. Available at https://www.dissentmagazine.org/article/the-welfare-state-and-its-neoconservative-critics.
———. 1984. *The New American Poverty*. New York: Henry Holt Publishing.
Hartz, Louis. 1995. *The Liberal Tradition in America*. New York: Harcourt Brace Jovanovich.
Hayek, Friedrich von. 1960. *The Constitution of Liberty*. Chicago: University of Chicago Press.
Heilbrunn, Jacob. 2008. *They Knew They Were Right: The Rise of the Neocons*. New York: Doubleday.
———. 2016. "The Neocons vs. Donald Trump." *New York Times*, March 10. Available at https://www.nytimes.com/2016/03/13/opinion/sunday/the-neocons-vs-donald-trump.html.
Herman, Susan N. 2011. *Taking Liberties: The War on Terror and the Erosion of American Democracy*. Oxford: Oxford University Press.
Himmelfarb, Gertrude. 1987. *The New History and the Old*. Cambridge, MA: Harvard University Press.
———. 1995. *The Demoralization of Society: From Victorian Virtues to Modern Values*. New York: Knopf.
Jaffa, Harry V. 1959. *Crisis of the House Divided: An Interpretation of the Lincoln-Douglas Debates*. Seattle: University of Washington Press.
———. 2000. *A New Birth of Freedom: Abraham Lincoln and the Coming Civil War*. Lanham, MD: Rowman & Littlefield.
Kagan, Donald, and Frederick W. Kagan. 2000. *While America Sleeps: Self-Delusions, Military Weakness, and the Threat to Peace Today*. New York: St. Martin's Press.
Kagan, Frederick W. 2007. *Choosing Victory: A Plan for Success in Iraq*. Washington, DC: American Enterprise Institute. January 5. Available at http://www.aei.org/publication/choosing-victory-a-plan-for-success-in-iraq/.
Kaplan, Robert. 1994. "The Coming Anarchy." *Atlantic Monthly* 273/2: 44–76.
———. 2003. *Paradise and Power: America and Europe in the New World Order*. London: Atlantic Books.
———. 2004. "America's Crisis of Legitimacy." *Foreign Affairs* 83/2: 65–87.
———. 2005. "A Matter of Record." *Foreign Affairs* 84/1: 170–73.
———. 2008. "The Case for a League of Democracies." *Financial Times*, May 13. Available at https://www.ft.com/content/f62a02ce-20eb-11dd-a0e6-000077b07658.
———. 2009. "Obama Siding with the Regime." *Washington Post*, June 17. Available at http://carnegieendowment.org/2009/06/17/obama-siding-with-regime-pub-23285.
Kagan, Robert, and William Kristol. 2004. "The Right War for the Right Reasons." *Weekly Standard*, February 23. Available at https://www.weeklystandard.com/robert-kagan-and-william-kristol/the-right-war-for-the-right-reasons.
Kaufman, Robert G. 2000. *Henry M. Jackson: A Life in Politics*. Seattle: University of Washington Press.
———. 2007. *In Defense of the Bush Doctrine*. Lexington, KY: University Press of Kentucky.
Kelman, Steven. 1987. "'Public Choice' and Public Spirit." *The Public Interest* (Spring): 80–94.

Kirk, Russell. 1953. *The Conservative Mind*. Chicago: Regency.
Kirkpatrick, Jeane. 1973. "The Revolt of the Masses." *Commentary*, February: 58–62.
———. 1982. *The Reagan Phenomenon—and Other Speeches on Foreign Policy*. Washington, DC: American Enterprise Institute Press.
———. 1990. "A Normal Country in a Normal Time." *The National Interest*, Fall: 40–43.
———. 2004. "Neoconservatism as a Response to the Counter-Culture." In *The Neocon Reader*, Irwin Stelzer, ed. New York: Grove Press. 234–40.
Kissinger, Henry. 1972. *A World Restored: Europe after Napoleon*. Gloucester, MA: Peter Smith.
———. 1994. *Diplomacy*. New York: Simon & Schuster.
———. 1999. "Between the Old Left and the New Right." *Foreign Affairs* 78/3: 99–116.
Kramer, Hilton. 1985. *The Revenge of the Philistines: Arts and Culture, 1972–1984*. New York: Free Press.
Kramer, Hilton, and Roger Kimball, eds. 1985. *The Betrayal of Liberalism: How the Disciples of Freedom and Equality Helped Foster the Illiberal Politics of Coercion and Control*. New York: Ivan R. Dee.
Krauthammer, Charles. 2004. "In Defense of Democratic Realism." *The National Interest*, Fall. Available at https://nationalinterest.org/article/in-defense-of-democratic-realism-699.
———. 2009a. "Hope and Change—But Not for Iran." *Jerusalem Post*, June 21. Available at https://www.jpost.com/Opinion/Op-Ed-Contributors/Hope-and-change-but-not-for-Iran.
———. 2009b. "Decline Is a Choice" *Weekly Standard*, October 19. Available at https://www.weeklystandard.com/charles-krauthammer/decline-is-a-choice-270813.
Kristol, Irving. 1963. "Facing the Facts in Vietnam." *The New Leader*, September 30.
———. 1965. "Teaching In, Speaking Out: The Controversy Over Vietnam." *Encounter*, August: 65–70.
———. 1968. "We Can't Resign as Policeman of the World." *New York Times Magazine*, May 12.
———. 1970a. "Urban Civilization and Its Discontents." *Commentary*, July: 34–35.
———. 1970b. "When Virtue Loses All Her Loveliness—Some Reflections on Capitalism and 'The Free Society,'" *The Public Interest* (Fall): 3–12.
———. 1975. "America Now: A Failure of Nerve?" *Commentary*, July: 16–98.
———. 1978a. "Capitalism, Socialism, and Nihilism." *Commentary*, April: 29–72.
———. 1978b. *Two Cheers for Capitalism*. New York: Basic Books.
———. 1979. "Confessions of a True, Self-Confessed Neoconservative." *Public Opinion*, October/November.
———. 1981. "Ideology and Supply-Side Economics." *Commentary*, April: 48–56.
———. 1983. *Reflections of a Neoconservative*. New York: Basic Books.
———. 1985. "Skepticism, Meliorism and *The Public Interest*." *The Public Interest*: 31–42.
———. 1990. "Defining Our National Interest." *The National Interest*, Fall: 16–25.
———. 1995a. "Memoirs of a Trotskyist." In *Neoconservatism: The Autobiography of an Idea*. New York: Free Press. 469–80.
———. 1995b. "My Cold War." In *Neoconservatism: The Autobiography of an Idea*. New York: Free Press: 481–86.
———. 1995c. "Adam Smith and the Spirit of Capitalism." In *Neoconservatism: The Autobiography of an Idea*. New York: Free Press. 258–299.
———. 1995d. *Neoconservatism: The Autobiography of an Idea*. New York: Free Press.
———. 1999. *Ex-Friends*. New York: Free Press.
———. 2003. "The Neoconservative Persuasion: What It Was and What It Is." *The Weekly Standard*, August 25. Available at https://www.weeklystandard.com/irving-kristol/the-neoconservative-persuasion.
———. 2004. "Neoconservatism: A Eulogy." In *The Norman Podhoretz Reader*, Thomas L. Jeffers, ed. New York: Free Press: 269–84.
———. 2010. *The Problem of Doing Good: Irving Kristol's Philanthropy*. Washington, DC: Hudson Institute.
Kristol, William. 2009. "Will Obama Save Liberalism?" *New York Times*, January 26. Available at https://www.nytimes.com/2009/01/26/opinion/26kristol.html.

Kristol, William, and Robert Kagan. 1996. "Toward a Neo-Reaganite Foreign Policy." *Foreign Affairs* 75/4: 18–32.

———. 2000a. "America Power–For What?" *Commentary*, January. Available at https://www.commentarymagazine.com/articles/american-power-for-what/.

———. 2000b. *Present Dangers: Crisis and Opportunity in American Foreign and Defense Policy*. San Francisco: Encounter.

Laqueur, Walter. 1973. "Kissinger and the Politics of Détente." *Commentary*, December: 46–53.

Latham, Robert. 1997. *The Liberal Moment: Modernity, Security, and the Making of Postwar International Order*. New York: Columbia University Press.

Lasch, Christopher. 1969. *The Agony of the American Left*. New York: Knopf.

Levy, Jacks S. 2007. "Preventive War and the Bush Doctrine." In *Understanding the Bush Doctrine: Psychology and Strategy in an Age of Terrorism*, Stanley A. Renshon and Peter Suedfeld, eds. New York: Routledge: 175–201.

Lieberman, Myron. 1989. *Privatization and Education Choice*. New York: Palgrave Macmillan.

———. 2002. "School Choice Schism." *The Public Interest* (Spring): 122–25.

Lilla, Mark. 2004. "Leo Strauss: The European." *The New York Review of Books*. October 21. Available at https://www.nybooks.com/articles/2004/10/21/leo-strauss-the-european/.

———. 2004. "The Closing of the Straussian Mind." *The New York Review of Books*, November 4. Available at https://www.nybooks.com/articles/2004/11/04/the-closing-of-the-straussian-mind/.

Lind, Michael. 2004. "A Tragedy of Errors." *The Nation*, February 5. Available at https://www.thenation.com/article/tragedy-errors/.

Lindberg, Tod. 2004. "Neoconservatism's Liberal Legacy." *Policy Review* (October 1). Available at https://www.hoover.org/research/neoconservatisms-liberal-legacy.

Lipset, Seymour Martin. 1976. "The Wavering Polls." *The Public Interest*: 70–90.

———. 1996. *American Exceptionalism: A Double-Edged Sword*. New York: W. W. Norton.

———. 1999. "Out of the Alcoves." *The Wilson Quarterly* 23/1: 37–48.

Mann, James. 2004. *The Rise of the Vulcans: The History of the Bush's War Cabinet*. New York: Viking, 2004.

McCormick, Thomas J. 1995. *America's Half-Century: United States Foreign Policy in the Cold War and After*. Baltimore: John Hopkins University Press.

Meier, Heinrich. 2006. *Leo Strauss and the Theologico-Political Problem*. Cambridge: Cambridge University Press, 2006.

Mills, Curt. 2017. "Are the Necons Finally with Trump?" *The National Interest*, October 17. Available at https://nationalinterest.org/feature/after-the-neocons-finally-trump-22767.

Moens, Alexander. 2004. *The Foreign Policy of George W. Bush: Values, Strategy, and Loyalty*. New York: Routledge.

Moynihan, Daniel Patrick. 1965. *The Negro Family: A Case for National Action*. Washington, DC: Office of Policy Planning and Research, US Department of Labor.

———. 1970. *Maximum Feasible Misunderstanding*. New York: Free Press.

———. 1973. *The Politics of Guaranteed Income*. New York: Vintage.

———. 1975. "The United States in Opposition." *Commentary*, March: 31–45.

———. 1976. *A Dangerous Place*. New York: Little, Brown.

Moynihan, Daniel, Patrick and Irving Kristol, eds. 1968. *Confrontation: The Student Rebellion and the Universities*. New York: Basic Books.

Muravchik, Joshua. 2009. "Operational Comeback." *Foreign Policy*, October 16. Available at https://foreignpolicy.com/2009/10/16/the-fp-memo-operation-comeback/.

Murray, Charles. 1984. *Losing Ground: American Social Policy, 1950–1980*. New York: Basic Books.

Murray, Douglas. 2006. *Neoconservatism: Why We Need It*. San Francisco: Encounter.

Nash, George. 1976. *The Conservative Intellectual Movement in America since 1945*. New York: Harper.

The National Commission on Terrorist Attacks. 2004. *The 9/11 Commission Report: Final Report of the National Commission on Terrorist Attacks upon the United States*. New York: W. W. Norton.
Niskanen, William A. 1988. *Reaganomics: An Insider's Account of Policies and the People* Oxford: Oxford University Press.
Norwood, Stephen H. 2013. *Anti-Semitism and the American Far Left*. Cambridge: Cambridge University Press.
Novak, Michael. 1991. *The Spirit of Democratic Capitalism*. Lanham, MD: Madison Books.
O'Neill, William. 1974. *Coming Apart: An Informal History of America in the 1960s*. New York: Times Books.
———. 2001. *The New Left: A History*. Wheeling, IL: Harlan Davidson.
Quester, George H. 1982. *American Foreign Policy: The Lost Consensus*. Santa Barbara, CA: Praeger.
Pangle, Thomas. 2006. *Leo Strauss: An Introduction to His Thought and Intellectual Legacy*. Baltimore: John Hopkins University Press.
Perle, Richard. 2009. "Ambushed on the Potomac." *The National Interest*, January–February. Available at https://nationalinterest.org/article/ambushed-on-the-potomac-2953.
Phillips, Kevin. 1970. *The Emerging Republican Majority*. New York: Anchor Books.
Plattner, Marc F. 1979. "The Welfare State vs. The Redistributive State." *The Public Interest* (Spring): 28–48.
Podhoretz, Norman. 1976. "Making the World Safe for Communism." *Commentary*, April: 31–42.
———. 1977. "The Culture of Appeasement." *Harper's*, October. Available at https://harpers.org/archive/1977/10/the-culture-of-appeasement/.
———. 1979. *Breaking Ranks: A Political Memoir*. New York: Harper and Row.
———. 1982. "The Neo-Conservative Anguish over Reagan's Foreign Policy." *New York Times Magazine*, May 2: 30–31.
———. 1989. "New Vistas for Neoconservatives." *Conservative Digest* 15: 56–7.
———. 2004. "World War IV: How It Started, What It Means, and Why We Have to Win." *Commentary*: 17–54
———. 2007. *World War IV: The Long Struggle Against Islamofascism*. New York: Doubleday.
Prewitt, Kenneth. 2005. "Political Ideas and a Political Science for Policy." *The Annals of the American Academy of Political and Social Science* 600/1: 14–29.
Rainwater, Lee, and William L. Yancey. 1976. *The Moynihan Report and the Politics of Controversy*. Cambridge, MA: MIT Press.
Ravitch, Diane. 2003. *The Language Police: How Pressure Groups Restrict What Students Learn*. New York: Knopf.
Renshon, Stanley A. 2007. "The Bush Doctrine Reconsidered." In *Understanding the Bush Doctrine: Psychology and Strategy in an Age of Terrorism*, Stanley A. Renshon and Peter Suedfeld, eds. New York: Routledge: 1–38.
Renshon, Stanley A., and Peter Suedfeld, eds. 2007. *Understanding the Bush Doctrine: Psychology and Strategy in an Age of Terrorism*. New York: Routledge.
Roch, Christine, Mark Schneider, Melissa Marschall, and Paul Teske. 1979. "School Choice Builds Community." *The Public Interest* (Fall): 86–90.
Rowen, Henry S., and Albert Wohlsetter. 1979. *US Non-Proliferation Strategy Reformulated* Los Angeles, CA: PAN Heuristics, August 29.
Roy, Oliver. 1996. *The Failure of Political Islam*. Cambridge, MA: Harvard University Press.
———. 2004. *Globalized Islam: The Search for a New Universal*. New York: Columbia University Press.
Rubin, Barry. 2002. "The Real Roots of Arab Anti-Americanism." *Foreign Affairs* 81/6: 73–85.
Sable, Marc Benjamin, and Angel Jaramillo Torres. 2018. *Trump and Political Philosophy: Patriotism, Cosmopolitanism, and Civic Virtue*. New York: Palgrave Macmillan.
Sanders, Jerry. 1983. *Peddlers of Crisis: The Committee on the Present Dangers and the Politics of Containment*. Boston: South End Press.

Schlesinger, Arthur M., Jr. 1949. *The Vital Center: The Politics of Freedom*. Boston: Houghton Mifflin.

———. 1992. "Reinhold Niebuhr's Long Shadow." *New York Times*, June 22. Available at https://www.nytimes.com/1992/06/22/opinion/reinhold-niebuhr-s-long-shadow.html.

Schiller, Bradley R. 1981. "Welfare: Reforming Our Expectations" *The Public Interest* (Winter): 55–65.

Schoenwald, Jonathan M. 2001. *A Time for Choosing: The Rise of Modern American Conservatism*. Oxford: Oxford University Press.

Shear, Michael D., and Jennifer Steinhauer. 2017. "Trump to Seek $54 Billion Increase in Military Spending." *New York Times*, February 27. Available at https://www.nytimes.com/2017/02/27/us/politics/trump-budget-military.html.

Smith, James A. 1991. *The Idea Brokers: Think Tanks and the Rise of the New Policy Elite*. New York: Free Press

Soma, John T., Maury M. Nichols, Stephen D. Rynerson, Lance A. Maish, and Jon David Rogers. 2005. "Balance of Privacy vs. Security: A Historical Perspective of the USA PATRIOT Act." *Rutgers Computer & Technology Law Journal* 31/2: 285–346.

Spörl, Gerhard. 2003. "The Leo-Conservatives." *The New York Times*, August 4. Available at https://www.nytimes.com/2003/08/04/international/europe/the-leoconservatives.html.

"Statement of Principles." 1997. Project for the New American Century. June. Available at https://web.archive.org/web/20130609011554/http://newamericancentury.org/.

Steiner, Gilbert Y. 1974. "Reform Follow Reality: The Growth of Welfare." *The Public Interest* (Winter): 47–65.

Steinfels, Peter. 1979a. *The Neoconservatives: The Origins of a Movement*. New York: Simon & Schuster.

———. 1979b. *The Neoconservatives: The Men Who Are Changing America's Politics*. New York: Simon & Schuster.

Strauss, Leo. 1953. *Natural Right and History*. Chicago: University of Chicago Press.

Students for a Democratic Society. 1962. *Port Huron Statement*, June 15, 1962. Available at https://archive.org/details/PortHuronStatement/page/n0.

Trepanier, Lee. 2017. "The Relevance of Political Philosophy and Political Science." In *Why the Humanities Matter Today: In Defense of Liberal Education*, Lee Trepanier, ed. Lanham, MD: Lexington Books: 127–44.

Trilling, Lionel. 1950. *The Liberal Imagination*. New York: Anchor Books.

Tucker, Robert W., and David C. Hendrickson. 2004. "The Sources of American Legitimacy." *Foreign Affairs* 83/6: 18–32.

United Nations Development Programme, 2002. *Arab Human Development Report 2002: Creating Opportunities for Future Generations*. New York: United Nations Publication.

Vaïsse, Justin. 2010. *Neoconservatism: The Biography of a Movement*. Cambridge, MA: Belknap.

Velasco, Jesus. 2010. *Neoconservatives in U.S. Foreign Policy under Ronald Reagan and George W. Bush: Voices behind the Throne*. Baltimore: John Hopkins University Press.

Voegelin, Eric. 1952. *The New Science of Politics*. Chicago: University of Chicago Press.

Wald, Alan M. 1987. *The New York Intellectuals: The Rise and Decline of the Anti-Stalinist Left from the 1930s to the 1980s*. Chapel Hill: University of North Carolina Press.

Wanniski, June. 1978a. *The Way the World Works*. New York: Gateway Books.

———. 1978b. "Taxes, Revenues, and the 'Laffer Curve.'" *The Public Interest* (Winter): 3–16

Waxman, Chaim I., ed. 1968. *The End of Ideology Debate*. New York: Funk and Wagnalls.

White, Theodore H. 1973. *The Making of the President 1972*. New York: Atheneum Publishers.

Wilson, James Q. 1972. "Liberalism versus Liberal Education." *Commentary*, June: 50–55.

———. 1985. *Thinking about Crime*. New York: Simon & Schuster.

———. 1993. *The Moral Sense*. New York: Free Press.

———. 1999. "Cultural Meltdown." *The Public Interest* (Fall): 99–104.

Winik, Jay. 1996. *On the Brink: The Dramatic, Behind-the-Scenes Saga of the Reagan Era and the Men and Women Who Won the Cold War*. New York: Simon & Schuster.

Wohlstetter, Albert. 1974. *Legends of the Strategic Arms Race*. Washington, DC: United States Strategic Institute, USSI Report 75–1, September.
———. 1979. "Can We Afford SALT?" *The New York Times*, March 25. Available at https://www.nytimes.com/1979/03/25/archives/foreign-affairs-can-we-afford-salt.html.
Wohlsetter, Albert, Fred Hoffman, R. J. Lutz, and Henry S. Rowen. 1954. *Selection and Use of Strategic Air Bases*. Santa Monica, CA: Rand Corporation, R-266.
Wohlsetter, Albert, Robert Wohlstetter, Gregory S. Jones, and Henry Rowen. 1979. *Towards a New Consensus on Nuclear Technology*. Los Angeles, CA: PAN Heuristics.
Wolfowitz, Paul. 2000. "Remembering the Future." *The National Interest*, Summer: 67–73.
———. 2009. "Think Again Realism." *Foreign Policy*, August 27. Available at https://foreignpolicy.com/2009/08/27/think-again-realism/.

Chapter Four

George Grant and Charles Taylor

Canadian Owls

Ron Dart

There has been an unfortunate historic tendency to falsely assume Canada has produced no serious philosophers or political philosophers. There have been various attempts to correct this obvious gaffe and misread of the Canadian intellectual tradition beginning with Leslie Armour's and Elizabeth Trott's *The Faces of Reason: An Essay on Philosophy and Culture in English Canada: 1850–1950*[1] and culminating in recent years in Robert Sibley's *Northern Spirits: John Watson, George Grant, and Charles Taylor: Appropriations of Hegelian Political Thought*;[2] Robert Meynell's *Canadian Idealism and the Philosophy of Freedom: C. C. Macpherson, George Grant, and Charles Taylor*;[3] and Ian Angus's *The Undiscovered Country: Essays in Canadian Intellectual Culture*.[4] The minimal yet emerging interest in the Maritime Hegelian, James Doull, must also be noted. The recent spate of interest in C. B. Macpherson cannot be ignored. I might add that, in most ways, Meynell's read of Hegel, Grant and Taylor is much more nuanced and truer to the layered way of all three political philosophers than is Sibley's (it was, in some ways, disappointing that Sibley did not deal with Macpherson). But the repartee between Meynell and Sibley on their conflicting interpretations of Hegel, Grant and Taylor does a superb job of walking the attentive reader into the clash between the classical-modern nationalist and cosmopolitan neoliberal ideological tendencies within the Canadian ethos and tradition.

The fact that there is much research and publishing being done on the Canadian ethos and intellectual-philosophical tradition means more and more literature is coming to the fore and George Grant (1918–1988) and Charles Taylor (b. 1931) are featured often in such a process. Grant, in most ways, embodied a classical Platonic High Tory approach to political philosophy, whereas Taylor is a subtle and nuanced defender of the modern Hegelian project. Needless to say, Taylor is much better known for the simple reason that he is an apologist for the modern liberal project, and there are those who would argue that Canada is, more than most cultures, Hegelian—such is the argument, for example, in David Macgregor's "Canada's Hegel"[5] or Philip Resnick's "Hegel's Canadian Heirs."[6]

There can be no doubt that Grant and Taylor, when younger, had many a literary and political engagement with leftist politics, given their nuanced reading of the Hegelian leftist tradition. Grant had been raised within a more liberal and progressive type of Presbyterian Hegelian liberalism; his close friendship with James Doull at Dalhousie in the 1950s (Grant taught philosophy, Doull Classics, their friendship going back to Oxford days and Doull a nuanced and sophisticated Hegelian) did much to shape his thinking at the time and Grant's 1961 article, "An Ethic of Community" in *Social Purpose for Canada* was part of a manifesto of sorts that bridged the older Co-operative Commonwealth Federation (CCF) to the updated leftist political party, the New Democratic Party (NDP). Grant worked with many social liberals such as Pierre Trudeau and Michael Oliver on such a project.[7]

Charles Taylor was a generation younger than Grant but he had decided leftist sympathies both when at Oxford (where he, like Grant, did his PhD) in the 1950s and in Canada in the 1960s. Taylor ran as an NDP candidate in the 1962, 1963, 1965 (where he ran against Trudeau the Liberal candidate), and the 1968 elections. Jack Layton (former head of the NDP) was a student of Taylor's. The publication of one of Taylor's earliest books, *The Pattern of Politics*[8] and his choice article, "The Agony of Economic Man" in *Essays on the Left*[9] reflect and embody Taylor's obvious commitment, in thought, word, and deed to a form of leftist political ideology from the 1950s to the 1960s and into the 1970s. Grant had turned away from the NDP by the 1963 Federal election when Tommy Douglas (NDP) and Joined forces with Lester Pearson (Liberal) to bring down the Conservative government of John Diefenbaker. In fact, it was the 1963 election and Grant's frustration with two forms of liberalism (NDP-Liberal) that birthed his classic 1965 Tory political manifesto, *Lament for a Nation: The Defeat of Canadian Nationalism*.[10]

GEORGE GRANT: CLASSICAL HIGH TORYISM AND LIBERALISM

The content of *Lament for a Nation* had been anticipated somewhat by Grant's lectures in the late 1950s that became his first main work in political philosophy, *Philosophy in the Mass Age*.[11] Grant tracked and traced, in this seminal work, the rise of liberalism from the English Puritans to Locke, Smith, Hume, and Burke to the emergence of the American liberal ethos and empire. There has been a tendency to see Burke as the conservative and

Hobbes, Paine, Smith, Hume, and Locke as variations of liberalism, but Grant, like C. B. Macpherson, rightly noted that Burke was a Rockingham Whig to the core.

This meant that other sources had to be mined for a more comprehensive and older High Tory vision. There were Coleridge, Swift, Johnson, and the judicious Hooker, each and all in their different ways, suspicious of the detrimental aspects of the market economy and holding a higher view of the state (and society) as agents of the commonwealth. This more historic and organic form of Toryism did emerge and veered in different directions than the diverse liberal family. It was this more communal, organic, and historic notion of the common good imperfectly delivered by the state that meant Grant had some affinities with Marxism (which he has a fine chapter on in *Philosophy in the Mass Age*).[12]

Grant was convinced, in this his earliest tome of sorts in political theory, that the liberalism of pre-Hegelian thought (Puritans and Locke and tribe) and the notion of "history as progress" of Hegel and post-Hegelian thought (and in action) was the true revolutionary position. This is why, at a certain point, Grant did part paths with Marx, but he did think Marx (and Rousseau in different ways) was much more conservative than was the set loose idea of the free individual making and shaping history and the future with few limitations and brakes on choice, liberty, and contractual relationships. In fact, Grant, more than most, by the late 1940s, was acutely aware that the Baconian epistemology and his reverence for science (and its impact on nature) had serious implications for the future. It was these deeper philosophical probes that took Grant to classical political philosophy and, in particular Plato and a form of Platonic Anglicanism. It also meant his turn to the Progressive Conservative Party for a couple of decades as a formal and material opposition to center and center left liberalism in the Canadian context and various forms of liberal imperialism in the United State. Such a turn highlighted Grant's High Tory nationalism that did not square well with various stages of the Hegelian tradition in both Canada and the United States.

I might add that Grant's contribution to *Social Purpose for Canada* (1961), as mentioned above, seemed to place him on the CCF-NDP left of center. The 1963 Federal election in Canada as mentioned above, for Grant, displayed, in many ways, the differences between his High Toryism and the New Left in Canada in the early 1960s. The Liberal Party of Lester Pearson and the NDP of Tommy Douglas voted to bring down the Progressive Conservative government of John Diefenbaker.

One of the core issues at the time was President John F. Kennedy's insistence that Canada take warheads for Bomarc missiles. Kennedy had clashed, again and again, with Diefenbaker on a variety of contentious issues, the underlying ideology about Canadian nationalism versus a more pro-American position on many issues. Pearson and Douglas (center and center left) defeated Diefenbaker and Grant took Diefenbaker's position in the 1965 clash, *Lament for a Nation: The Defeat of Canadian Nationalism*, the High Tory contra leftist manifesto of sorts. But the New Left in Canada would not let Grant go so easily.

Gad Horowitz (New Left) argued, at the time, that Grant's form of conservatism (contra Goldwater) was unique within the Canadian historic context. It was this "Tory Touch" or what Horowitz called "Red Toryism" that highlighted the affinities between the distinctive Canadian Left and Anglo-Canadian conservativism.[13] Grant was wary of being called a "Red Tory" (given its socialist and nationalist tendencies) but there can be no doubt that the organic nature of past, present, future, and the notion of the commonweal (and the role of the state in protecting such a common good) within historic conservatism have some convergences with the political Left.

It should also be noted that Grant was one of the few professors in Canada in the 1960s that dared to explicitly critique the Vietnam War at public teach-ins. It was, mostly, those on the political Left that opposed the war and Grant stood by their side in a variety of ways. Grant also questioned the direction that public universities were going with their excessive commitment to the growing knowledge industry, skill training, techne, and power, and an excessive addiction to the scientific method—this meant, for Grant, an undermining of a classical education in the humanities and learning as wisdom and insight.

The New Left was drawn to Grant for the simple reason that he seemed to hold a peace position higher than an aggressive war position and his notion of education linked, to some degree, peace and wisdom as a way of knowing and being—such a commitment knit Grant to the New Left in the 1960s and early 1970s in a substantive way and manner. The fact, I might add, that the New Left viewed Grant as one of their own did not mean Grant was an uncritical devotee of the New Left. In fact, his *Sic et Non* attitude to the New Left was best articulated in his two reflections in 1966, "A Critique of the New Left" and "The Value of Protest."

Many within the New Left in Canada continued to hold Grant high until his work in the 1980s on abortion and euthanasia made them see his classical vision could not be co-opted by the Right or Left (interestingly yet predictably so the political Right held him high in the 1980s). I might also add that the secular Left was wary of religion and Grant's thinking and life was rooted and grounded in a deeper and fuller notion of the contemplative, communal, and public dimensions of religion (Anglicanism being his hearth and home for many a decade). Indeed, the New Left did part paths with Grant on the abortion, euthanasia, and religious issue but they still honored his incisive probes on the American military industrial complex, multinational corporations, and the merging, within liberalism, of liberty, power, and willing.

It should be noted that Grant's much older Canadian High Toryism had substantive theological, philosophical, literary, economic, and political roots that saw, in the liberal and modern American experiment, the clearcutting of an older and deeper way of being. The historic Anglo-Canadian Tory tradition has had an abiding distrust of the American commitment to the liberal way. This historic ethos has been articulated and described well by S. W. Wise and Robert Craig Brown in their 1967 *Canada Views the United States: Nineteenth-Century Political Attitudes*[14] and Wise's more comprehensive 1993 book, *God's Peculiar Peoples: Essays on Political Culture in Nineteenth-Century Canada*.[15]

Grant imbibed such a heritage and a great deal of his suspicion of the American enterprise had much to do with his deeper philosophic opposition to Hegelian liberalism as embodied in the United States (in both its republican and democratic forms). It is interesting that Grant, in this sense, has many an affinity with the controversial Canadian political theorist, Shadia Drury, in her recent Ted Talk lecture in Calgary, "Socratic Mischief: How Human Civilization Went Astray" (January 14, 2019). Grant and Drury would differ on aspects of their read of Classical thought, but would both concur about their path parting with Hegel and the connection between Hegel and American liberalism and empire.[16]

There was, indeed, many an affinity with Grant (in his many missives and tracts for the times) with the emerging and more substantive work of Alasdair MacIntyre. I remember when doing my PhD studies in Religious Studies (the department Grant founded in the early 1960s and which became a model for many in Canada) at McMaster University in the early-mid 1980s, MacIntyre's books being primary and often sole texts for some courses. *After Virtue* was a portal into many of MacIntyre's larger and more developed positions.[17] Grant was more Platonic than MacIntyre's more Aristotelian lens but both Plato and Aristotle had much more in common than both did with the modern and postmodern project. I might add, though, that MacIntyre's "Revolutionary Aristotelianism" as reflected upon in *Alasdair MacIntyre: Revolutionary Aristotelianism: Virtue and Politics* would part paths with Grant on the idealizing of sorts of society and communities of virtue and a demeaning of the state.[18]

Grant would definitely and decidedly agree with MacIntyre's critique of capitalism (and the way the market economy destroys communities and centralizes power), but Grant would have a higher view of the state as a corrector and balancer of the impact of multinational corporations. It is somewhat significant that MacIntyre's contrast between the good of communities-society and the questionable interests of corporate capitalism-state, at a more sophisticated and philosophical level, reflects and echoes Philip Blond's *Red Tory: How Left and Right Have Broken Britain and How We Can Fix It*.[19]

Grant and MacIntyre share a commitment to the classical tradition in opposition to the modern liberal Hegelian project, but the fact that Grant turns to Plato rather than Aristotle does make a substantive difference when they apply their classical reads to contemporary political thought and action. Needless to say, Grant and MacIntyre differ with Taylor's misread of the classical tradition of Plato-Aristotle and his sophisticated read of the modern liberal tradition (but more on this later). It is interesting, though, that all three thinkers have critical affinities with Marx contra Smith, Hobbes, Locke, and Burke.

Grant's turn to Plato and Platonic Anglicanism (a worthy and historic line and lineage) had much to do with what he saw as the liberal commitment to liberty, history as progress, and the fusion of willing-liberty in contrast to the classical notion of the "moving image of eternity" as embodied in the ancient notion of the good, true, and beautiful (and how such ultimate realities are lived forth in the penultimate world of time and history). There were two thinkers that Grant questioned and opposed in the late 1960s and 1970s, in different ways, as reflecting versions of a worrisome form of liberalism: Nietzsche and Rawls. Grant gave the CBC Massey Lectures in the late 1960s on Nietzsche, and his lectures were published in 1969 as *Time as History*.[20] Each of these lectures, step by step, ponders both the appeal of Nietzsche and the trajectory his thinking takes the unwary. Grant's turn to Rawls in 1974 in *English Speaking Justice*,[21] which clarified, in a succinct and compact manner, how and why Rawls notion of justice could become a plaything of the deeper liberal will to power, the language of justice being but an arbitrary and contractual reality that can become whatever the free thinking individual defines it as. Grant summed up the problem well when he suggested:

> The view of traditional philosophy and religion is that justice is the overriding order which we do not measure and define, but in terms of which we are measured and defined. The view of modern thought is that justice is a way which we chose in freedom, both individually and publically, once we have taken our fate into our own hands, and known that we are responsible for what happens.[22]

Grant's focus on Nietzsche and Rawls (often not seen walking the same pathway) meant that Grant saw the deeper meaning of liberalism in a way few did—liberty, will, power merging in a shaping, making contractual manner, Nietzsche more blunt and Rawls more subtle in delivery and application. Grant turned, near the end of journey, to Heidegger and Heidegger's separation of Being from Justice, pre-Socratic openness to Being rather than the more substantive Platonic vision of the good meant, for Grant, Heidegger, like Nietzsche, although seeming to mine the ancient contra modernity epitomized the modern and postmodern tendencies. In short, neither Nietzsche nor Heidegger, at a deeper level, was conservative: they were sly moderns that used the classical tragic and pre-Socratic ethos to legitimate the will to power at the core of modernity, the language of tolerance, multiculturalism, pluralism, etc., being but protean rhetoric to obscure a more insidious reality.

Much of Grant's final reflections were on technology and techne as a will to power way of being modern. The publications of *Technology and Empire: Perspectives on North America*[23] and *Technology and Justice*[24] illuminate and enucleate how and why Grant transcended the culture wars of his time, realizing only too acutely, that the Left and Right, could both indulge in a variety of will to power decisions that had serious impacts on the unborn, environment, communities, religion, families, society, and the state. Grant seemed to be on the Right when he defended religion and the sacred contra secularism, questioned the pro-choice and pro-euthanasia movements, defended the significance of the family and friendships, and he seemed to be on the political Left, when he opposed the market economy, capitalism, multinational corporations, American military industrial complex, American imperialism and held a high view of the state as a needful agent of the commonwealth.

Much of Grant's thinking, at center and core, is more about pondering what we, as moderns, are enfolded within and what such enfolding means when unfolded. It is not very liberal of a liberal not to critique liberalism (such is ideology), but Grant, given his deeper historic roots as a classical Canadian High Tory, could see such liberalism for what it actually was (at core and the more popular and populist rhetorical fringes). But, what has this to do with Charles Taylor?

CHARLES TAYLOR: APOLOGIST FOR MODERNITY

I have had an interest in the work of Taylor for decades, and in an earlier article of mine, "Charles Taylor and the Hegelian Eden Tree: Canadian Compradorism," I reflected on both the appeal yet worrisome dimensions of Taylor's thinking and insights.[25] There is much about Taylor in which the booster stance should win the day, but there is a legitimate place, given his popularity, for a more critical and knocker stance also. It is essential to note, though, that Taylor's more nuanced read of the layered ideology of the Enlightenment offers a needful corrective to simplistic and reactionary reads of it such as the work of John Gray's *Enlightenment's Wake: Politics and Culture at the Close of the Modern Age.*[26] There are many like Gray who selectively pick and choose from the Enlightenment, then either curtly dismiss or uncritically genuflect before such an agenda—such is not Taylor's probing way.

If George Grant was a defender of the classical vision, Plato being his guide, the Christian Platonic notion of the good, true, and beautiful his pathway, the historic Canadian Anglican ethos his ecclesial home, Taylor is, in most respects, a prominent apologist, in a subtle and sophisticated way, of the modern project. Grant turned his back on Hegel and Hegel's read of the classical tradition and held Plato and Hegel at odds. Taylor, like Hegel, has attempted to synthesize, in the finest dialectical manner, the best of the rationalist and romantic traditions in a full humanist notion of the meaning of the self, society, and politics. Taylor is very much a post–Vatican II Roman Catholic, and in the Canadian context, he has much affinity with the more theological yet political Gregory Baum. Taylor's centrist Hegelianism, needless to say, moved him in the 1970s, increasingly so, from his more committed (in thought, word, and deed) leftist Hegelianism to a more centrist and less ideological leftist political stance. Much of this move had significant input from Taylor's ongoing interaction with Gadamer.

The publication of *Hegel* in 1975 and *Hegel and Modern Society* in 1979 are must-reads to get a fix and feel for Taylor's deeper and deepening understanding of the ongoing relevance of Hegel for the unfolding of the modern liberal project in Canada and beyond. I should add that where Hegel, Grant, and Taylor do concur is that a form of ideological secularism (a blend of scientism and rationalism) that negates and closes off both the significance of the sacred and dialogue of the Spirit (*Geist*) in time and history is foreign to the finest aspects of both the Classical and Enlightenment traditions.

Both Taylor and Grant have respect for aspects of reason, empiricism, inductive and deductive ways of knowing, but both realize, only too well, the reductionistic, one-dimensional and imperial tendencies of such ways of knowing being. The differences between Grant and Taylor is that Grant was committed to the Christian Platonic way whereas Taylor, following Hegel, viewed such an approach as an earlier phase of the dialectical and emerging consciousness of freedom and liberty.

It is this very point that separates the older and deeper conservatism from the more modern liberalism of Hegel-Taylor. The question that Grant would put to Hegel-Taylor is simply this: Is your read of the Classical Tradition and Plato a misread and caricature that distorts such an ethos and tradition to serve the emerging liberal ideology and agenda? I, for one, tend to find both Hegel and Taylor somewhat amiss in their read of the more nuanced nature of classical thought and, in particular, Plato. What difference does such a different interpretation make?

I mentioned above that Taylor's more engaged read of Hegel in the 1970s did move him in a different direction than his more committed leftist thinking and activism of the 1950s and 1960s. This merging of Hegel and Gadamer, and the difference it makes, was pondered thoughtfully and succinctly by Ronald Beiner in his essay, "Hermeneutical Generosity and Social Criticism" in *Philosophy in a Time of Lost Spirit: Essays on Contemporary Theory*.[27] Beiner makes the telling point that in Taylor's more ideological leftist phase, his analysis of the economic and political situation was clean and clear—the center and center right distorted reality to serve a questionable agenda.

But, the more Taylor was impacted by Gadamer (and others) a form of hermeneutical generosity emerged in which diverse and divergent ways of knowing and being rerouted Taylor's thinking and multicultural activism. This did not mean that Taylor slipped into sheer relativism or became an uncritical fan of postmodernism. It did mean, though, that Taylor was less inclined (in thought and deed) to be uncritical of the leftist and NDP positions of his younger years. This does not mean that Taylor genuflected to the political Right. In fact, there is a centrist and humanistic Hegelianism in Taylor that refuses to go too far to the political Right or Left. The earlier Marxism is somewhat softened but there is certainly no uncritical turn to the ideological neo-Liberalism of Thatcher, Reagan, and Mulroney.

The 1980s was a period of time in which Taylor turned more and more to the dialogue within the Western Tradition regarding various approaches to understanding and defining the self—his summa of sorts that ended such a decade, *Sources of the Self: The Making of Modern Identity*[28] was a packed tome, and the more abridged and *Readers Digest* version was delivered as the CBC Massey lectures and published as *The Malaise of Modernity*.[29] It is significant, when reading both the larger text and shorter version, how Taylor defends the layered and complex modern notion of the Self against what he sees as its limitations and closing off discussion in classical thought and a too open-ended approach of postmodern ideology. This is Taylor doing his Hegelian via media between the ancients and the postmoderns. The question, as raised above is this: Did Hegel and Taylor misread the classical notion of the self as a limited and inadequate notion of liberty to serve the more modern liberal version? And, what might be the implications of such a misread and problematic hermeneutic? In short, does Taylor lack a certain hermeneutical generosity toward the Classical Tradition and Plato? And, if so, why?

The Sources of the Self was somewhat thinned out in nature and content, given Taylor's attitude to the classical ethos, yet the main themes remained unchanged when Taylor delivered the 1991 CBC Massey Lectures that was published as *Malaise of Modernity*. There are some significant points of convergence between Taylor's notion of "malaise" that the most sensitive in the modern and postmodern ethos experience and Grant's notion of "intimations of betrayal." Both men, from different angles and perspectives, concur on the fact that something is seriously missing in how the West conceives and understands the self and identity. Much is promised but little of substantive depth is delivered for the longing and thirsting soul. Taylor noted this malaise and Grant highlighted the fact that many are those of much sensitivity and insight that have intimations of being betrayed by hopes and dreams offered, and a table spread lacking the goods and nutrition for the soul.

Both Grant and Taylor, for different reasons and from different perspectives, refused to bend the knee to a narrow notion of reason (rationalism being the issue) and science (scientism being the problem). The fact that classical thought, classical Christian philosophy-theology, the romantic-humanist branches of the Enlightenment project and the postmodern critique of "logocentrism" (which is meant as a deconstructionist approach to rationalism and scientism) have an openness to spirituality and religion means that reductionistic nature of ideological secularism conceals much more than it reveals.

Taylor's earlier missives, *A Catholic Modernity?*[30] and *Varieties of Religion Today: William James Revisited*[31] and his much larger and more demanding tome of a read, *A Secular Age* (winner of the 2007 Templeton Prize)[32] illuminate, for the attentive reader, Taylor's nuanced approach to the religious issue and the challenge of secularism. *A Secular Age* thoughtfully and nimbly, in a historic manner, clarifies why secularism emerged, how religion contributed to the rise of secularism but the limitations of secularism as an ideology that negates or caricatures religion. *A Secular Age*, needless to say, did not please the hardline leftist secularists, and as there has been an unfortunate tendency for the Left to equal Secularism (Marx and tribe), Taylor's deeper Roman Catholic commitments (and his approval and support of religion and spirituality through a deeper delving in James) was suspected by the Left which once held him near and dear. Does this mean that Taylor's openness to spirituality and religion placed him on the Right?

The fact that the best of the Enlightenment project was supportive of spirituality and religion (Hegel, like Taylor, synthesized, in a dialectical manner, the wisest and most mature elements of the rational and romantic vision into a full-bodied humanistic vision) means that the extreme right of the Enlightenment (ideological secularism and, for that matter, the New Atheism) does not even represent, in a minimal way, the sheer catholic synthesis of the best of the modern Enlightenment project that Hegel and Taylor warmly welcome. I mentioned at the beginning of this essay, that Taylor is one of the finest apologists of the modern liberal enlightenment project and it is his deep understanding of such a layered tradition that gives him credibility when interpreting it against those who would reduce and restrict it in such a way that negates spirituality and religion (such as those who see religion as a problem that negates freedom and a being enlightened in a more rational and scientific way and manner).

The challenge for Taylor, of course, as a booster for the Enlightenment project is to clarify, beyond the religious pluralism of the Enlightenment, the relationship between Christianity and other religions. There has been, obviously, post–Vatican II thinking on contemplative interfaith dialogue and Taylor has pointed in such a direction but more demanding questions still remain. Is process or procedural liberalism (or dialogue) the end point of interfaith engagement? Is pluralism or some form of sophisticated syncretism the new ideology in a post-Christendom, postscientific, post-secular era? Are these the new absolutes that cannot be questioned? It is these sorts of questions that Grant and Taylor faced (Grant founded one of the finest Inter-Faith Religious Studies Departments in Canada) when dealing with the larger and perennial issues that the political Left and variations of secular liberalism often negate.

GRANT AND TAYLOR: CANADIAN OWLS

There can be no doubt that Grant and Taylor are agents of a wisdom tradition and like the philosophic owls there is a breadth and depth to them. Both men have been on the political Left but both men have questioned and distanced themselves from a secular and ideological form of the Left. This does not mean that they are on the conservative or republican right; both men are too wise for such a commitment. Grant was much more grounded in the classical tradition and ethos and suspicious of the subtle form of modernity that Taylor embraces. Grant often pitted Plato against Hegel and, in this sense, if Grant were alive, he would have serious questions about Taylor's thoughtful modernity.

Grant had many owls in his home and he very much embodied the wisdom way of the ancients. Taylor, like Hegel, is a philosophic owl and wisdom figure within the Enlightenment ethos; he brings sanity, poise, and moderation to those who would reduce the fullness of such a project to a single vision and one-dimensional approach. Grant and Taylor, in their different ways, embody the best of the Canadian philosophic tradition and, as such, deserve to be lauded as Canadian owls.

NOTES

1. Leslie Armour and Elizabeth Trott, *The Faces of Reason: An Essay on Philosophy and Culture in English Canada, 1850–1950* (Waterloo: Wilfrid Laurier University Press, 1981).

2. Robert C. Sibley, *Northern Spirits: John Watson, George Grant, and Charles Taylor: Appropriations of Hegelian Political Thought* (Montreal and Kingston: McGill-Queen's University Press, 2008).

3. Robert Meynell, *Canadian Idealism and the Philosophy of Freedom: C. B. Macpherson, George Grant and Charles Taylor* (Montreal and Kingston: McGill-Queen's University Press, 2011).

4. Ian Angus, *The Undiscovered Country: Essays in Canadian Intellectual Culture* (Vancouver: University of British Columbia Press, 2013).

5. David MacGregor, "Canada's Hegel," *Literary Review of Canada*, February 1994, available at https://reviewcanada.ca/magazine/1994/02/canadas-hegel/.

6. Philip Resnick, "Hegel's Canadian Heirs," *Literary Review of Canada*, May 2008, available at http://marklovewell.com/articles/lovewell_lrc08may.pdf.

7. Michael Oliver, ed. *Social Purpose for Canada* (Toronto: University of Toronto Press, 1961).

8. Charles Taylor, *The Pattern of Politics* (Toronto: McClelland Limited, 1970).

9. Laurier LaPierre, Jack McLeod, Charles Taylor, and Walter Young, eds. *Essays on the Left: Essays in Honour of T. C. Douglas* (Toronto: McClelland and Stewart Limited, 1971).

10. George Grant, *Lament for a Nation: The Defeat of Canadian Nationalism* (Ottawa: Carleton University Press, 1995a).

11. George Grant, *Philosophy in the Mass Age* (Toronto: The Copp Clark Publishing Company, 1959), chapters IV, VI, VII & VIII.

12. Ibid., v.

13. Ron Dart, *The Red Tory Tradition: Ancient Roots, New Routes* (Dewdney, BC: Synaxis Press, 1999), chapter 3.

14. S. W. Wise and Robert Craig Brown, *Canada Views the United States* (Toronto: Macmillan of Canada, 1967).

15. S. W. Wise, *God's Peculiar Peoples: Essays on Political Culture in Nineteenth-Century* (Ottawa: Carleton University Press, 1993).

16. Shadia Drury, "Socratic Mischief: How Human Civilization Went Astray," *Ted Talk in Calgary*. January 14, 2019, available at https://www.youtube.com/watch?v=0R367Q4zBQI.

17. Alasdair MacIntyre, *After Virtue: A Study in Moral Theory* (Notre Dame: University of Notre Dame Press, 1981).

18. Paul Blackledge and Kelvin Knight, eds., *Virtue and Politics: Alasdair MacIntyre's Revolutionary Aristotelianism* (Notre Dame: University of Notre Dame Press, 2011).

19. Phillip Blond, *Red Tory: How Left and Right Have Broken Britain and How We Can Fix It* (London: Faber and Faber, 2010).

20. George Grant, *Time as History* (Toronto: University of Toronto Press, 1995b). I might add that Grant's deeper concerns with the thinking and popularity of Nietzsche and Heidegger is amply pondered, reflected upon, and developed in Ronald Beiner's most recent missive, *Dangerous Minds: Nietzsche, Heidegger, and the Return of the Far Right* (Philadelphia: University of Philadelphia Press, 2018).

21. George Grant, *English Speaking Justice* (Toronto: Anansi, 1974).

22. Ibid., 74.

23. George Grant, *Technology and Empire: Perspectives on North America* (Toronto: Anansi, 1969).

24. George Grant, *Technology and Justice* (Concord/Ontario: House of Anansi Press Limited, 1986).

25. Dart, *The North American High Tory Tradition*, 197–205.

26. John Gray, *Enlightenment's Wake: Politics and Culture at the Close of the Modern Age* (London: Routledge, 1995). I might add that although Gray has soared in popularity most of his writings tend to read and interpret the modern Enlightenment project through reductionistic eyes.

27. Ronald Beiner. *Philosophy in a Time of Lost Spirit: Essays on Contemporary Theory* (Toronto: University of Toronto Press, 1997), 151–66.

28. Charles Taylor, *Sources of the Self: The Making of the Modern Identity* (Cambridge: Harvard University Press, 1989).

29. Charles Taylor, *The Malaise of Modernity* (Concord/Ontario: Anansi, 1991).

30. Charles Taylor, *A Catholic Modernity?* (New York: Oxford University Press, 1999).

31. Charles Taylor, *Varieties of Religion Today: William James Revisited* (Cambridge: Harvard University Press, 2002).

32. Charles Taylor, *A Secular Age* (Cambridge: The Belknap Press of Harvard University Press, 2007).

BIBLIOGRAPHY

Angus, Ian. 2013. *The Undiscovered Country: Essays in Canadian Intellectual Culture*. Vancouver: University of British Columbia Press.

Armour, Leslie, and Elizabeth Trott. 1981. *The Faces of Reason: An Essay on Philosophy and Culture in English Canada, 1850–1950*. Waterloo: Wilfrid Laurier University Press.

Beiner, Ronald. 1997. *Philosophy in a Time of Lost Spirit: Essays on Contemporary Theory*. Toronto: University of Toronto Press.
———. 2018. *Dangerous Minds: Nietzsche, Heidegger, and the Return of the Far Right*. Philadelphia: University of Philadelphia Press.
Blackledge, Paul, and Kelvin Knight, eds. 2011. *Virtue and Politics: Alasdair MacIntyre's Revolutionary Aristotelianism*. Notre Dame: University of Notre Dame Press.
Blond, Phillip. 2010. *Red Tory: How Left and Right Have Broken Britain and How We Can Fix It*. London: Faber and Faber.
Dart, Ron. 1999. *The Red Tory Tradition: Ancient Roots, New Routes*. Dewdney, BC: Synaxis Press.
Drury, Shadia. 2019. "Socratic Mischief: How Human Civilization Went Astray." *Ted Talk in Calgary*. January 14. Available at https://www.youtube.com/watch?v=0R367Q4zBQI.
Grant, George. 1959. *Philosophy in the Mass Age*. Toronto: The Copp Clark Publishing Company.
———. 1969. *Technology and Empire: Perspectives on North America*. Toronto: Anansi.
———. 1974. *English Speaking Justice*. Toronto: Anansi.
———. 1986. *Technology and Justice*. Concord/Ontario: House of Anansi Press Limited.
———. 1995a. *Lament for a Nation: The Defeat of Canadian Nationalism*. Ottawa: Carleton University Press.
———. 1995b. *Time as History*. Toronto: University of Toronto Press.
Gray, John. 1995. *Enlightenment's Wake: Politics and Culture at the Close of the Modern Age* London: Routledge.
LaPierre, Laurier, Jack McLeod, Charles Taylor, and Walter Young, eds. 1971. *Essays on the Left: Essays in Honour of T. C. Douglas*. Toronto: McClelland and Stewart Limited.
MacGregor, David. 1994. "Canada's Hegel." *Literary Review of Canada*, February. Available at https://reviewcanada.ca/magazine/1994/02/canadas-hegel/.
MacIntyre, Alasdair. 1981. *After Virtue: A Study in Moral Theory*. Notre Dame: University of Notre Dame Press.
Meynell, Robert. 2011. *Canadian Idealism and the Philosophy of Freedom: C. B. Macpherson, George Grant and Charles Taylor*. Montreal and Kingston: McGill-Queen's University Press.
Oliver, Michael, ed. 1961. *Social Purpose for Canada*. Toronto: University of Toronto Press.
Resnick, Philip. 2008. "Hegel's Canadian heirs." *Literary Review of Canada*, May. http://marklovewell.com/articles/lovewell_lrc08may.pdf.
Sibley, Robert C. 2008. *Northern Spirits: John Watson, George Grant, and Charles Taylor: Appropriations of Hegelian Political Thought*. Montreal and Kingston: McGill-Queen's University Press.
Taylor, Charles. 1970. *The Pattern of Politics*. Toronto: McClelland Limited.
———. 1989. *Sources of the Self: The Making of the Modern Identity*. Cambridge: Harvard University Press.
———. 1991. *The Malaise of Modernity*. Concord/Ontario: Anansi.
———. 1999. *A Catholic Modernity?* New York: Oxford University Press.
———. 2002. *Varieties of Religion Today: William James Revisited*. Cambridge: Harvard University Press.
———. 2007. *A Secular Age*. Cambridge: The Belknap Press of Harvard University Press.
Wise, S. W. 1993. *God's Peculiar Peoples: Essays on Political Culture in Nineteenth-Century*. Ottawa: Carleton University Press.
Wise, S. W., and Robert Craig Brown. 1967. *Canada Views the United States*. Toronto: Macmillan of Canada.

Chapter Five

Alasdair MacIntyre's Revolutionary Peripateticism

Kelvin Knight

In the summer of 2007, Alasdair MacIntyre strode to a podium at Britain's most troubled university.

> Before I even begin, let me say that among the elements in the conference's title is the word resistance and I've been asked by the union to talk . . . about the boycott which they are asking faculty and others to observe over a variety of functions because of the failure of London Metropolitan University to negotiate adequately with or to recognize the union adequately and to use this to cut jobs. I want to say that this is a form of resistance that I think everyone ought to agree with.[1]

Almost forty years before, when he moved from the United Kingdom to the United States, British universities were altogether more exclusive institutions. Then, it was affluent students, largely straight from "public," fee-paying schools, mostly male and almost exclusively white, who resisted the new, academic authority to which they were subject. MacIntyre understood them well, since he came from a similar background and had himself become a Marxist and member of the Communist Party of Great Britain when an undergraduate. This was some twenty years earlier, after the Second World War's defeat of fascism, and after the beginning of the Cold War between the communist East and capitalist West. Politics was then an utterly serious business, in a threatening new world of nuclear weapons. He had worked as a political activist, as an academic, and for the Workers' Education Association, teaching older, employed students who lacked the privileges of those brought up to enter Oxford or Cambridge, the London School of Economics (LSE), or Essex.

In 2007, MacIntyre walked into the industrial conflict of a very different university. It was, and remains, a university with Britain's largest proportion of black and minority ethnic students, many of whom have to work full-time in order to try to study full-time. It was a university to which he would return many times, both to teach and research, unpaid, flying across the Atlantic and staying in London, all at his own expense. His moral commitments remained as they had been over forty years earlier.

In the audience on this first visit was the leading theorist of Britain's Socialist Workers Party (SWP), which occupied the position on Britain's Far Left that the Communist Party had once enjoyed. MacIntyre had himself been one of the group's leading members, long before. He, Alex Callinicos now alleged, had deserted the Left. The deserter could take that head-on:

> I don't know how to [change the social system] but then I don't think that you do either, and I think it's very important that if you don't know how to do it you shouldn't talk as though you do. That's to say, it would be indeed wonderful if we had a theory and a practice related to contemporary capitalist social order which would do for us what Marxist parties once hoped to do—but we don't.[2]

This problem had been at the forefront of MacIntyre's mind for forty years. When he left Essex for Massachusetts, he had indeed flown away from the British Left. He had never joined the American Left, and he had never joined any American political party. Merely criticizing capitalist social order was a world away from changing it. Indeed, mere demonstration of dissent seemed a displacement activity by those unable even to theorize how change might be enacted. Like them, MacIntyre wanted a theory and a practice related to contemporary capitalism which would do what he had once hoped would be done by Marxist parties; unlike the most committed of them, he, after much revolutionary theorizing and attempted practice, had acknowledged that no group could do what he still thought it would be indeed wonderful to do.

In America, MacIntyre tried to work through the problem, not just with contemporary capitalist social order, which he thought obvious, but with the theory and practice of those who wished for its replacement. What was most obviously wrong with Marxism was that it lacked a moral theory of its own. When Marxists had to decide what was to be done, and to justify their actions to themselves and others, they had to resort either to simulacra of Kantianism or "a means-end morality" that MacIntyre often characterized as "a crude utilitarianism."[3] This could be blamed on Marx, who had impatiently walked away from philosophy before he had a theory adequate to any revolutionary practice. Therefore, if there was to be any hope of doing what Marxist parties had once hoped to do, then what had first to be done was to make good Marx's error and return to serious philosophizing. In America, MacIntyre became a full-time philosopher.

Over a decade passed before MacIntyre, in 1981, presented *After Virtue: A Study in Moral Theory*. The focus of his critique had hardly shifted but had sharpened upon the modern moral philosophy that legitimated capitalism. Legitimation occurred by simultaneously maintaining incompatible moral theories. The moral ideals of utility and freedom that had divided Marxists had first divided modernity, between the utilitarianism that justified the bureaucratic state and the rights that justified capitalist competition and property. The interminability of modern moral debate, and consequent incoherence of modern morality, was due to modernity's social structure. A similar incoherence afflicted modern social science. To this extent, he took himself to still be following Marx. The third of Marx's *Theses on Feuerbach* recognized

> that the Enlightenment's mechanistic account of human action included both a thesis about the predictability of human behavior and a thesis about the appropriate ways to manipulate human behavior. As an observer, if I know the relevant laws governing the behavior of others, I can whenever I observe that the antecedent conditions have been fulfilled predict the outcome. As an agent, if I know these laws, I can whenever I can contrive the fulfilment of the same antecedent conditions produce the outcome. What Marx understood was that such an agent is forced to regard his own actions quite differently from the behavior of those whom he is manipulating. For the behavior of the manipulated is being contrived in accordance with his intentions, reasons and purposes; intentions, reasons and purposes which he is treating, at least while he is engaged in such manipulation, as exempt from the laws which govern the behavior of the manipulated.[4]

The pity was that, having recognized this, Marx abandoned philosophy and attempted to make a comprehensive social and historical science out of political economy. With such a science, Marxists would deceive themselves into thinking that they could use state power to manipulate their way to communism. The end, they supposed, justified their means and, of course, their power. On the analysis of both MacIntyre and the SWP, what Stalinists had instead created was a state capitalism.

MacIntyre's analysis of modernity, both Western and Eastern, criticized not only workers' exploitation but also their institutionalized manipulation. In this, he continued the line of thought that he had developed with the likes of E. P. Thompson and Charles Taylor in what history knows as Britain's First New Left.[5] What such anti-Stalinist, humanist Marxists criticized as workers' systemic alienation from their own activity, he now attacked as managerial manipulation warranted by the contradictions of modern moral and social theory. The problem was no longer reducible to an impersonal capitalist mode of production, as the subject for scientific study by what had become Marxist theory. Ethically, it was a problem of identifying ideas capable of motivating resistance to institutions that empower some to dominate and manipulate others. In the Stalinist East, Marxist ideas had led to all power being institutionalized in the party and state. In the more economically successful West, ideas of private enterprise, property, and rights had institutionalized power in private corporations. In both, workers were demoralized and manipulated by professional managers.

Capitalist modernity would remain the object of MacIntyre's critique as much as ever. His great difference from the revolutionary Left was that he did not share its belief that the French Revolution, which it supposed had instituted a permanent change from feudal to capitalist rule, or the Russian Revolution, which it supposed had instituted a change from class to classless rule, provided any model for the successful institutionalization of a liberatory socialism. Without abandoning hope for some such change, he accepted that there was no adequate reason to suppose that it would occur of historical necessity or that it could occur by substituting one group of rulers for another. What the experience of twentieth-century Russia and China, and of mid-twentieth-century British and European social democracy, seemed to evince was that the bureaucratic state was as crucial to maintaining exploitation and manipulation as was capital's private ownership. What the subsequent failure of those revolutionary and reformist socialist experiments suggested was that even if the state were to be directed by some socialist party it would not suffice to actualize socialism's theoretical ideal.

If any hope for any kind of revolutionary change for the better were to be sustained, then serious theorizing was necessary. Such theorizing must try to comprehend real social practice, in a way that what MacIntyre criticized as the Enlightenment project in moral theory failed to do. What Bentham said of the purposive pursuit of welfare was fine, in theory. What Kant said of the moral obligatoriness of treating everyone as an end in themselves was excellent, so long as one was prepared to isolate moral ideals from empirical reality. As he would later make explicit,[6] MacIntyre's critique of the Enlightenment's moral theories was not with their morality but with their detachment of philosophical theory from everyday practice. In Marx's term, his critique targeted them as ideology. In practice, they functioned to legitimate an order to which they failed to correspond. For intellectuals, they became the heart of an otherwise heartless world, the soul of soulless conditions. For MacIntyre, they are the sigh of the oppressed creature. As expressed in the language of human rights, they are the last utopia to be unmasked. What, for him, remains the greatest hope expressed by Marx was of a different kind. It was the hope to theorize practice so realistically that the theory really was, is, and will be enacted. Marx's most genuinely revolutionary insight was that the standpoint of modern "civil society cannot be transcended, and its limitations adequately understood and criticized, by theory alone, that is, by theory divorced from practice, but only by a particular kind of practice, practice informed by a particular kind of theory rooted in that same practice."[7] The task MacIntyre set himself in walking away from the British Left to the American academy was to try to think through what such praxis might be.

After Virtue shocked MacIntyre's audiences with its journey all the way back to Aristotle. Only relatively less shocking was his suggestion that the alternative terminus was not Marx but Nietzsche. Unlike Marx, Nietzsche placed no hope in social revolution. What MacIntyre valued in Nietzsche was the radicalism of his philosophical critique of all modern hopes, including those for socialism. If there was no other ground for hope than those offered by modern moral and social theorists, then no will to truth could be any more than an agonistic will to power. Indeed, behind modern ideologies and institutions, modern social reality seemed to be as Nietzsche described the human condition. If one were to continue looking for hope after Nietzsche's devastating deconstruction of its modern forms, then one would have to look elsewhere. Having done so, MacIntyre announced that hope could still be found in Aristotelian ethics. In *After Virtue*, his caveat was that what he called Aristotle's metaphysical biology had to be discarded in order to properly focus on what is of continuing value in Aristotle's philosophy of practice. Thus trimmed, Aristotelianism's conceptual scheme involves

> a fundamental contrast between man-as-he-happens-to-be and man-as-he-could-be-if-he-realized-his-essential-nature. Ethics is the science which is to enable men to understand how they make the transition from the former state to the latter.... The precepts which enjoin the various virtues and prohibit the vices which are their counterparts instruct us how to move from potentiality to act, how to realize our true nature and to reach our true end. To defy them will be to be frustrated and incomplete, to fail to achieve that good of rational happiness which is peculiarly ours as a species to pursue. The desires and emotions which we possess are to be put in order and educated by the use of such precepts and by the cultivation of those habits of action which the study of ethics prescribes; reason instructs us both as to what our true end is and as to how to reach it.[8]

After Virtue identified a number of ways in which this scheme has been retheorized through Western history. It then theorized the scheme in contemporary terms. One step was psychological, in showing how it was possible to interpret and narrate one's sense of identity, one's various aims, interests, and ambitions and one's experiences in terms of that scheme. Another step was historical. Here, MacIntyre refused to imitate Marx and Hegel in theorizing history as a teleological totality of progress. Instead, he reflected on the changing Aristotelian tradition of ethical theorizing about social practice. It was this second-order theorizing that would most excite the critical faculties of most other professional philosophers, and that would preoccupy MacIntyre in his next two books: *Whose Justice? Which Rationality?* and *Three*

Rival Versions of Moral Enquiry. Each of these is an important work in the philosophy of the history of philosophy. Each says much, philosophically, about practice. Even so, neither book focused upon what was essential to his original task. Indeed, in elaborating on virtues and vices, on movement from potentiality to act, and on reasoning about action and the ordering of ends, he argued for the historical and philosophical significance of Thomas Aquinas's synthesis of Aristotelianism with Augustinian Christianity. Still more notoriously, he practiced what he theorized in becoming a Roman Catholic. So far as politics and ethics were concerned, this digression allowed political philosophers to categorize him as a communitarian critic of Rawls's liberalism and moral philosophers to categorize him as a virtue ethicist.

Having, in *After Virtue*, identified his philosophical position within a longer Aristotelian tradition, the two subsequent books distinguish this tradition from rivals. Incisive though these exercises in intellectual history are, they are philosophically complex in at least two ways.

One complication is due to his admission, in *After Virtue*, that "a tradition is sustained and advanced by its own internal arguments and conflicts."[9] If *Whose Justice?* tried to establish that the most plausible kind of Aristotelianism derived from the work of Aquinas, *Three Rival Versions* admitted that there have been incompatible variants even of a specifically Thomistic Aristotelianism. In further books—*Dependent Rational Animals: Why Human Beings Need the Virtues* (1999), *Edith Stein: A Philosophical Prologue, 1913–1922* (2005), *God, Philosophy, Universities: A Selective History of the Catholic Philosophical Tradition* (2009), and his contributions to *Intractable Disputes about the Natural Law: Alasdair MacIntyre and Critics* (2009)—his principal concern was to elaborate the case for his unconventional version of Thomistic Aristotelianism, as an undogmatic kind of intellectual enquiry into social practice. The earliest, *Dependent Rational Animals*, is certainly the one that has continued to have the widest appeal, in part because its concern with Thomism's internal arguments and conflicts is less apparent there than are his points against non-Thomistic Aristotelians and non-Aristotelian philosophers. Nonetheless, the book renounces his previous dismissal of Aristotle's metaphysical biology in order to elaborate a Thomistic naturalism that is at once teleological and sociological. This naturalism is incompatible with the dualistic personalism that allowed Jacques Maritain—one of two philosophers for whom MacIntyre had expressed "the greatest respect and from whom I have learned most,"[10] as an Aristotelian—to theorize human rights and facilitate Catholicism's mid-twentieth-century accommodation to liberalism.[11] Having abandoned Marxism because its theoretical lacunae rendered its attempted challenge to capitalism and liberal ideology inadequate, he had to adopt novel positions regarding Aquinas and Aristotle in order to sustain a challenge to capitalism and liberalism in their names.

If this theoretical complication was something entirely new in MacIntyre's philosophy, the second and more elemental complication in his account of Aristotelianism as a tradition has clear origins in his earlier Marxism. As a Marxist, he was always keen to emphasize ideas in Marx and Marxism which resisted theory's reification from labor and action. Socialist consciousness, he wrote, is aware of work's potential to remake external nature "into the image of man by means of art and science."[12] Against attempts to subject artists and scientists to state diktat, he argued that "art and science move by their own laws of development."[13] Marxism, he had wanted to argue, was, at its best, the coherent theorization of shared human practice that no capitalist ideology could be. This was a fine thought, and a fine theoretical aspiration, but one that proved impossible to justify. Now, with Aristotelianism, he had another go. His paradigmatic Aristotelian is not a professional theorist but an artist, scientist or some other kind of worker, or the fulfiller of other social roles, who understands her own good to be realized through such fulfillment insofar as the roles are ones that allow her to manage her own actions and, therefore, to achieve excellence in their performance.[14] Certainly, this idea of personal virtue and of its necessary social conditions is recognizable in Aristotle, certainly it was rendered less elitist by Aquinas, and certainly MacIntyre's adaption of their arguments to his purposes is, or would be, contested by most students of both Aristotle and Aquinas. As is now acknowledged by most students of his own work, the idea combines elements from Aristotle, Aquinas, and Marx. It does so in order to try to pick up from where, following the "Theses on Feuerbach," Marx abandoned philosophy.

The first step that *After Virtue* took in retheorizing Aristotelianism's conceptual scheme in modern and post-Marxist terms was neither psychological nor historical. Rather, "the first stage requires a background account of what I shall call a practice."[15] This basic step was sociological and socialist, or, as American political philosophers preferred, communitarian. MacIntyre's objection to liberalism was to Kant, Mill and Locke long before it was to anything written by Rawls (of whom he had been an early, appreciative reader)[16], and it was more to the Enlightenment's project of high moral theory than to analytic philosophers' attempts to salvage something from that project's failure. Even so, that objection was indeed to the individualist presuppositions of a long liberal tradition that Rawls had himself retheorized. MacIntyre's starting point was not the metaphysically or hypothetically abstracted, sociologically and psychologically incredible, individual of classical and Kantian liberalism. Nor was it the social totality of what became Marxist theory, capable of causally determining individuals' behavior. Rather, it was what he called *a* practice.

Ideas of shared practice had informed the most important moves in philosophy in the decades following the shock of the First World War. Nietzsche's denial of moral rationality was extended to the irrationality of states. Morally and politically, Europe's Age of Reason was clearly over. In Germany, Heidegger made extraordinary moves in rethinking what Aristotle said of being, time, and individuals' thought and actions apart from his compatriots' neo-Kantianism. In Britain, Wittgenstein increasingly contemplated thought and action as matters of custom, habit, and rule-following. Philosophers generally despaired of states as instruments of their rational ideals and policies. Many who understood why European liberalism had been defeated, but who still aspired to change the world for the better, looked to Marx. When one of those came to despair also of Marx, seeing neither the atomized individual not the social totality as an adequate starting point, he instead took as a more modest starting point the philosophical idea of shared practice.

A practice, on MacIntyre's account, is distinguished by a good which its participants characteristically try to achieve. It is in respect of this shared goal that participants reason with one another about their actions as practitioners. While not determining individuals' intentions, reasons, or purposes, each practice gives individuals reasons for action. This was not a surprising thought for analytic philosophers, one of whom, Peter Geach—the other philosopher for whom MacIntyre expressed great respect and gratitude—reinstilled objective, attributive meaning to linguistic usage of "good." Even so, such thoughts appeared to represent a retreat from politics and purposiveness. If they had any political implication it was conservative: since rational action is grounded in customary rules, custom should be conserved. This rationale was reversed by MacIntyre's introduction of Aristotle's teleological explanation of action by reference to the goods that it was intended to actualize. Whereas Aristotle had discriminated between the instrumental function of production and the rational purposiveness of action or *praxis*, MacIntyre generalized about a multiplicity of productive practices, retaining Aristotle's judgment that the highest, most architectonic practice was politics.

Shared practices, on MacIntyre's account, are the schools of the virtues. They educate individuals into the qualities that enable them to get along with others and into standards of excellence that enable them to actualize their own good, as social beings, as well as good products. Practices are the ways in which individuals are socialized into reasoning with others, into recognizing goods greater than that of satisfying their own immediate desires, and into working with others for the sake of those common goods. By tutoring individuals in the idea of goods greater than themselves, social practices endow individuals' actions with a sense of purposiveness and meaning that can furnish their understanding of themselves, their past actions and future intentions, with a narrative unity that is communicable to, and recognizable by, others.

What gives a sharply and distinctively critical edge to MacIntyre's concept of social practices is his clear juxtaposition of practices to institutions.

This is what his current Aristotelianism most importantly owes to his past Marxism. Unlike Marx's supposedly scientific juxtaposition of labor to capital, MacIntyre's juxtaposition is expressly ethical. Whereas the young Marx complained that capital's employment of labor alienated workers from that productive activity which is most essentially human, the mature MacIntyre protests that corporate institutions' domination of purposive practices denies practitioners rational, cooperative, and ethically educative direction of their own actions. It is this juxtaposition that most clearly reverses the conservative, rule-following rationale of what is more familiarly said of practice and tradition:

> Practices must not be confused with institutions. Chess, physics and medicine are practices; chess clubs, laboratories, universities and hospitals are institutions. Institutions are characteristically and necessarily concerned with . . . external goods. They are involved in acquiring money and other material goods; they are structured in terms of power and status, and they distribute money, power and status as rewards. Nor could they do otherwise if they are to sustain not only themselves, but also the practices of which they are the bearers. For no practices can survive for any length of time unsustained by institutions. Indeed so intimate is the relationship of practices to institutions—and consequently of the goods external to the goods internal to the practices in question—that institutions and practices characteristically form a single causal order in which the ideals and the creativity of the practice are always vulnerable to the acquisitiveness of the institution, in which the cooperative care for common goods of the practice is always vulnerable to the competitiveness of the institution. In this context the essential function of the virtues is clear. Without them, without justice, courage and truthfulness, practices could not resist the corrupting power of institutions.[17]

For most chess players, physicists, and medics, most of the time, all may feel fine. After all, if any practice is to progress toward its distinctive good, it requires organization or institutionalization. So long as the chess club, laboratory, university, or hospital enables them to pursue the good internal to chess, physics, or medicine, then even great inequalities in the distribution of money, power, and status between nurses, trainee doctors, and senior consultants may be justified by reasoning about pursuit of their shared good as participants in the practice. So long as the senior managers of a university or hospital allow for pursuit of that good, allow the physicists or medics to reason how best to pursue it, and allow such reasoning to, at least, affect their own decision-making about how to distribute resources, then all may indeed be fine. Conversely, insofar as those managers allow their decision-making to be determined by other considerations, or by other individuals or institutions with greater money, power, or status and with no part in the practices they rule, then practitioners and managers will conflict.

It was such a conflict into which MacIntyre walked in addressing the 2007 conference. Even so, it was fought between rival institutions. What he supported was the demand of one institution, the University and College Union (UCU), to be properly recognized and negotiated with by another, the university. On the virtues of this form of resistance, by a labor union in industrial conflict with a corporate employer, he and the SWP could agree. Indeed, once the university management had terminated all lectureships in philosophy, history, and a few other disciplines, it made redundant the SWP member who was the leading, surviving UCU activist. MacIntyre would also agree with the SWP that such resistance should be informed by aims additional to the defense of jobs and incomes. Here, though, they would disagree about what those aims should be. For one, the aim is to gain recruits with whom to build the party, on the supposition that this is the means to revolution; for MacIntyre, the aim is to defend personal vocations, educative disciplines, and the pursuit of common goods.

Out of the 2007 conference emerged two new institutions. One was an International Society for MacIntyrean Enquiry, in which MacIntyre himself plays no part. It was formed by conferees from the political Left, Right, and Center, from universities across Europe and America, and from departments of philosophy, politics, sociology, and what has become the distinct academic discipline of theorizing management. Each of these disciplines may, like physics, be understood as a distinct practice. A major concern of conferees' was to continue debating the implications and applications of MacIntyre's juxtaposition of institutions to practices. Creation of their own institution facilitated their cooperative, international, and interdisciplinary work, which continues.[18]

The second institution has a similar aim.[19] Joined by MacIntyre, the Centre for Contemporary Aristotelian Studies in Ethics and Politics has been based at the troubled university. His research project there was into "common goods and political reasoning." His express aim was

> to complete what has been an ongoing project concerned with Aquinas's conception of the common good of political societies, as he developed it from Aristotle's account of the good of political community, and with whether and in what ways this conception might find application in the politics of modern societies. A major aim of the study is to identify the different types and styles of political reasoning that are at home in contemporary politics in advanced societies and to compare them with the type and style of reasoning which is needed, if one is to identify and achieve the common goods of political societies.

The conclusions he anticipated were

that the institutional prerequisites for effective political reasoning aimed at achieving the common good of political societies are not just different from, but incompatible with the institutional structures of the modern state and of the advanced economies with which the activities of the modern state are increasingly integrated.[20]

What became *Ethics in the Conflicts of Modernity* achieves all this and far more besides. In many ways, the 2016 book marks his return to the original task and ethical argument of *After Virtue*. Now, however, he considers it an Aristotelian insight "that it is through conflict and sometimes only through conflict that we learn what our ends and purposes are," while repeating "that moral education goes on and . . . the virtues come to be valued and redefined" under conditions of conflict.[21] As anticipated, it turns out that his Thomistically Aristotelian conception of the political good cannot find application within the electoral politics or bureaucratic institutions of modern states. For this reason, it makes little sense to locate his type of political reasoning anywhere along liberal democracy's political spectrum—left, right, or center.

This does not entail that his kind of political reasoning can have no contemporary application. To the contrary, he restates his academically notorious proposition that such reasoning is institutionalizable within certain local communities, citing as examples, Thorupstrand, a Danish fishing village, and Monte Azul, a Brazilian favela or slum.[22] These are political societies in the sense that they are rationally run by their participants in pursuit of discursively ordered common goods, conducive to the flourishing of those inhabitants. Such communities differ in scale, in their lack of military defense, and in other ways, from those states over the government of which parties of left and right contend.

Ethics in the Conflicts of Modernity concludes by exploring the political reasoning exemplified in the decisions and actions of four individuals: Vasily Grossman, a Soviet writer, Sandra Day O'Connor, a conservative Supreme Court Justice, C. L. R. James, a Trotskyist in Trinidad, America and Britain, and Denis Faul, a Catholic priest who mediated between state and rebels in The Troubles endured by Northern Ireland. It is in these various narratives that MacIntyre most closely analyzes types and styles of political reasoning which have been sustained, commendably, within modern societies.

The longest narrative is that recounted of Grossman; the shortest, that of O'Connor. What is likely to be most striking to an American reader is the extent to which MacIntyre defends the USSR against Grossman and the extent to which he criticizes O'Connor for her unquestioning attitude toward American institutions. While unstintingly critical of Stalin, of "Stalinist Russia," *and* of the later USSR, he applauds the insistence of "Victor Serge, custodian of the ideals of 1917," that Bolshevism "could have developed very differently, that there was no inevitability in the move from Lenin to Stalin."[23] Conversely, he himself insists against O'Connor

> that the United States is in fact governed by economic, financial, political, and media elites who determine the peculiarly limited set of alternatives between which voters are allowed to choose in state and federal elections, that money functions in American political life, so that the United States is in some respects not a democracy, but a plutocracy, and that the United States in recent decades has been a too often destructive force in world affairs.[24]

He judges O'Connor to have been incapable of entertaining such thoughts because they are precluded by the unquestioned presuppositions into which she was socialized, and judges her incapable of questioning her presuppositions because they belong to a tradition of American conservatism committed to "a false opposition between abstract reasoning on the one hand and reckoning with the particularities of social life on the other."[25] What enabled Grossman and James to put their beliefs and priorities in question was, however, much more than a Marxism which, for Grossman, attempted an institutional prohibition of all questioning. It was, in part, a number of changes in conditions that confronted both the Soviet and the Trinidadian Marxist with dilemmas which obliged them to reason about the goods that they pursued. Such dilemmas were absent from O'Connor's career progression, notwithstanding the sexist prejudice that, as MacIntyre emphasizes, she had to overcome.[26] What helped Grossman and James to make rational choices when faced with their personal dilemmas was also what complemented their Marxism as a source of questions, and what gave them external resources with which to put even their Marxism in question. For James, this included a firm family upbringing and a kind of formal education similar to that from which MacIntyre himself benefitted. For both James and Grossman, it also included the practice of an art. Grossman's art was literary, enabling him to pursue truth in an additional way to that of Marxist enquiry. That this should be so, Grossman should have learned from Marxists who were no less anti-Stalinist in art's defense[27] than would be the Trotskyist MacIntyre. What MacIntyre now adds, citing D. H. Lawrence and Oscar Wilde, is that such guidance can be theoretical as well as practical.[28] More practical guidance can be gained from other practices and arts. James benefitted especially from participation in what he (and now, following him, MacIntyre has) called the art of cricket—as a schoolboy and adult player, as a journalistic commentator and, eventually, as a moral critic. For him, as against anyone with an amoral will to win, to cheat was to deny oneself the ability to reason practically.[29] He had been brought up to acknowledge that to break the rules of a shared practice was simply (to use an expression that, in his time, was widely applied) "not cricket."[30]

The British Empire was thought by many of its administrators to have been won on the playing fields of Eton and Rugby public schools. Those bureaucratic managers were taught to be team players and rule followers, not individualists. Beneficiaries of such an ethical education, gained through the practice of play that was taught as a good in itself with the successful aim of building character and cultivating virtue, also populated such elite institutions as T. H. Green's Oxford. There, philosophical reflection on such ethically educative practice led to identification of Aristotle as its theorist, in rejection of utilitarians' means-end morality. Consequently, at the same time that Thomism was revived in Italy, Aristotelianism was revived in Britain and its empire. While James's life was informed by an ethics and a politics that might well seem to have pulled in different directions, MacIntyre's radicalization of Aristotelian practical reasoning aspires to point them toward a common good. The kind of ethic once instilled into those charged with imposing alien institutions upon imperial subjects is a kind of ethic that can also motivate resistance to institutions' corrupting effect, among those whose behavior institutions' managers are charged with manipulating.

The morally educative value of practices was famously illustrated in *After Virtue*, in fine Wittgensteinian style, with the hypothetical example of an initially candy-desiring and progressively chess-playing child. She learns to subordinate her untutored desire for candy to a new desire to excel by the standards internal to the practice of chess. As with James's cricketers, MacIntyre's chess player internalizes the game's prohibition of cheating. The good internal to chess, as a shared practice, is incompatible with any means-end rationality that warrants winning at any cost, whether or not one thereby also wins some candy. An institutional point is that if people internalize a common good as a personal aim, it can be more effectively pursued than by deployment of mere sticks or carrots. Even Stalinists encouraged "socialist emulation." Against Stalinists and others, MacIntyre's general point is that morally educative common goods are goods internal to shared practices; they are not goods imposed by alien institutions. Even so, shared goods may be imposed by necessity and, if they are to be actualized, their pursuit must be institutionalized. As MacIntyre now says of Russia's Great Patriotic War, Grossman and his compatriots shared an "overriding good to which all other goods [had] to be subordinated," exercising their practical reasoning "in solidarity . . . with all those engaged in the same enterprise."[31] His sociological and economic claim is that, between the extremity of war and the relative triviality of games, a vast expanse of everyday social life consists of practices and goods to which individuals can similarly devote their reasoning. Where work's institutionalization allows, "primary responsibility for the quality of the end products of the work lies with the workers, who in this respect are . . . agents with rational and aesthetic powers, even though their labor is still exploited."[32] His moral claim is that this is beneficial to themselves and to others. His theoretical claim is that Aristotelianism's conceptual scheme articulates what is "expressed in and presupposed by a wide range of activities, responses, and judgments, and this because it . . . captures certain truths about human beings, truths that we acknowledge in our everyday practices."[33] His political claim is that "the ethics-of-the-state and the ethics-of-the-market"[34] conflict with this ethics of common goods and shared practices. As in those industrial conflicts which he, alongside the SWP, can still support, justice, courage, and truthfulness are required if practices are to resist the corrupting power of modernity's dominant state and corporate institutions.

What then was it that MacIntyre walked away from, when he abandoned the British Left? Even if he did not dissociate himself from all of the picket lines, it was at least the meetings of those Marxists who talk as though they have a theory and a practice capable of replacing capitalism with an emancipatory and egalitarian socialism. To this extent, his path was the same as that taken by millions of others in the twentieth century, disillusioned by the institutionalized practice of actually existing socialist states and parties. It was also Marxism as a tradition of reasoning that he abandoned. What he did not at all abandon was the questioning of contemporary capitalist social order that he had previously conducted from within that tradition. As he says in recounting the narrative of his own intellectual life, "it was on the basis of Marxist insights into the nature both of morality and of moral philosophy" that he pursued the enquiry into conflicting traditions of moral enquiry that he still pursues now, and he still remains "convinced of the truth and political relevance of Marx's critique of capitalism."[35]

MacIntyre abandoned Marxism as a tradition of practical as well as theoretical reasoning. He judged it to have failed because it was concerned only with institutionalized social relations and not with individuals' goods and desires. If Marxists wished to criticize comrades' moral crimes and irrationalities, they had to look back beyond "the Marxist view of things"[36] for moral views acquired through participation in other practices. To think that one's only responsibility was to emulate Bolshevik practice by effecting revolution and building socialism was to participate in moral error. Even so, he did not walk away from Marxism entirely. In both *After Virtue* and *Ethics in the Conflicts of Modernity* he represents the tradition by reference to persons more than institutions. Stalin was simply bad; Lenin, Trotsky, Serge, and James were not. In the USSR, Trotskyism represented socialists' questioning of Stalinism's "moral crimes and irrationalities."[37] For Serge and James, and for himself, Trotsky represented an option that Russia had not taken.

MacIntyre's departure from Marxism differs from that of those who walked into Marxism as middle-class students, only to walk away when building their graduate careers. They, like MacIntyre, abandoned a theory that reduced all of the dilemmas and conflicts of modernity to a conflict between workers and employers. If they were brought up to cultivate a moral conscience, they could always ease it by espousing liberal causes. To do so would be to have abandoned the kind of questioning in which James and Grossman persisted and in which O'Connor never engaged. If they were to take the dilemmas and conflicts of modern life more seriously, then they could, as MacIntyre has long put it, become Nietzschean. Consistent Nietzscheans, on this view, are those who aspire to reject all moral traditions and exercise their will to domination through modernity's various institutionalized means. With Marxists, MacIntyre still observes capitalism's "opportunities for managerial and professional careers" and for "extraordinary rewards for those able to set others to work and to appropriate the surplus value of their labor."[38]

With Nietzsche and against many Marxists, MacIntyre observes that claims to a revolutionary theory and practice provide opportunities for "the exercise of power within the group over the group."[39] Such awareness of the moral dangers in a politics of outright opposition to the dominant order also informs his narrative of Denis Faul's political reasoning. Faul was opposed to what he understood as Britain's imperial rule of Northern Ireland at a time when resistance to it moved from the demand for civil rights to the violence of the Provisional Irish Republican Army. He supported both the original demands and the families of those imprisoned as IRA members. For such members, as for the wartime Grossman, "there was a single overriding good to be achieved," whereas "for Father Faul there were a number of different goods to be taken into account" and rationally ordered.[40] As a Catholic priest, Faul's reasoning about politics was relatively free from conflict with the kind of intimate relationships with which Grossman, O'Connor, and James had to contend. It was a kind of political reasoning to which MacIntyre was otherwise close, and the philosopher speaks with the priest in condemnation of "the manipulative and deceitful use of power" by the rebels' leaders. That "handful" of leaders who made out of the conflict's settlement grounds for their own successful political careers he condemns as "rampant scoundrels."[41]

Revolutionary types of practical reasoning need to be questioned as much as do reformist and conservative styles. They need to be questioned not only about their efficacy in achieving their proposed ends but also about the desirability of those ends, and about their relation to other human goods. Conflicts between goods, including the goods of money, power, and status, are forced upon practical reasoners. If no theory can yet guide even the soundest such reasoners beyond the conflicts of modernity to a revolutionary transformation of society, MacIntyre nonetheless proposes Aristotelianism as a type of reasoning capable of pointing to the transformation of desires and selves. On his Aristotelian account, still more than on that of earlier academic Aristotelians, individuals' fulfillment of their human potential is conditional on the transformation of social conditions. In this, his aspirations for both theory and practice remain revolutionary.

NOTES

1. Alasdair MacIntyre, transcribed from the recording of the "Alasdair MacIntyre's Revolutionary Aristotelianism: Ethics, Resistance and Utopia" conference held at London Metropolitan University, June 29 to July 1, 2007.
2. Ibid. For Callinicos's critique, see Alex Callinicos, "Two Cheers for Enlightenment Universalism: Or, Why It's Hard to Be an Aristotelian Revolutionary," in *Virtue and Politics: Alasdair MacIntyre's Revolutionary Aristotelianism*, Paul Blackledge and Kelvin Knight, eds. (Notre Dame: University of Notre Dame, 2011), 54–78. For historical and intellectual context, see Paul Blackledge and John Gregson, *Marxism, Ethics and Politics: The Work of Alasdair MacIntyre* (London: Palgrave Macmillan, 2019).
3. Alasdair MacIntyre, "Notes from the Moral Wilderness," in *The MacIntyre Reader*, Kelvin Knight, ed. (Notre Dame: University of Notre Dame Press, 1998a), 36, 49. Most recently, see Alasdair MacIntyre, *Ethics in the Conflicts of Modernity: An Essay on Desire, Practical Reasoning, and Narrative* (Cambridge: Cambridge University Press, 2016), 280.
4. Alasdair MacIntyre, *After Virtue: A Study in Moral Theory* (Notre Dame: University of Notre Dame, 2007a), 84.
5. Jason Blakely, *Alasdair MacIntyre, Charles Taylor, and the Demise of Naturalism: Reunifying Political Theory and Social Science* (Notre Dame: University of Notre Dame, 2016), 24–37.
6. Alasdair MacIntyre, "Some Enlightenment Projects Reconsidered," in *Ethics and Politics: Selected Essays, Volume 2* (Cambridge: Cambridge University Press, 2006).
7. Alasdair MacIntyre, "The *Theses on Feuerbach*: A Road Not Taken," in *The MacIntyre Reader*, 225.
8. MacIntyre, *After Virtue*, 52–53.
9. Ibid., 260.
10. Ibid.
11. Thaddeus J. Kozinski, *The Political Problem of Religious Pluralism: And Why Philosophers Can't Solve It* (Lanham, MD: Lexington Books, 2010); Kelvin Knight, *Freedom's Useful Name: Politics and Philosophy in the Emergence of Human Rights* (forthcoming).
12. Alasdair C. MacIntyre, *Marxism: An Interpretation* (London: SCM Press, 1953), 53.
13. Alasdair MacIntyre, "Freedom and Revolution," in *Alasdair MacIntyre's Engagement with Marxism: Selected Writings, 1953–1974*, Paul Blackledge and Neil Davidson, eds. (Leiden: Brill, 2008), 132.
14. Alasdair MacIntyre, "Plain Persons and Moral Philosophy: Rules, Virtues and Goods," in *The MacIntyre Reader*.
15. MacIntyre, *After Virtue*, 186–87.
16. Alasdair MacIntyre, *A Short History of Ethics: A History of Moral Philosophy from the Homeric Age to the Twentieth Century* (London: Routledge, 1967), 241; Kelvin Knight, "Rules, Goods, and Powers," in *Powers and Capacities in Philosophy: The New Aristotelianism*, Ruth Groff and John Greco, eds. (London: Routledge, 2013), 319, 324.
17. MacIntyre, *After Virtue*, 194.
18. See, for example, Kelvin Knight, "Introduction," in *The MacIntyre Reader*, Kelvin Knight, ed. (Notre Dame: University of Notre Dame Press, 1998), 10–27; Ron Beadle, "The Misappropriation of MacIntyre," *Reason in Practice* 2/2 (2002): 45–54; Kelvin Knight, *Aristotelian Philosophy: Ethics and Politics from Aristotle to MacIntyre* (Cambridge: Polity Press, 2007), 124–89; Ron Beadle, "Why Business Cannot Be a Practice," *Analyse & Kritik* 30/1 (2008): 227–41; Kelvin Knight, "Practices: The Aristotelian Concept," *Analyse & Kritik* 30/2 (2008): 317–29; Kelvin Knight, "Revolutionary Aristotelianism," in *Virtue and Politics: Alasdair MacIntyre's Revolutionary Aristotelianism*, Paul Blackledge and Kelvin Knight, eds. No-

tre Dame: University of Notre Dame: 20–34; Paul Blackledge, "Alasdair MacIntyre: Social Practices, Marxism and Ethical Anti-Capitalism," *Political Studies* 57/4 (2009): 866–84; Keith Breen, *Under Weber's Shadow: Modernity, Subjectivity and Politics in Habermas, Arendt and MacIntyre* (Aldershot: Ashgate, 2012), 177–88; Ron Beadle and Geoff Moore, "MacIntyre, Neo-Aristotelianism and Organization Theory," *Research in the Sociology of Organisations* 32 (2011): 85–121; Ron Beadle, "Managerial Work in a Practice-Embodying Institution: The Role of Calling, the Virtue of Constancy," *Journal of Business Ethics* 113/4 (2013): 679–90; Geoff Moore, Ron Beadle, and Anna Rowlands, "Crowding in Virtue: A MacIntyrean Approach to Business Ethics," *American Catholic Philosophical Quarterly* 88/4 (2014): 779–805; Gregory R. Beabout, *The Character of the Manager: From Office Executive to Wise Steward* (Basingstoke: Palgrave Macmillan, 2013); Caleb Bernacchio and Robert Couch, "The Virtue of Participatory Governance: A MacIntyrean Alternative to Shareholder Maximisation," *Business Ethics: A European Review* 24/S2 (2015): 130–43; Geoff Moore, *Virtue at Work: Ethics for Individuals, Managers, and Organizations* (Oxford: Oxford University Press, 2017); Ron Beadle, "On Running Away to the Circus," *Politics & Poetics* 4 (2017a): 349–642; Caleb Bernacchio, "Networks of Giving and Receiving in an Organizational Context: *Dependent Rational Animals* and MacIntyrean Business Ethics," *Business Ethics Quarterly* 28/4 (2018): 377–400; Ron Beadle, *Virtuous Circles: What Everyone Could Learn from the Circus* (forthcoming). For a wider literature review, see Ron Beadle, "MacIntyre's Influence on Business Ethics," in *Handbook of Virtue Ethics in Business and Management*, Alejo José G. Sison, Gregory R. Beabout, and Ignacio Ferrero, eds. (New York: Springer, 2017b), 57–67.

19. A third, lesser institution is the Contemporary Aristotelian Studies "specialist group" of the UK's Political Studies Association. An altogether more ambitious attempt to establish such a group within the American Political Science Association was supported by Ronald Beiner and led by Philip de Mahy.

20. Alasdair MacIntyre, "Common Goods and Political Reasoning: Proposal for a Research Project," Centre for Contemporary Aristotelian Studies in Ethics and Politics, London Metropolitan University, 2010, available at https://www.londonmet.ac.uk/research/centres/centre-for-contemporary-aristotelian-studies-in-ethics-and-politics/.

21. MacIntyre, *After Virtue*, 165, 171.

22. MacIntyre, *Ethics in the Conflicts of Modernity*, 176–83; also see Alasdair MacIntyre, *Dependent Rational Animals: Why Human Beings Need the Virtues* (Chicago: Open Court, 1999), 142–45.

23. MacIntyre, *Ethics in the Conflicts of Modernity*, 247, 260–61.

24. Ibid., 266.

25. Ibid., 272.

26. Ibid., 265–66, 310.

27. Ibid., 249–51.

28. Ibid., 141–50.

29. Ibid., 288–93.

30. C. L. R. James, *Beyond a Boundary* (New York: Random House, 2005), 217–54.

31. MacIntyre, *Ethics in the Conflicts of Modernity*, 253.

32. Ibid., 131.

33. Ibid., 201–2.

34. Ibid., 124.

35. Alasdair MacIntyre, "On Having Survived the Academic Moral Philosophy of the Twentieth Century," in *What Happened in and to Moral Philosophy in the Twentieth Century? Philosophical Essays in Honor of Alasdair MacIntyre*, Fran O'Rourke, ed. (Notre Dame: University of Notre Dame Press, 2013), 20.

36. Ibid., 277.

37. Ibid., 247.

38. Ibid., 120.

39. Ibid., 282. For a defense of Marxism from MacIntyre, see Paul Blackledge, "Through a Glass Darkly: Alasdair MacIntyre, Karl Marx, and C. L. R. James," *International Critical Thought* (forthcoming).

40. *Ethics in the Conflicts of Modernity*, 306.

41. Ibid., 307, 309.

BIBLIOGRAPHY

Beabout, Gregory R. 2013. *The Character of the Manager: From Office Executive to Wise Steward*. Basingstoke: Palgrave Macmillan.
Beadle, Ron. 2002. "The Misappropriation of MacIntyre." *Reason in Practice* 2/2: 45–54.
———. 2008. "Why Business Cannot Be a Practice." *Analyse & Kritik* 30/1: 227–41.
———. 2013. "Managerial Work in a Practice-Embodying Institution: The Role of Calling, the Virtue of Constancy." *Journal of Business Ethics* 113/4: 679–90.
———. 2017a. "On Running Away to the Circus," *Politics & Poetics* 4: 349–642.
———. 2017b. "MacIntyre's Influence on Business Ethics." In *Handbook of Virtue Ethics in Business and Management*. Alejo José G. Sison, Gregory R. Beabout, and Ignacio Ferrero, eds. New York: Springer. 57–67.
———. Forthcoming. *Virtuous Circles: What Everyone Could Learn from the Circus*.
Beadle, Ron, and Geoff Moore. 2011. "MacIntyre, Neo-Aristotelianism and Organization Theory." *Research in the Sociology of Organisations* 32: 85–121.
Bernacchio, Caleb. 2018. "Networks of Giving and Receiving in an Organizational Context: *Dependent Rational Animals* and MacIntyrean Business Ethics." *Business Ethics Quarterly* 28/4: 377–400.
Bernacchio, Caleb, and Robert Couch. 2015. "The Virtue of Participatory Governance: A MacIntyrean Alternative to Shareholder Maximisation." *Business Ethics: A European Review* 24/S2: 130–43.
Blackledge, Paul. 2009. "Alasdair MacIntyre: Social Practices, Marxism and Ethical Anti-Capitalism." *Political Studies* 57/4: 866–84.
———. Forthcoming. "Through a Glass Darkly: Alasdair MacIntyre, Karl Marx, and C. L. R. James," *International Critical Thought*.
Blackledge, Paul, and John Gregson. 2019. *Marxism, Ethics and Politics: The Work of Alasdair MacIntyre*. London: Palgrave Macmillan.
Blakely, Jason. 2016. *Alasdair MacIntyre, Charles Taylor, and the Demise of Naturalism: Reunifying Political Theory and Social Science*. Notre Dame: University of Notre Dame.
Breen, Keith. 2012. *Under Weber's Shadow: Modernity, Subjectivity and Politics in Habermas, Arendt and MacIntyre*. Aldershot: Ashgate.
Callinicos, Alex. 2011. "Two Cheers for Enlightenment Universalism: Or, Why It's Hard to Be an Aristotelian Revolutionary." In *Virtue and Politics: Alasdair MacIntyre's Revolutionary Aristotelianism*. Paul Blackledge and Kelvin Knight eds. Notre Dame: University of Notre Dame. 54–78.
James, C. L. R. 2005. *Beyond a Boundary*. New York: Random House.
Knight, Kelvin. 1998. "Introduction." *The MacIntyre Reader*. Kelvin Knight ed. Notre Dame: University of Notre Dame Press. 1–30.
———. 2007. *Aristotelian Philosophy: Ethics and Politics from Aristotle to MacIntyre*. Cambridge: Polity Press.
———. 2008. "Practices: The Aristotelian Concept." *Analyse & Kritik* 30/1: 317–29.
———. 2011. "Revolutionary Aristotelianism." In *Virtue and Politics: Alasdair MacIntyre's Revolutionary Aristotelianism*. Paul Blackledge and Kelvin Knight, eds. Notre Dame: University of Notre Dame. 20–34.
———. 2013. "Rules, Goods, and Powers." In *Powers and Capacities in Philosophy: The New Aristotelianism*. Ruth Groff and John Greco, eds. London: Routledge. 319–34.
———. Forthcoming. *Freedom's Useful Name: Politics and Philosophy in the Emergence of Human Rights*.
Kozinski, Thaddeus J. 2010. *The Political Problem of Religious Pluralism: And Why Philosophers Can't Solve It*. Lanham, MD: Lexington Books.
MacIntyre, Alasdair. 1953. *Marxism: An Interpretation*. London: SCM Press.
———. 1967. *A Short History of Ethics: A History of Moral Philosophy from the Homeric Age to the Twentieth Century*. London: Routledge.

———. 1998a. "Notes from the Moral Wilderness." In *The MacIntyre Reader*. Kelvin Knight, ed. Notre Dame: University of Notre Dame Press. 31–52.

———. 1998b. "Plain Persons and Moral Philosophy: Rules, Virtues and Goods." In *The MacIntyre Reader*. Kelvin Knight ed. Notre Dame: University of Notre Dame Press. 136–54.

———. 1998c. "The *Theses on Feuerbach*: A Road Not Taken." In *The MacIntyre Reader*. Kelvin Knight, ed. Notre Dame: University of Notre Dame Press. 223–34.

———. 1999. *Dependent Rational Animals: Why Human Beings Need the Virtues*. Chicago: Open Court, 1999.

———. 2006. "Some Enlightenment Projects Reconsidered." In *Idem, Ethics and Politics: Selected Essays, Volume 2*. Cambridge: Cambridge University Press. 172–85.

———. 2007a. *After Virtue: A Study in Moral Theory*. Notre Dame: University of Notre Dame.

———. 2007b. "Alasdair MacIntyre's Revolutionary Aristotelianism: Ethics, Resistance and Utopia Conference Transcription." June 29–July 1. London Metropolitan University.

———. 2008. "Freedom and Revolution." In *Alasdair MacIntyre's Engagement with Marxism: Selected Writings, 1953–1974*. Paul Blackledge and Neil Davidson, eds. Leiden: Brill. 123–34.

———. 2010. "Common Goods and Political Reasoning: Proposal for a Research Project." Centre for Contemporary Aristotelian Studies in Ethics and Politics, London Metropolitan University. Available at https://www.londonmet.ac.uk/research/centres/centre-for-contemporary-aristotelian-studies-in-ethics-and-politics/.

———. 2013. "On Having Survived the Academic Moral Philosophy of the Twentieth Century." In *What Happened in and to Moral Philosophy in the Twentieth Century?: Philosophical Essays in Honor of Alasdair MacIntyre*. Fran O'Rourke, ed. Notre Dame: University of Notre Dame Press. 17–36.

———. 2016. *Ethics in the Conflicts of Modernity: An Essay on Desire, Practical Reasoning, and Narrative*. Cambridge: Cambridge University Press.

Moore, Geoff, Ron Beadle, and Anna Rowland. 2014. "Crowding in Virtue: A MacIntyrean Approach to Business Ethics." *American Catholic Philosophical Quarterly* 88/4: 779–805.

———. 2017. *Virtue at Work: Ethics for Individuals, Managers, and Organizations*. Oxford: Oxford University Press.

Chapter Six

Benedict Ashley's Reappraisal of Marxism

Christopher S. Morrissey

Benedict Ashley (1915–2013) was born in Kansas and grew up in a socially conscious home, sensitive to racial injustice.[1] Although in his youth he was a committed atheist and communist, he converted to Catholicism while studying at university.[2] Later on in life, after he was ordained a Dominican priest in 1948, he became an influential theologian and philosopher, thanks to his academic writings and his work as a consultant for the United States Conference of Catholic Bishops.[3] The path to his conversion from Marxism opened up when he was a student at the University of Chicago in the 1930s. In that milieu, Ashley had become part of a group of graduate research assistants working for the controversial philosopher and educational reformer Mortimer Adler.[4]

At the time, Adler was working on his never-published *Summa Contra Marxistes*, a book in which Adler planned to build bridges between Marxism and Thomism. In those years, Ashley was a Trotskyite, passionately committed to world revolution, because he considered the Trotskyites, who were opposed to Stalin's Russian nationalism, to be the true Marxists. But unexpectedly, in a strange turn of events, Adler's university seminars influenced Ashley's intellectual development in a deep and lasting way. By exposing Ashley to arguments in Aristotle and Aquinas for the existence of God and the immortality of the human soul, Adler set the stage for Ashley himself to become convinced of the truth of these arguments. Interestingly, Ashley would later come to disagree with Adler about the probative force of these arguments. Adler would eventually go on to consider them as merely probable, but Ashley continued to deepen his conviction about their certainty. In fact, Ashley built his later academic work on the foundation of a detailed understanding of the scientific status of the proofs' logic. This subsequent development entailed the articulation of some highly distinctive Thomistic interpretations on Ashley's part, which we will explore in this chapter in relation to his biography.[5]

It seems that Ashley's change of direction from Marxism to Aristotelian Thomism occurred in light of three main issues: first, his own religious experience, which involved grappling with the proofs for God's existence; second, maturing concerns for social justice, and what that realistically requires; and third, the place for teleological metaphysics within an overall understanding of history. The slow and careful evolution of Ashley's intellectual views is indicated by the fact that when he became a Catholic in 1938 he still remained a Trotskyite.[6] In this chapter, we will explore how Ashley's religious conversion on the basis of Aquinas's proofs is intimately bound up with the other two key aspects of Ashley's reappraisal of Marxism's "dialectical materialism": first, the development of his views on social justice, from his commitment to world revolution to Catholic social teaching; and second, the sublation of his fascination with Marxism's materialist teleology of history, transforming it into his distinctive interpretation of Thomistic metaphysics, in which the material dimension of reality was to play an emphatically more important role than in any of the conventional Thomisms of the twentieth century. We shall consider these two key aspects of his thought in detail below, and we designate them respectively as "the dialectic of social justice," and "the metaphysical priority of the material." In doing so, we aim to uncover how the story of Ashley's life is indelibly marked by his reappraisal of the "dialectical materialism" of his early Marxism, a reappraisal made in light of Aquinas's famous proofs.

PART ONE: THE DIALECTIC OF SOCIAL JUSTICE

After he was convinced by the Aristotelian-Thomistic proofs for God's existence and the immortality of the soul, which led him to abandon his atheism, Ashley nonetheless clung to a conviction that atheism was really not essential to the social theories of Marx. He initially judged Marxism as eminently compatible with what he then knew about Catholic social teaching. Although he was first attracted by the inevitability of progress proclaimed by the Marxist dialectics of history, Ashley would soon replace that problematic metaphysics with metaphysical views of his own, which he developed as he learned more in his studies about Thomism. Interestingly, Ashley went on to criticize the dominant metaphysical trends in the Thomism of the twentieth century, by eventually coming to propound an alternative Thomistic view of natural science, which he considered to be truer to Aquinas.[7]

Ashley would go on to do a second PhD in philosophy, but his Chicago years set him on the path to his first PhD in political science, for which he ended up writing a dissertation on the idea of natural slavery in Aristotle and Aquinas.[8] Although at first Ashley blended his Marxist social views with an early version of his Aristotelian-Thomistic metaphysics, Ashley claims in his autobiography that he repudiated Marxism because of its incorrigibly materialistic metaphysics. Yet there are two ways in which we wish to qualify his claim, and to thereby bring a deeper perspective to bear upon his reappraisal of the influence of Marxism in his life. The second way concerns the role of the material in his metaphysical thought, which we have said we will discuss later, in the next section of this chapter. But the first way concerns the manner in which his passionate youthful activism for social justice remained as a permanent feature of his life. We must note that Ashley never abandoned the radical conclusions of his first dissertation, which he wrote under the conviction that Marxist theory needed to be clarified "in the light of the Aristotelian tradition and disciplines."[9]

In fact, despite his critique of the metaphysics of Marxism, Ashley never repudiated his view that the problem of economic slavery remains perennial among human beings. Even if economic exploitation is not described by using the name "slavery," the injustice of such exploitation is still a contemporary reality, argued Ashley, even though the reality is "covered up by democratic slogans," in an America that is not really a democracy.[10] Therefore, since this conviction never changed, let us begin our study of Ashley's reappraisal of Marxism by looking first to the ways in which his Marxist views did become modified.

The decisive impetus for change can be illustrated by the story of how Ashley once irritated the famous Thomist Etienne Gilson. Ashley asked him a question after a lecture given by Gilson on "Christian Philosophy," in which Ashley heard Gilson assert that Aquinas's Five Ways never convinced anyone who was not already a believer. Ashley raised his hand during the question period and offered his own life as evidence to the contrary, since Ashley had until very recently been an atheist, but had been convinced otherwise by Aquinas's proofs during his Marxist student years with Adler.[11] It was through studying philosophy that Ashley came quite early on to abandon the atheist component of his concern for social justice. Yet he spent many years thereafter, as a Dominican priest, studying Aristotelian-Thomistic metaphysics, in order to develop what turned out to be a much more robust philosophical support for his critical views concerning contemporary economic injustice.

Let us look now a bit more closely at precisely how Ashley came to change his mind about atheism and God's existence. Ashley arrived at the University of Chicago in 1933.[12] He was impressed with what he found:

> The University of Chicago in the period just before World War II was a very exciting venue because of the activities of its brilliant young president, Robert Maynard Hutchins (1899–1977) and his philosopher friend Mortimer Jerome Adler (1902–2001).[13]

Their program of great books and great ideas challenged the pragmatism of John Dewey, which had previously dominated the university. Although Allan Bloom defended the classicism of Hutchins and Adler in his 1987 best-seller *The Closing of the American Mind*, Ashley makes the critical observation that Bloom

> no longer put the same stress on the typically Catholic thought of St. Thomas Aquinas that Hutchins and Adler had done. The index of his book cites Aquinas only once and then only to show that great books are profitably studied even in translation.[14]

Moreover, even though Hutchins seemed to be an unconvinced Christian, Ashley notes that

> he and his friend Mortimer Jerome Adler, a non-religious Jew, had come to believe that Aristotle and his Catholic commentator St. Thomas Aquinas were central to the classical tradition of the "Great Books." Hence Hutchins and Adler looked to a Roman Catholic saint and theologian for guiding principles for education in the face of Dewey's relativism and pragmatism, which they thought had undermined high intellectual standards in American culture.[15]

The university faculty, however, fiercely resisted their efforts. One side effect was that St. John's College in Annapolis was founded by those of like mind as the ideal place to unfold their educational utopia, which had met with resistance in Chicago. Adler also went on to found his Institute for Philosophical Research (which Ashley in his autobiography incorrectly calls the "Center for Philosophical Research,"[16] even though one of Ashley's greatest students, John Deely, got his first job there, working for Adler).

In his freshman year, Ashley's intellectual horizons were suddenly expanded upon hearing Adler's lecture, "Have There Been Any New Ideas in the Last Five Hundred Years?" Adler debunked the myth of progress, and argued that only three ideas in the last five hundred years (from Spinoza, Freud, and Marx, respectively) were worth calling "new." For Ashley, the import of this provocative thesis was that wisdom was to be found in a vast tradition that long preceded today's intellectual preoccupations. Hearing Adler discuss Spinoza's "modes" of God, Freud's theory of the unconscious, and Marx's theory of surplus value, Ashley was impelled to consider that the study of antiquity should rather be his preferred path toward the goal of wisdom:

> What struck me was not whether these were the only good new ideas, but that old, old ideas may still be valuable, though today often obscured by intellectual fads and unexamined prejudices. That opened wide to me the treasures of tradition without closing to me the door to future search for wisdom.[17]

Ashley therefore chose to subject himself to the Great Books seminars of Hutchins and Adler in his sophomore and junior years, seminars that employed an innovatively rigorous method of Socratic dialogue that caused "not a few" students to drop out along the way. Ashley was also exposed to Adler's argument that the Bible cannot be fully understood except in light of its claim to be the Word of God (whether or not that claim is true) and that religion was about revelation and not simply "great, ancient literature."[18]

Interestingly, it was Richard McKeon who had introduced Adler to reading Thomas Aquinas, a discovery that rescued Adler from the relativism that Adler had argued for in his first book, *Dialectic*.[19] But Aquinas seemed not to have had the same salutary influence on McKeon himself, whom Ashley considered to be "a bit sinister person, who seemed unwilling to commit himself to any specific position or program, let alone a religious affiliation."[20] Ashley says that for McKeon, "all the classic philosophers were equally true and equally false," or (in Adler's own description of McKeon's views), "All philosophical system are equally valid, but incommensurable."[21]

Ashley was thrilled by Adler's relentless use of dialectic in the classroom. It was an acquired taste, but Ashley had the right background. "One of the best things of my childhood was arguing with my father, so I loved Adler for his logic," writes Ashley; "While I think Adler did sometimes abuse logic by setting up rigid dichotomies contrary to the evidence, I loved him and still love him for his logic and for his courage in exposing academic fraud."[22] Ashley's unusual upbringing had taught him to be conscious of racial injustice, and in his Chicago years we see him trying to fit his social concerns with his thoughts on Marxist revolution. He once wrote a poem in which we can observe him trying to reconcile a devotion to Marx with an interest in jazz music, which Ashley and his friends (Leo Shields and Quentin "Bud" Ogren) all had:

> We three students sit inside our room in a bookish maze,
> working on philosophy and Marx, with a leaflet to write
> and a poster to make for a meeting tomorrow night.
> Oh, on the radio
> a clarinet swinging!
>
> Masses swing on down
> with blood and brain,
> dancing in the little room so narrow,
> while we three dance only in our minds and marrow,

> trying to discern the meaning of the music:
> Is it the waking cry of revolution
> the clarion of resolution?
> Or just the moan
> of blue despair?[23]

Looking back, Ashley confesses that he and his Trotskyite friends probably didn't really ever attain any concrete political accomplishments, "either for good or ill,"[24] even though they spent countless hours on ceaseless activism, which included weekly meetings, passing out pamphlets, picketing at strikes, and attending other student meetings (wherever they could have a chance to propagate their views). Ashley seems to think that the most important concrete intervention they made at the time was to petition Robert Hutchins, the university president, "to increase the meager representations of black students at the University," even though Ashley sadly notes that their protest seemed to have had "no effect."[25]

Ashley's activism did result, however, in his name being placed in FBI files, due to the fact that he was "editor of a journal of the Young Socialist League magazine, *Soapbox*."[26] When Ashley subsequently joined the Dominicans, after the war the FBI used to visit him at the Dominican monastery to question him about his previous associates, whenever conducting checks about security clearance for prospective government employees. Ashley would answer truthfully the questions they posed to him, but was greatly amused by their cluelessness about communism:

> I was always amazed at how ignorant these FBI agents seemed to be of the real facts about communism, as also appeared to be the notorious Senator McCarthy whose televised investigations I watched. He was exposing Communism without any real understanding either of its aims or its tactics. From what I saw—of course my experience was very limited—Communism did make real inroads only in a few unions, such as the Electrical Workers and Longshoremen's unions and the Trotskyites among the Teamsters. Furthermore, from the first I believed in the guilt of Alger Hiss. . . . I do not believe that Marxism was ever a real threat in this country, as it truly was in some European and other countries. Its number of supporters here was always small, and its political tactics easily exposed and unacceptable to American culture. Yet the media often inflated this feeble and confused movement into a monster menace. . . . The university officials were well aware that the radical students, although annoying, were an insignificant minority. . . . I would estimate that the American Student Union, concerned mainly to oppose the draft, had only about 350 members, with probably only half of them active. Of these 40–80 were Communists, of whom 50 to 25 were active. We Trotskyites were certainly not more than 25.[27]

What was it, then, that so appealed to Ashley about the movement of which he was a part? Even at the time he was not unaware of how small and seemingly insignificant its influence was. The answer lies in the seductive intellectual appeal of the comprehensive Marxist understanding of the teleological meaning of history:

> One of the ideas of Marxism that most appealed to me was that it was based on the inevitability of the dialectics of history. Today this seems to me the source of all Marx's errors. He borrowed it from Hegel and the Enlightenment myth of inevitable progress and its appeal arises from the fact that it is a rationalized (Hegel) or secularized (Marx) substitute for the Christian concept of Divine Providence and Predestination. Since, however, it is either atheistic (Marx) or pantheistic (Hegel) and knows nothing of a God who freely created the world, it is self-contradictory.[28]

Here Ashley is retroactively criticizing Marx's atheism as flowing from his teleological materialism, but at the time of his conversion Ashley saw no necessary connection between atheism and this metaphysics of inevitable historical progress. Moreover, we must note that Ashley's socialist ideals were something that he saw as eminently compatible with his nascent Catholicism:

> I had never thought atheism was essential to the social theories of Marx and I thought the social doctrine of the Church with its rejection of laissez faire capitalism might be reconciled with Marxist economics. But as soon as the Socialist Workers Party heard of my conversion they expelled me. As I became better acquainted with Catholic social doctrine and of modern economic theory the fallacies of Marx became obvious to me. Yet I continued to believe and still do believe that social justice requires very profound changes in the capitalist economic system that now dominates the world and reflects the dominance of secular humanism.[29]

But while Ashley characterizes the fallacies of Marx as eventually "obvious" to him, we should consider that Ashley's interest in a comprehensive metaphysics stayed with him his whole life. In fact, it is my contention that his early fascination with the scientifically knowable causal order of the material world never left him. It became a distinctive feature of his interpretation of Thomist metaphysics, because it was central to his unusual interpretation of Aquinas's Five Ways (those proofs that were so important at triggering Ashley's own conversion to Catholicism).

While Ashley says that he is unsure, he estimates that his thoughts on the probative force of Aquinas's proofs came clearly into focus for him between his sophomore year and junior year. He does remember announcing to a friend in the spring that he found the proofs unconvincing, but then pondered them over the summer, eventually concluding that they were "inescapably true."[30] The problem of evil did not present Ashley with any grave difficulties, since he considered it only logical that there is "no contradiction in an absolutely good God causing physical evils or permitting (not causing) spiritual evil, i.e., sin, for a greater good," even if we remain ignorant about what the greater good might be.[31] Our ignorance can hardly be considered to be a contradiction when placed beside God's providence. The poetic side of Ashley also seemed to find the drama of history to be its own justification, as he seems to suggest with his rhetorical question: "Would we like to be players in a game without excitement?"[32]

One of Ashley's unfinished projects was a collection of poems called *Live Fight Know Delight*, to which he wrote a preface in the form of a letter once drafted for his longtime friend Ruth. It gives a very clear picture of his exact state of mind in 1938, apparently just before he converted to Catholicism. It is worth quoting at length because it contains much crucial personal testimony for our argument:

> I am a graduate student with an M.A. degree at the University of Chicago. I am twenty-two and live in an apartment in an old building where many literary bohemians have lived. My two roommates are named Leo and Bud or Quentin. Leo is a Catholic from Salt Lake where I spent Christmas vacation. Strangely enough he is a good Trotskyite revolutionist too. Bud is a Comrade also who got me into the Movement as I got Leo. He is a very good speaker, Swedish, tall, and glad-handed. Leo is Irish and thin and dark. All three of us are living on fellowships while we work on a philosophic work which may be important. It is a clarification of Marxist theory in the light of the Aristotelian tradition and disciplines. We are all very interested in the philosophy of St. Thomas Aquinas, but Bud and I have no religions. I believe in God. He believes the existence of God can be demonstrated, and so do I. We are writing the book for Dr. Adler, a Jew interested in Thomism and Truth and convinced that a revolution is at hand. We however are working for the proletarian revolution as members of the Socialist Workers' Party. We like it and feel sure it is worth doing all our lives. It is strange too that we touch the perennial stream of philosophy here.[33]

Paradoxically, while "the perennial stream of philosophy" allowed them to come into contact with never-changing eternal truths, Ashley was not unaware of how seemingly marginal their contingent political efforts were:

> We Trotksyites are pariahs. The Communists, I have known them for so long, will not speak to us. Most of us have no philosophy but Marxism but a few now see Marxism through the clear intellectual light of Thomism. We all have the problem of learning how to act as Marxist revolutionaries with the proletariat who know the difference between a boss and a worker without knowing philosophy. All these schisms and controversies are funny. The question is as serious as Pilate's and mostly asked as falsely. We must answer the question the right way. We must act rightly. We must make the right revolution in the best way: the way on the left. To find that way much of our time is spent in meetings and some of it in agitation and organization. . . . We are still Marxists

trying to be Bolshevists as well. In our apartment I have painted two murals, one called Theory, one called Practice. Over our mantle are the portraits of Marx, Lenin, and Trotsky. Our party is called the Socialist Workers Party and is a section of the Fourth International.[34]

Yet note here also how Ashley characteristically places his religious thoughts side-by-side with his philosophical conviction about the "physical world of changing matter":

> Leo and Bud and I do pretty much the same things, study philosophy and do our Party Work. Leo goes to Mass every morning at 6:30. Bud has a job distributing Beechnut Gum samples. He is the best sampler in any college in the United States. He is in love but not doing well. . . . I am not in love and neither is Leo. We have many friends of many kinds. I write and am worried about this religion business. Marx saw how superstition held workers back from taking what they had made and he explained there is a physical world of changing matter. I am sure of this too. But God made it, as you used to tell me. What we want to do is to understand things thoroughly and act rightly. I want delight too, that is happiness. Leo says it is beatitude and so says St. Thomas. We all want happiness and are trying to get it.[35]

We should appreciate that the undeniable fact of the "physical world of changing matter" is one of the foundational premises to Aquinas's First Way toward proving God's existence. In Ashley's mind, it is always absolutely crucial, in terms of intellectual integrity, to take the rational truth about matter as the basis for any serious worldview. He would even go on later to write that if Catholicism were "ever shown to be false or without rational grounds, I would be morally obliged to reject it" and to leave the priesthood.[36] Therefore, what we can see here in his testimony from 1938 is how, at the time of his religious conversion, he was struggling, in his highly characteristic way, to solve the "physical" puzzle of the place of "changing matter" within the meaning of the universe.

In an interview with a school paper, Ashley notes that he "never did join the Communist Party."[37] But after Ashley was baptized on Palm Sunday, April 10, 1938, the momentous event very quickly led to his being expelled from the Socialist Workers Party. And yet Ashley continued working with his friend Leo on Adler's *Contra Marxistes* project. However, they were now critical of Marxist fallacies in economics, and both were liberal supporters of the New Deal, and also pacifists opposed to fascism and Franco: "Within the year after my baptism, when I had become better informed on the social teachings of the Church, I repudiated my Marxism. Leo also gradually withdrew from it."[38]

After the funding for Adler's *Contra Marxistes* project came to an end, the two of them were confronted with the problem of securing scholarship money to allow them to complete their doctorates in political science, but their past association with Adler created some difficulties in that regard. However, the department chair, Jerome Kerwin, a Catholic sympathetic to Ashley's postbaptismal interest in Catholic social theory, tipped them off that the University of Notre Dame now had scholarships available for a new graduate program. And so, when this new funding was secured, they left the University of Chicago after the 1938–1939 academic year, going in 1939 to South Bend, Indiana.[39] Perhaps this geographical relocation can be seen as parallel to the intellectual relocation that the two friends also underwent at the time:

> For Leo and me Marxism was finally exorcised by the realization that it is essentially totalitarian because of its materialism. Thus we had formerly been very much mistaken to think that one can separate Marx's social theory from his atheism, since for Marx the aim of human social life is the same as that of laissez faire capitalism, a material not a spiritual common good.[40]

And yet this retrospective reinterpretation by Ashley of his intellectual trajectory is, we believe, not the full story. For the condemnation of materialism is made far too simply here. After all, Ashley went on to incorporate, into his Thomistic metaphysics, a much subtler version of his early convictions about the indispensable basis that the material world must supply to any serious thinker. Thus, while Ashley is right to note here that he rejected materialism as the *last word* in metaphysics, he nonetheless continued to regard materialism as the indispensable *first step* in any sound metaphysics, and so we must turn now to study this interesting subsequent development in his thinking, which we believe has gone unappreciated for what it is: namely, an essential outgrowth of Ashley's reappraisal of Marxism.

PART TWO: THE METAPHYSICAL PRIORITY OF THE MATERIAL

After he joined the Dominicans, Ashley would soon replace the problematic materialism of Marxist metaphysics with highly refined, materially based metaphysical views of his own. He wove his keen interest in the truth about the material world into everything else he learned in his studies about Thomism. Ashley disagreed in an important way with the most influential Thomists of the day.[41] This disagreement is well symbolized by the memorable encounter, which we mentioned earlier, with Gilson, whom he publicly contradicted over the Five Ways of Aquinas. For Ashley, these ways are foundational for any rational metaphysics, but only so on the basis of an interpretation that puts him at odds with the dominant metaphysical trends in twentieth-century Thomism. Claiming his interpretation to be truer to Aquinas, Ashley went on to write important metaphysical reappraisals of our modern need for materialist science as a solid foundation for metaphysics, in books such as *The Way toward Wisdom* and *Theologies of the Body*.[42] On our reading of this evidence, we believe Ashley consistently wrote under the impetus of his youthful conviction that Marxist theory needed to be clarified in the light of the Aristotelian tradition, which he judged to supply a better metaphysics for philosophers concerned with social justice.[43]

An essential influence on Ashley was William Humbert Kane, OP,[44] who taught him a key insight that Kane himself had learned during his own doctoral studies in Rome: "the realization that, contrary to the views of most twentieth-century Thomists, the metaphysics of Aquinas, if it is not grounded in a sound natural science, lacks a critical foundation."[45] Without establishing a solid foundation on the basis of materialistic science, metaphysics will be vulnerable to the charge of being nothing more than a game of words. Ashley came to realize that modern Thomists either wrongly considered modern science to have destroyed the general Aristotelian philosophy of nature, or wrongly separated this philosophy of nature from modern natural science, in order to pursue the futile task of constructing metaphysics independently of modern science. What most contemporary Thomists were doing wrong, therefore, was to make metaphysics a kind of untouchable prequel to science, as if science somehow needed it for its necessary foundations. But what Ashley was convinced was truer to Aristotle and Aquinas, was to view the role of metaphysics rather as subsequently *coordinating* any solid results of science by the use of philosophically reflective *critical* thinking. Thanks to Kane, "I became thoroughly convinced of this interpretation of Aquinas that remains the core of my philosophical reflections," affirms Ashley.[46]

Ashley's first PhD was in political science, but his second PhD was in philosophy, writing a dissertation on "Aristotle's Sluggish Earth," in which he examined the (outdated) physics, astronomy, chemistry, and biology in Aristotle's special physical science, but in their precise relations to the (still relevant) general science of nature of Aristotle, in order to clarify how science could be better understood philosophically. Ashley argued that the careful analysis contained within his dissertation reveals not only the falsity of the older criticisms of Aristotle as antiempirical, but also of the newer charge that he neglects mathematics and controlled experiment. It is shown that these latter methods play a real though small role in his science, not because he is ignorant of their value, but because he perceived that they cannot form the main structure of a strictly physical science. Aristotle saw that their true value lies in their role as indirect and dialectical procedures which prepare and complement genuine physical analysis and proof, but which cannot replace them:

> Aristotle's special physical science thus emerges not only as fully comparable to the hypothetical systems of Newton and of Einstein, but also as methodology superior to them in its rigorous adherence to a strictly physical viewpoint,

which includes but subordinates mathematization and controlled experiment to direct qualitative observation and direct analysis of sensible nature. As such it remains a valuable model and outline of physical problem for modern scientists.[47]

Most of Ashley's important research in this dissertation was published in serial issues of the journal *The New Scholasticism*, which were also reprinted in a special edition.[48] Moreover, this research stands at the basis of all his later convictions about the only tenable way to do Thomistic metaphysics: namely, in light of modern science properly understood (which is: in light of Aristotle's unsurpassed general science of nature).[49]

We may note how Ashley's confidence in reason and modern science fits with his own positive experience, where reason, under the guidance of Adler and Aquinas, had led him to an abstract but unshakeable conviction about God's existence, unavoidable as the indisputable source of our evolving material universe.[50] Eventually, Ashley and Kane would found the Albertus Magnus Lyceum along with Fr. Raymond Jude Nogar, OP, in order to promote dialogue along these lines between philosophy and science.[51] The effort seemed to meet with limited immediate success,[52] but paradoxically the efforts of these Dominicans would still endure, becoming well known as the critical "River Forest" school of Thomism, which criticized the dominant contemporary schools of Thomism in light of modern science.[53] Perhaps some of Ashley's most interesting teachings within this movement are his brilliant explanations of why "one" is not a number,[54] and also why evolution demonstrates the need for an "elaboration and application of the proofs of the existence of God" that must also consider the probable existence of angels to coordinate evolution's unfolding.[55]

But let us conclude our analysis with a more focused spotlight on Ashley's distinctive interpretation of the Five Ways of Aquinas, in order to illustrate what we have characterized as an intellectual development being driven by his reappraisal of Marxist materialism. Scholars debate whether Aristotle's proof in *Physics*, Book VIII, for God's existence is a physical argument for the necessity of a First Mover, or a natural theology proof indebted to a metaphysical teleology. Ashley's interpretation makes its stand, however, within a certain Dominican strain of the Thomistic commentatorial tradition that could implicitly reconcile both sides of this apparently irreconcilable modern debate. Along with some of his confreres, Ashley maintains that metaphysics is not established in existence as a real science unless physics can first prove the existence of immaterial being as a really existing subject matter.[56]

Ashley's harmonization for the debate (concerning the status of Aristotle's proofs as either physical or metaphysical) comes by understanding *Physics*, Book VIII, as Aristotle's proof that the First Mover must be the first *efficient* cause of motion in our universe, but *Metaphysics*, Book XII, as his proof from *final* causality that the First Mover must be the cause of motion in any possible universe. For Ashley and the "River Forest" Dominican school, the *physical* proof from efficient causality must come first in the order of scientific knowledge, otherwise we can have no assurance that such a discipline as metaphysics even exists with its own distinctive subject matter (which is: being, considered both as material and immaterial). The proof from final causality is, by contrast, a *metaphysical* proof, because teleology is considered in any possible universe, a question which can only be raised after metaphysics is firmly established beforehand on the basis of a scientific analysis of the efficient causality of motion. Ashley therefore would always argue

> the demonstration of the existence of a first immaterial cause given in *Physics* VIII . . . cannot be metaphysical, but is presupposed to metaphysics, that is, First Philosophy. . . .
>
> No step in this argument requires a metaphysical notion of Being as *ens commune*, but only the analysis of *ens mobile* proper to natural science. If the argument were proper to metaphysics, it would be circular, since metaphysics presupposes the argument's conclusion, namely, that immaterial being exists.[57]

Ashley thus viewed Aquinas's First Way as being the "more evident" way (as Aquinas says: "*manifestior*") because it establishes the existence of the subject matter of metaphysics on the scientific basis of efficient causality. Moreover, on Ashley's interpretation, the Second and Third Ways also proceed with a similarly physical analysis of efficient causality. The Fourth and Fifth Ways, however, subsequently move on to metaphysical proofs:

> The second way from *efficient agency* and the third from *necessity* are variations on this first way. Once we understand the first way based on the observed effect that is motion, the second way argues from the *agents* or moved movers that cause the motion. Furthermore, if we consider the efficient causality of these agents, we see that the action of the first immaterial cause is *necessary* if they are to act, since the fact that they as moved movers are in act is merely *contingent*; and this is the third way. Thus the first three of the five ways are based on three effects, all related to efficient causality: (1) the effect of *motion*, (2) the effect of *agency* of the moved movers, and (3) the *necessity* of the first cause for these contingent agents to act and produce the observed motion. . . . The other two of the five ways . . . namely, those through formal and final causality . . . [pertain] more properly not to natural science but to First Philosophy.[58]

Ashley also usefully summarizes the main lines of his interpretation at the end of his magnum opus on metaphysics:

Aristotle, after proving in natural science the existence of a God of motion and its immateriality and hence the need and validity of a Metascience broader in scope than natural science itself, left a deeper consideration of this problem to Metascience. Aquinas completed Aristotle's discussion by his famous *Quinque Viae* or Five Ways of proving God's existence. Of these Five Ways the first is rated by Aquinas as "the first and more evident (*manifestior*) because it is taken from motion," the type of change most evident to our senses and proper to natural science. [*S.Th.* I, 2, 3] This implies that the other four ways somehow epistemologically presuppose the first, not as if they are its corollaries, but because it precedes them in the order of the intuitive evidence of the middle terms that are their premises.

Thus the *Physics* first intuits the existence of motion from sensible observation and then by analysis of motion arrives at the notion of the four causes. The second and third way, presupposing the proof from motion, derive their middle terms from *efficient* causality: the second from the series of efficient causes that produce motion, the third from the possibility or necessity of the effects of efficient causality. The fourth way, however, no longer argues from efficient causality but from *formal* causality (degrees of perfection) and the fifth way from *final* causality. Final causality, however, is nothing but the predetermination of the efficient cause to produce the perfect actualization of the formal cause.

No argument from *material* causality is possible since God is the Unmoved Mover, which is Pure Act, while a material cause must be in potency. Yet in all five proofs the notion of being as not only actual but as changing and thus also potential enters into the demonstration, and this concept of potential being is derived from material causality.[59]

The impossibility of understanding God in terms of material causality flows from what we can learn from the material structure of our universe: namely, the asymmetry between potency and actuality. This asymmetry essentially rules out any kind of philosophical monism as being a viable scientific option:

> Our knowledge of God also excludes any possibility that he could be an *intrinsic* material cause of his effects since he is utterly free of potentiality. Nor, since he is Pure and Necessary Act, can he be the *intrinsic* formal cause or act of anything that is contingent and thus somehow potential. Thus the language sometimes used in monistic worldviews that speaks of the Absolute as the "ground of all beings," as if the Absolute were the matter out of which phenomenal things are made, or as the "soul of the universe," as if the Absolute were a form in matter, can only be understood as metaphors and not proper analogies. Yet the Stoics and other more spiritual monists have called God the Logos, or Energy, or Force, or Soul that animates the material cosmos. For Plotinus too the World Soul was the Third God. But an intrinsic formal cause is correlative to the matter that it informs, and if God were such he would depend for his existence on matter and would not be its free Creator.[60]

Thus, Ashley's consistent philosophical view, ever since his intellectual conversion as instigated by the Five Ways, was that the physical universe is capable of introducing us to its metaphysical dimension. The basis for this view lay in his understanding of Aristotle's causal analyses, which show how physical knowledge of efficient causality must open us up to considering the correlatively metaphysical implications of final causality:

> Just as matter and form are correlative so that they complement each other, so efficient causality, if it has regular, productive effects that maintain the natural order, is correlative to final causality; and all natural science explanations through law-like efficient causality must also be through final causality, that is, they must be teleological (or "teleonomic") . . . since nothing occurs in natural processes except through efficient causes that are predetermined to produce effects that have the regularity of a predictable probability.[61]

Therefore, it is this, Ashley's unified vision of causality, which he learned from his study of Aristotle and Aquinas, which was able give him a philosophical matrix for understanding any possible discovery in natural science. Not only that, this unified theory of causality shows how the concerns of science are correlative to those of metaphysics, provided that we allow science to illuminate the full meaning of Thomism's traditional metaphysical vocabulary:

> The natural unit has (1) some organization or order (formal cause) and (2) at the same time has potentiality (material "cause") for becoming other than it is. (3) This potentiality is actualized from outside by another natural unit (efficient cause), and this actualization is either destructive of the unit, or actualizes it in its own line of stability and actuality, and hence is (4) teleological (final "cause").[62]

This remarkable intellectual achievement of Benedict Ashley—a unique and all-embracing understanding of matter, indebted to a tenaciously scientific interpretation of Aristotle and Aquinas—is something we are inclined to see as a visionary gift to anyone seeking to bring together modern science, philosophy, and theology in a vision of wisdom.[63] Could Ashley ever have arrived at such an eloquent lifelong articulation of this vision had he not converted to Catholicism precisely from his Marxist materialism? No, we believe it would not have been possible, for Ashley's life embodied an incredible providential turn. Thanks to his origins, he became the twentieth-century's greatest Thomistic proponent of a most unusual paradox:[64] the importance of materialist science, as what alone can provide metaphysics with a scientific foundation, for ascending further to better understand the God who actually exists. For Ashley, the dialectic of social justice pointed beyond this material world to a transcendent providence, acting as the ultimate efficient cause in history. But the metaphysical priority of the material demanded that philosophy and theology become better acquainted with modern science, if only to know God better.

NOTES

1. Benedict M. Ashley, OP, *Barefoot Journeying: The Autobiography of a Begging Friar* (Chicago: New Priory Press, 2013a), 1–38.
2. Ashley, *Barefoot*, 95–130.
3. Ashley, *Barefoot*, 173–372. See, for example, the book he co-authored with Jean Deblois and Kevin D. O'Rourke, *Health Care Ethics: A Catholic Theological Analysis*, Fifth Edition (Washington, DC: Georgetown University Press, 2006); as well as his *Choosing a World-View and Value-System: An Ecumenical Apologetics* (Staten Island: Alba House, 2000); and *Living the Truth in Love: A Biblical Introduction to Moral Theology* (Staten Island: Alba House, 1996).
4. Ashley, *Barefoot*, 93. See also Mortimer Adler, *Philosopher at Large: An Intellectual Autobiography* (New York: Macmillan, 1977); *A Second Look in the Rearview Mirror: Further Autobiographical Reflections of a Philosopher at Large* (New York: Macmillan, 1992); *The Paideia Proposal: An Educational Manifesto* (New York: Simon & Schuster, 1982); *Paideia Problems and Possibilities: A Consideration of Questions Raised by the Paideia Proposal* (New York: Macmillan Publishing Company, 1983); and *Reforming Education: The Opening of the American Mind* (New York: Macmillan, 1988).
5. Ashley, *Barefoot*, 39–138; Cf. Mortimer Adler, *How to Prove There Is a God* (Chicago: Open Court, 2012).
6. Ashley, *Barefoot*, 93.
7. Cf. Benedict Ashley, "Does Natural Science Attain Nature or Only the Phenomena?" in *The Philosophy of Physics*, Vincent Edward Smith, ed. (Jamaica: St. John's University Press, 1961), 63–82.
8. Benedict M. Ashley, "The Theory of Natural Slavery According to Aristotle and St. Thomas," PhD Thesis, Notre Dame University, South Bend, Indiana, 1941.
9. Ashley, *Barefoot*, 107.
10. Ibid., 146.
11. Ibid., 96–97.
12. Ibid., 39.
13. Ibid., 41.
14. Ibid., 41–42.
15. Ibid., 42.
16. Ibid., 42.
17. Ibid., 43.
18. Ibid., 43.
19. Ibid., 45.
20. Ibid., 44.
21. Ibid., 45.
22. Ibid., 49–50.
23. Ibid., 68.
24. Ibid., 88.
25. Ibid.
26. Ibid., 91.
27. Ibid., 91–93.
28. Ibid., 93.
29. Ibid.
30. Ibid., 96.
31. Ibid., 99.
32. Ibid., 99.

33. Ibid., 107.
34. Ibid.
35. Ibid.
36. Ibid., 187.
37. Ibid., 124.
38. Ibid., 128.
39. Ibid., 137–38.
40. Ibid., 148.
41. Cf. Jacques Maritain, *The Degrees of Knowledge* (New York: Charles Scribner's Sons, 1938); and Etienne Gilson, *The Christian Philosophy of St. Thomas Aquinas* (New York: Random House, 1956).
42. *The Way toward Wisdom: An Interdisciplinary and Intercultural Introduction to Metaphysics* (South Bend: University of Notre Dame Press, 2006b); and *Theologies of the Body: Humanist and Christian* (Braintree: The Pope John Center, 1985). See also the "crash course" in Ashley's distinctive interpretation of Aristotelian Thomism found in chapter 2 of his *Healing for Freedom: A Christian Perspective on Personhood and Psychotherapy* (Washington, DC: Catholic University of America Press, 2013b), 31–94.
43. To establish this consistency, one may compare his "Research into the Intrinsic Final Causes of Physical Things," *Proceedings of the American Catholic Philosophical Association* 26 (1952): 185–94, and his *Are Thomists Selling Science Short?* (River Forest: Albertus Magnus Lyceum, 1958a), with his "The End of Philosophy and the End of Physics: A Dead End," in *Postmodernism and Christian Philosophy*, Roman Ciapalo, ed. (Washington, DC: Catholic University of America Press, 1997), 12–22.
44. For representative writings, see William H. Kane, "Introduction to Philosophy," *The Thomist* 1 (1939): 193–212; "The Nature and Extent of Philosophy of Nature," *The Thomist* 7 (1944): 204–32; "The First Principles of Changeable Being," *The Thomist* 8 (1945): 27–67; "Abstraction and the Distinction of the Sciences," *The Thomist* 17 (1954): 43–68; "The Subject of Metaphysics," *The Thomist* 18 (1955): 503–21; "The Naturalistic Approach to Natural Science Through Motion and Matter," *The Thomist* 19 (1956): 219–31; and "Introduction to Metaphysics," *The Thomist* 20 (1957): 121–42.
45. Ashley, *Barefoot*, 174.
46. Ashley, *Barefoot*, 175.
47. Ashley, *Barefoot*, 201. Cf. his tribute to Kane at 218–25.
48. *Aristotle's Sluggish Earth: The Problematics of the De Caelo* (River Forest: Albertus Magnus Lyceum, 1958b).
49. Cf. Vincent Edward Smith, *The General Science of Nature* (Milwaukee: Bruce Publishing Co., 1958).
50. Cf. Ashley, *Barefoot*, 203. Cf. also Ashley's "Causality and Evolution," *The Thomist* 36/2 (1972): 199–230; and his "Change and Process," in *The Problem of Evolution*, John Deely and Raymond J. Nogar, eds. (New York: Appleton-Century-Crofts, 1973a), 265–94.
51. Ashley, *Barefoot*, 218–25. Cf. Benedict M. Ashley, "St. Albert and the Nature of Natural Science," *Albertus Magnus and the Sciences: Commemorative Essays 1980*, in James A. Weisheipl, ed. (Toronto: Pontifical Institute of Mediaeval Studies, 1980), 73–102.
52. Ashley, *Barefoot*, 220. Cf. William H. Kane, John D. Corcoran, Benedict M. Ashley, and Raymond J. Nogar (eds.), *Science in Synthesis: A Dialectical Approach to the Integration of the Physical and Natural Sciences* (River Forest: Dominican College of St. Thomas, 1952).
53. Cf. Benedict Ashley, "The River Forest School and the Philosophy of Nature Today," in *Philosophy and the God of Abraham: Essays in Memory of James A. Weisheipl, OP*, R. James Long, ed. (Toronto: Pontifical Institute of Mediaeval Studies, 1991), 1–15.
54. Ashley, *Barefoot*, 231–32.
55. Ashley, *Barefoot*, 314–15. Cf. *The Ashley Reader: Redeeming Reason* (Naples: Sapientia Press of Ave Maria University, 2006a), 47–59.
56. This tradition of interpretation is also disputed within the Dominicans. See Lawrence Dewan, OP, "St. Thomas, Physics, and the Principle of Metaphysics," *The Thomist* 61 (1997): 549–66; Ashley's reply to Dewan is found in *The Way toward Wisdom* (Notre Dame: University of Notre Dame Press, 2006b), 146–53. Cf. also Ashley's detailed reply to Dewan in the

Addendum to "The Validity of Metaphysics: The Need for a Solidly Grounded Metaphysics," a paper Ashley read at the Jacques Maritain Center's Thomistic Institute on July 18, 1999. Available at https://web.archive.org/web/20170314020439/http://www2.nd.edu/Departments/Maritain/ti99/ashley.htm.
57. Ashley, *The Way toward Wisdom*, 95–96.
58. Ibid., 100–101.
59. Ibid., 421.
60. Ibid., 422.
61. Ibid., 324.
62. Benedict Ashley, "Change and Process," in *The Problem of Evolution*, John N. Deely and Raymond J. Nogar, eds. (New York: Appleton-Century-Crofts, 1973), 267–78, 294.
63. Cf. Benedict M. Ashley and John Deely, *How Science Enriches Theology* (South Bend: St. Augustine's Press, 2012).
64. Also of towering stature is the Galileo specialist, William A. Wallace, OP, who also wrote important works propounding the "River Forest" view of the philosophy of nature; most importantly, *The Modeling of Nature* (Washington, DC: Catholic University of America Press, 1996); Cf. Benedict M. Ashley and Eric A. Reitan, "On William A. Wallace, OP, *The Modeling of Nature*," *The Thomist* 61 (1997): 625–40.

BIBLIOGRAPHY

Adler, Mortimer. 1977. *Philosopher at Large: An Intellectual Autobiography*. New York: Macmillan.

———. 1982. *The Paideia Proposal: An Educational Manifesto*. New York: Simon & Schuster.

———. 1983. *Paideia Problems and Possibilities: A Consideration of Questions Raised by The Paideia Proposal*. New York: Macmillan Publishing Company.

———. 1988. *Reforming Education: The Opening of the American Mind*. New York: Macmillan.

———. 1992. *A Second Look in the Rearview Mirror: Further Autobiographical Reflections of a Philosopher at Large*. New York: Macmillan.

———. 2012. *How to Prove There Is a God*. Chicago: Open Court.

Ashley, Benedict M. 1941. "The Theory of Natural Slavery According to Aristotle and St. Thomas." PhD Thesis. Notre Dame University, South Bend, Indiana.

———. 1952. "Research into the Intrinsic Final Causes of Physical Things." *Proceedings of the American Catholic Philosophical Association* 26: 185–94.

———. 1958a. *Are Thomists Selling Science Short?* River Forest: Albertus Magnus Lyceum.

———. 1958b. *Aristotle's Sluggish Earth: The Problematics of the De Caelo*. River Forest: Albertus Magnus Lyceum.

———. 1961. "Does Natural Science Attain Nature or Only the Phenomena?" In *The Philosophy of Physics*, Vincent Edward Smith, ed. Jamaica: St. John's University Press. 63–82.

———. 1972. "Causality and Evolution." *The Thomist* 36/2: 199–230.

———. 1973. "Change and Process." In *The Problem of Evolution*, John N. Deely and Raymond J. Nogar, eds. New York: Appleton-Century-Crofts. 265–94.

———. 1980. "St. Albert and the Nature of Natural Science." In *Albertus Magnus and the Sciences: Commemorative Essays 1980*, James A. Weisheipl, ed. Toronto: Pontifical Institute of Mediaeval Studies. 73–102.

———. 1985. *Theologies of the Body: Humanist and Christian*. Braintree: The Pope John Center.

———. 1991. "The River Forest School and the Philosophy of Nature Today." In *Philosophy and the God of Abraham: Essays in Memory of James A. Weisheipl, OP*, R. James Long, ed. Toronto: Pontifical Institute of Mediaeval Studies. 1–15.

———. 1996. *Living the Truth in Love: A Biblical Introduction to Moral Theology*. Staten Island: Alba House.

———. 1997. "The End of Philosophy and the End of Physics: A Dead End." In *Postmodernism and Christian Philosophy*, Roman Ciapalo, ed. Washington, DC: Catholic University of America Press. 12–22.

———. 1999. "The Validity of Metaphysics: The Need for a Solidly Grounded Metaphysics." Jacques Maritain Center's Thomistic Institute. July 18, 1999. Available at https://web.archive.org/web/20170314020439/http://www2.nd.edu/Departments/Maritain/ti99/ashley.htm.

———. 2000. *Choosing a World-View and Value-System: An Ecumenical Apologetics*. Staten Island: Alba House.

———. 2006a. *The Ashley Reader: Redeeming Reason*. Naples: Sapientia Press of Ave Maria University.

———. 2006b. *The Way toward Wisdom: An Interdisciplinary and Intercultural Introduction to Metaphysics*. South Bend: University of Notre Dame Press.

———. 2013a. *Barefoot Journeying: The Autobiography of a Begging Friar*. Chicago: New Priory Press.

———. 2013b. *Healing for Freedom: A Christian Perspective on Personhood and Psychotherapy*. Washington, DC: Catholic University of America Press.

Ashley, Benedict, M., and Eric A. Reitan. 1997. "On William A. Wallace, OP, *The Modeling of Nature*." *The Thomist* 61: 625–40.

Ashley, Benedict, M., Jean Deblois, and Kevin D. O'Rourke. 2006. *Health Care Ethics: A Catholic Theological Analysis*. Fifth Edition. Washington, DC: Georgetown University Press.

Ashley, Benedict, M., and John Deely. 2012. *How Science Enriches Theology*. South Bend: St. Augustine's Press.

Dewan, Lawrence, OP. 1997. "St. Thomas, Physics, and the Principle of Metaphysics." *The Thomist* 61: 549–66.

Gilson, Etienne. 1956. *The Christian Philosophy of St. Thomas Aquinas*. New York: Random House.

Kane, William H. 1939. "Introduction to Philosophy." *The Thomist* 1: 193–212.

———. 1944. "The Nature and Extent of Philosophy of Nature." *The Thomist* 7: 204–32.

———. 1945. "The First Principles of Changeable Being." *The Thomist* 8: 27–67.

———. 1954. "Abstraction and the Distinction of the Sciences." *The Thomist* 17: 43–68.

———. 1955. "The Subject of Metaphysics." *The Thomist* 18: 503–21.

———. 1956. "The Naturalistic Approach to Natural Science Through Motion and Matter." *The Thomist* 19: 219–31.

———. 1957. "Introduction to Metaphysics." *The Thomist* 20: 121–42.

Kane, William H., John D. Corcoran, Benedict M. Ashley, and Raymond J. Nogar, eds. 1952. *Science in Synthesis: A Dialectical Approach to the Integration of the Physical and Natural Sciences*. River Forest: Dominican College of St. Thomas.

Maritain, Jacques. 1938. *The Degrees of Knowledge*. New York: Charles Scribner's Sons.

Smith, Vincent Edward. 1958. *The General Science of Nature*. Milwaukee: Bruce Publishing Co.

Wallace, William A., OP. 1996. *The Modeling of Nature*. Washington, DC: Catholic University of America Press.

Chapter Seven

Christopher Lasch

A Reconsideration

Jeremy Beer

Had nature taken a more typical course, Christopher Lasch would still be with us.[1] Only sixty-one years old when on Valentine's Day, 1994, he succumbed to cancer in his Pittsford, New York, home, Lasch died while still in his intellectual prime. The book for which he may be remembered longest, *The True and Only Heaven: Progress and Its Critics,* had appeared just three years earlier. And he had just finished, with the aid of his daughter Elisabeth, the manuscript of *The Revolt of the Elites and the Betrayal of Democracy,* a book in which he attempted to bring into focus the problems posed for authentic democracy—the health of which, as we shall see, was always Lasch's overriding concern—by the detachment of the new privileged classes, both physically and ideologically, from common men and women.[2]

In *The Revolt of the Elites* Lasch foretold the political divide that would preoccupy political commentators a decade later. "The new elites are in revolt against 'Middle America,'" he warned, "imagined by them to be technologically backward, politically reactionary, repressive in its sexual morality, middlebrow in its tastes, smug and complacent, dull and dowdy."[3] This would seem to be the lament of a cultural conservative, and in fact, by the end of his life Lasch wore that label fairly comfortably, hewing to a populism that emphasized the need to nurture the institutions and practices associated with traditional communities and, especially, the need to acknowledge human limits. He realized that it was against such an acknowledgment that the entire modern project had set its face, "that the normal rebellion against dependence" which our religious tradition teaches is common to all men had been "sanctioned by our scientific control over nature" In an age that fancies itself as disillusioned, this is the one illusion—the illusion of mastery—that remains as tenacious as ever," especially among those cosmopolitan, hypermobile, liberated elites who had consolidated their control over politics, economics, and culture.[4]

But Lasch had once been closely associated with the political Left, and part of what made, and continues to make, his analysis so arresting is that he never entirely disavowed such influences as progressivism, Marx, Freud, and the Frankfurt School. Unlike the Left's other postwar exiles, he never underwent a Damascene ideological conversion, but rather gradually and reluctantly came to shed certain leftist presuppositions and preoccupations. Lasch never become a Cold Warrior, in contrast to those of his peers who migrated from *Partisan Review* to some form or other of neoconservatism. Nor did he ever blunt his critique of economic and political centralization and the technological rationality that sustained them: unlike Irving Kristol, he was not prepared to muster even one cheer for capitalism. It might be said that Lasch did not so much repudiate his mentors on the Left as combine their insights with those of others—including, to name just a few, Orestes Brownson, Henry George, Lewis Mumford, Jacques Ellul, Reinhold Neibuhr, and Philip Rieff—to create a very original and potent critical brew. It might also be said that his work confirms the truth of T. J. Jackson Lears's observation that "the most profound radicalism is often the most profound conservatism."[5]

That is one reason, perhaps, that it seems Lasch's popularity is now on the rise, especially among those for whom the partisan narratives of the culture wars have lost much of their credibility.[6] Certainly, to turn to Lasch's oeuvre today is to be struck forcefully by its refreshing independence. Lasch managed to be at once both democratic and anti-liberal. Negatively, his criticism was founded on a theoretically rich, psychologically informed understanding of the interrelated histories and effects of class, consumer capitalism, therapeutic culture, and technology. Positively, it was based on a respect for—and an ardent wish to defend—the unenlightened, traditional values and preferences of the petit bourgeois: family, hard work, loyalty, craftsmanship, voluntary association, ethnicity, sport, moral clarity, and faith. It all added up to, in his words, a thoroughly "unclassifiable political equation."[7]

Robert and Zora (Schaupp) Lasch, both born in Nebraska, were impeccably progressive intellectuals. Robert, some nine years younger than Zora, attended Oxford as a Rhodes Scholar from 1928 to 1930 and went on to work for most of his life as an editorialist at Midwestern newspapers, including the *Chicago Sun* and *Sun-Times* and the *St. Louis Post-Dispatch*.[8] Zora took her doctorate in philosophy from Bryn Mawr College in 1925. She spent most of her career as a social worker but later taught logic at Washington University and a couple of other schools. Good logician that she was, Zora, as her son recalled, "had a no-nonsense approach to ideas, which it took me some time to learn to appreciate."[9]

Robert and Zora's first child, Robert Christopher Lasch, was born on June 1, 1932. The Omaha, Nebraska, household into which he arrived was not only highly political and intellectual but, in his own recollection, militantly secular. Young Christopher used to enjoy unsettling the sons and daughters of his Republican neighbors by poking fun at their religious beliefs and "flaunting" his atheism.

Christopher enrolled at Harvard (where he roomed for at least two years with John Updike) in the fall of 1950 and emerged four years later with an AB in history and the Bowdoin Prize for his honors senior thesis. Columbia, with its renowned history department, was the next stop. Lasch entered in the fall of 1954 and finished his dissertation in 1961 under the direction of William Leuchtenburg. Richard Hofstadter, however, emerged as the faculty member who would exert the largest influence on Lasch, even though Lasch's only formal association with him was as a research assistant one summer. As different as Lasch's own version of American history and culture would become, Hofstadter remained one of those figures with whose ideas Lasch felt he had to grapple for the rest of his life.

While at Columbia, Lasch married Nell Commager, daughter of historian Henry Commager Steele. Before finishing his dissertation Lasch taught history at Williams College and Roosevelt University. After taking his doctorate, he secured an appointment as assistant professor of history at the University of Iowa. Just two years later, in 1963, he was made associate professor.

Until arriving at Iowa, Lasch had thought of himself as working within the liberal tradition. Besides Hofstadter, he was attracted to thinkers like Lionel Trilling, George Kennan, and Walter Lippmann. But the deepening freeze of the Cold War and Lasch's Midwestern populist-progressive instincts ultimately made it impossible for him to accept what he saw as the hard-edged and seemingly hard-hearted anti-democratic elitism of the anticommunists' "realist" foreign policy. It seems to have been while at Iowa that Lasch's growing disillusionment with the liberal Cold Warriors led him to become interested in the burgeoning "Madison school" of diplomatic history then enjoying popularity in radical circles. The University of Wisconsin historian William Appleman Williams was especially influential on Lasch, not least because Williams led him to Marx.[10]

In 1966, Lasch moved to Northwestern University, where he was made full professor just five years after completing his doctorate. But his stay was brief. Eugene Genovese had just been tapped to turn around the aging and fractious history department at the University of Rochester. Deemed virtually unhireable by American universities because he had very publicly espoused the cause of the Vietcong, Genovese had been serving out his exile in Montreal. Now he was back, and he wanted, in Lasch's words, "to shape a department that would be fairly explicitly committed to the enterprise of historically informed social criticism and at the same time not committed to any specific form of it." Marxian critics were certainly welcome. Genovese soon convinced Lasch to come on board, and he arrived in the fall of 1970.[11] Lasch would remain at Rochester until he died nearly twenty-four years later.

Before he became a radical historian, Christopher Lasch (or Kit, as he was known by his friends, family, and colleagues) was an insightful historian of radicalism—and also liberalism and progressivism. Lasch's first book, a revised version of his dissertation, appeared in 1962 as *The American Liberals and the Russian Revolution.* By that time he had published over twenty pieces, but most of these were reviews that had appeared in his father's *St. Louis Post-Dispatch.*[12] It was with this book that he began to make his academic reputation.

The specific subject of this book—the crisis caused by the Russian revolution and its consequences for liberals' belief in progress and the natural goodness of man—was not one to which Lasch was often to return. But even here, though he was not ready to take seriously either the Marxist or conservative alternatives, Lasch had identified fundamental flaws in liberalism, especially its complacent optimism and messianism.[13] In many ways, *American Liberals* marked the beginning of the end of his identification with liberalism. Now at Iowa, he was becoming increasingly attracted to the Marxism he had so recently dismissed. In 1962, Lasch published a short but portentous review in the school newspaper, the *Daily Iowan.* The book under consideration was *Eros and Civilization,* by Herbert Marcuse. In Marcuse, Lasch encountered both Freud and Marx through the lens of the Frankfurt Institute for Social Research's most famous expositor. Over the next twenty years, at least, no two thinkers were more important to Lasch's intellectual development.

Lasch's next book was *The New Radicalism in America, 1889–1963: The Intellectual as a Social Type* (1965). Although Lasch was becoming increasingly familiar with the work of Freud and Marx and their epigones, Freudian and Marxian categories did not yet figure prominently in his analysis. For this reason, and because it engages the same themes, this book can be viewed as a counterpart to *The Revolt of the Elites,* which would appear nearly thirty years later. Indeed, in *The New Radicalism* Lasch foretold the detached class of elites that he would target for blistering condemnation in *Revolt.*

Through biographical studies of Jane Addams, Randolph Bourne, Mable Dodge Luhan, Lincoln Steffens, and other early-twentieth-century figures of the Left, Lasch contended in *The New Radicalism* that the appearance of the "intellectual" in America had coincided with the development of radicalism, and therefore that "modern radicalism or liberalism" is a phase in the "social history of the intellectuals."[14] For Lasch, the rise of an intellectual class was problematic because it reflected—was in fact a consequence of—"that cultural fragmentation that seems to characterize industrial and postindustrial societies."[15] The radical intellectuals saw themselves as a distinct class standing against the bourgeoisie, whose educational practices, culture, and sexual relations it intended to reform. By contrast, the progressive tradition had been more populist and middle-class in origin and style; it was interested in generating greater political and economic equality, not cultural transformation.

The bigoted elitism of the new radicals, argued Lasch, in words not very different than those he would use three decades later, consigned them to political ineffectuality. "In the people as a whole—'the people,' in whose interests the new radicals so often professed to speak—they aroused indifference at best and resentment at worst." And their obsession with overcoming the intangible repression that they believed characterized the bourgeois family made them nearly incomprehensible to laymen: "The revolt of the intellectuals had no echoes in the rest of society."[16]

On the contrary, far from being too powerful, for Lasch it was the very weakening of the traditional family brought about by the growth of the state and the industrial economy that generated the revolt of the intellectuals and their free-floating anxiety. His basic thesis, which he would seek to refine for the rest of his life, was the following:

> When government was centralized and politics became national in scope, as they had to be to cope with the energies let loose by industrialism, and when public life became faceless and anonymous and society an amorphous democratic mass, the old system of paternalism (in the home and out of it) collapsed, even when its semblance survived intact. The patriarch, though he might still preside in splendor at the head of his board, had come to resemble an emissary from a government which had been silently overthrown. The mere theoretical recognition of his authority by his family could not alter the fact that the government which was the source of all his ambassadorial powers had ceased to exist.[17]

The Agony of the American Left (1969) and *The World of Nations* (1973), both primarily composed of reworked articles, essays, and reviews, marked the high point of Lasch's Marxist phase.[18] In the former book, Lasch lamented that the radical Left had no realistic "program for change" because its intellectuals had been co-opted by the government and the corporations and had accepted the premises of the Cold War. He saw hope in the revival of prematurely abandoned mass-based radical movements of the earlier twentieth century, such as populism and socialism, especially if these were infused with a Marxist understanding of class interests. In the latter volume he dealt again with the inherent flaws of liberal reform movements and liberalism itself. Even here, where Lasch continues to employ Marxian social analysis, it is easy to see how unorthodox his Marxism was in his very un-Marx-like view of history. For Lasch admitted to a "long-standing antipathy to Whiggish or progressive interpretations of history. I have never found very convincing those explanations of history in which our present enlightenment is contrasted with the benighted conditions of the past; in which history is regarded as "marching," with occasional setbacks and minor reverses, toward a better world."[19] Of course, Lasch's skepticism toward Whig historiography would culminate in *The True and Only Heaven*, published eighteen years later.

The publication of *Haven in a Heartless World*, however, marked a new phase in Lasch's work.[20] With *The Culture of Narcissism* and *The Minimal Self*, it represents the first entry in Lasch's trilogy of psychological critiques of late-twentieth-century culture. Drawing heavily on Freud and the Frankfurt School (Herbert Marcuse, T. W. Adorno, Max Horkheimer, and followers), and intended as a "theoretical introduction to a historical study of the family," *Haven* also represented a substantial loosening of Lasch's always somewhat tenuous ties with left-wing orthodoxy.

Ironically, as Lasch later recalled, he was steeled in his break by reading some of the later essays of Horkheimer, one of the authors of *The Authoritarian Personality*. Horkheimer, in Lasch's account, had had the courage to change his mind about the patriarchal family after he emigrated to America "and encountered a type of family that seemed to produce individuals lacking a sense of purpose or direction, unable to commit themselves to anything or to take an interest in anything beyond their immediate pleasure, driven by ill-formed and contradictory desires, and lacking any attachment to the past or future or to the world around them." Lasch's own growing "doubts about the desirability or even the feasibility of an open-ended experimental approach to sexuality, marriage, and childrearing" were confirmed in Horkheimer's analysis. More importantly, Horkheimer's "willingness to modify his theoretical and ideological preconceptions in the light of empirical evidence" provided Lasch with "a model of intellectual integrity and courage, at a time when such models were in short supply." It was the Left, he argued in the preface to the paperback edition, that had undergone a "major reorientation" in the 1970s, not him.

Haven attempted to defend the family on the basis of two premises: the first was that the family has a crucially important role in the shaping of personality; the second was that certain personality traits are more compatible with different kinds of sociopolitical arrangements than others. Thus, wrote Lasch, embedding his argument within an elaborate apparatus of psychological theory, those economic, cultural, and political forces which have weakened the bourgeois, nuclear family have had profound consequences because they have also altered the personality development of the rising generation. Lasch emphatically did not believe that the family was a "haven in a heartless world," as is often thought (a misreading, or rather non-reading, of his book that he lamented), but rather that this had been the conventional myth of the family since the American industrial revolution of the late nineteenth century. Lasch believed precisely the opposite: that the conditions of modern life—its wars, commerce, politics, social decay—were such that the family was less able than ever to serve as a refuge from the outside world, even as that role was more necessary than ever.

Lasch believed that the family had been in a state of decline for a hundred years or so. This decline, one of the primary characteristics of modern society, was the result of the expropriation by larger social institutions of activities once undertaken by families. Industrial capitalism took production out of the household. Capitalism then appropriated workers' skills and knowledge, replacing them with scientific management and an efficiently structured, bureaucratic, hierarchical work environment. At the same time, workers' private lives came increasingly under the control of medical, social, and governmental authorities. The result was that people had become highly dependent on corporations and the centralized state in nearly all matters, which reduced them to a degree of servitude incompatible with the ideals of democracy. The most important of such changes, for Lasch's purposes in *Haven,* was "the expropriation of child rearing by the state and by the health and welfare professions." But he insisted that the socialization of reproduction was intrinsically related to the socialization of production.

The Culture of Narcissism built on the psychological argument offered in *Haven* by applying its insights to American culture's "current malaise," the latter a word that would attach itself with merciless persistence to the Carter years. A true virtuoso performance, one of those rare books that manages to sustain real originality for several hundred pages, *The Culture of Narcissism* was nonetheless very much a book of its time—not only in the cultural subjects to which Lasch paid critical attention, but also in its despairing, pessimistic tone. Though he tried to muster some reasons for hope, things did not seem to be going well in American society—or, as the second sentence of Lasch's preface put it, "Those who recently dreamed of world power now despair of governing the city of New York."[21] Liberal culture, which seemed "in its decadence to have carried the logic of individualism to the extreme of a war of all against all," seemed to be on the verge of suicide. Furthermore, the liberationist critiques of both radicals and Marxists had become irrelevant, speaking as they did to the conditions that pertained under the reign of "economic man" but not "psychological man," the characteristic human type of the new therapeutic age who had been effectively liberated from the allegedly repressive, authoritarian bourgeois order only to find himself enslaved by his own seeming ethereality and the paternalistic state.[22]

The defining characteristic of psychological man, the apotheosis of advanced capitalism, was his anxious *narcissism.* Lasch used the psychoanalytic understanding of this term to describe a new, socially pervasive (if often subpathological) personality structure that was the consequence of "quite specific changes in our society and culture—from bureaucracy, the proliferation of images, therapeutic ideologies, the rationalization of the inner life, the cult of consumption, and in the last analysis from changes in family life and from changing patterns of socialization."[23] Characterologically, narcissism manifested itself in "profusion in the everyday life of our age," wrote Lasch. Individually, its symptoms included "dependence on the vicarious warmth provided by others, combined with a fear of dependence, a sense of inner emptiness, boundless repressed rage, and unsatisfied oral cravings," not to mention, less directly, "pseudo self-insight, calculating seductiveness, nervous, self-deprecatory humor." So much was understood by a number of psychoanalytic theorists. Lasch's contribution was to reveal the extent to which contemporary social conditions both helped create (e.g., by undermining and dispersing parental authority, which made it "almost impossible for the young to grow up")—and reflected (e.g., in "the intense fear of old age and death, altered sense of time, fascination with celebrity, fear of competition, decline of the play spirit, deteriorating relations between men and women") the rise of the narcissistic personality.[24]

In essence, Lasch contended, given current social conditions—"lawless, violent, and unpredictable"—the feelings of helplessness and dependence associated with narcissism were rational. More than ever, the individual found himself entirely exposed to the power of the state, distant corporations, and their seemingly unaccountable bureaucracies. Lasch's goal was to show that the therapeutic response to this situation is self-defeating.[25] "Arising out of a pervasive dissatisfaction with the quality of personal relations, it advises people not to make too large an investment in love and friendship, to avoid excessive dependence on others, and to live for the moment,"—in other words, it tends to reinforce the very sort of narcissistic traits "that had created the crisis of personal relations in the first place."

In the final pages of this rich and densely argued book, Lasch distinguishes his critique from that of conservatives, whom he faults for refusing to connect the social and personality changes described by Lasch with "the rise of monopoly capitalism."[26] Libertarian conservatives like Ludwig von Mises exaggerated the personal autonomy made possible by the free market in the same way that they exaggerated the extent to with the state was fundamentally at odds with capitalist enterprise. In fact, therapeutic and consumer culture are intrinsically—and historically—related via their connection to the rise of corporate capitalism. "The same historical development that turned the citizen into a client transformed the worker from a producer into a consumer." The result, to which conservatives' pro-capitalist ideology blinds them, is that to struggle against the narcissistic dependence associated with the new therapeutic bureaucracy will mean to resist also the dependence created by capitalism itself. Lasch concludes by exhorting his readers to look to the "traditions of localism, self-help, and community action," or, in other words, to resist the forces of narcissism by seeking "to create their own 'communities of competence.'"[27]

The timing—and title—of *The Culture of Narcissism* could not have been better. Not only did it become a best-seller; it also caught the attention of Patrick Caddell, Jimmy Carter's pollster and trusted advisor (Carter himself had supposedly speed-read the book). Thus did it happen that in May 1979, Christopher Lasch arrived at the White House for a private dinner with the president. He had been summoned, along with a half-dozen or so other academics, activists, and journalists (including Daniel Bell, Jesse Jackson, and Bill Moyers), to discuss the state of the nation with President Carter.

The early summer of 1979 was a difficult one for the president. The energy crisis was at its peak, and Carter had decided to regroup by inviting a stream of "prominent citizens" to give their two cents on how he ought now to address the issue. To Carter's mind, these prominent citizens confirmed what Caddell had argued in a long memo, namely, that a spiritual "malaise" lay at the root of the nation's many practical difficulties. It was this condition that the nation's leader needed to address.

On July 15, 1979, Carter delivered the televised address that would come to be known as the "malaise" speech (even though Carter—unlike Lasch—never did use the word "malaise"). Needless to say, the speech did not prove especially popular with a public that wanted "answers," not a sermon, and certainly not a sermon that scolded them for their selfishness while predicting that a more austere future lay ahead (among other things, Carter had lamented that "too many of us now tend to worship self-indulgence and consumption"). Lasch was not terribly impressed himself, subsequently writing Caddell to urge the president to "temper his appeal for national sacrifice with some kind of assurance that those most vulnerable—the poor and disadvantaged—wouldn't be asked to carry a disproportionate burden."[28] He lamented that his psychoanalytically sophisticated use of the concept of "narcissism" had been understood to mean simply that Americans were "selfish" or "egoistic" when he had meant to convey something very different, that the contemporary self is so contracted that it is "uncertain of its own outlines" and hence tends either to "remake the world in its own image"—the Promethean error that is reflected in the cult of unlimited technological development—or else "to merge into its environment in blissful union," which requires a radical or absolute denial of selfhood.[29] To attack the problem of consumerism required not the moralism reflected in Carter's speech but rather seeing it as a consequence of the degradation of work. Mass production and mass consumption, Lasch contended, depend on social arrangements that "tend to discourage initiative and self-reliance and to promote dependence, passivity, and a spectatorial state of mind both at work and at play."[30] In other words, these arrangements, fundamentally anti-democratic in their implications, are the source of our contemporary malaise.

Whether or not Carter or Caddell or anyone else interpreted it correctly, with *The Culture of Narcissism* Lasch achieved national stature as a culture critic. *The Culture of Narcissism* was comparable in its popular penetration to later works like Allan Bloom's *Closing of the American Mind* or Robert Putnam's *Bowling Alone*. Almost everyone had heard of it; many bought it; few bothered to read it; and even fewer understood it.

If anything, *The Minimal Self,* perhaps Lasch's most underrated book, is more fulfilling than its two predecessors. In this book Lasch links his critique of therapeutic culture with the problems of environmental exploitation, industrialism, and technology. Lasch criticizes the social movements of the Left—the environmental, women's, and peace movements—for, among other things, misunderstanding the teachings of psychoanalysis, which teaches that human happiness, or at least "ordinary unhappiness," lies in achieving a balance between "separation and union, individuation and dependence."[31] Psychoanalysis "refuses to dissolve the tension between instinct and culture."[32] Its beauty, in a way, is that it doesn't "work." In making self-knowledge its goal, it rejects the technological approach to the self inherent in other therapeutic approaches. Psychoanalysis is a most inefficient technology—perhaps its chief recommendation.

Freud attempted to strengthen the self, typically by bringing subconscious impulses and desires into consciousness, where they can be dealt with more constructively. In contrast, many among the environmental, feminist, and peace movements advocated the abandonment of the concept of the individual self and its fusion with nature or the social whole, an approach that to Lasch vitiated their otherwise useful critiques of instrumental reason. Authentic selfhood, argued Lasch, lies in the awareness of one's divided nature, in the "awareness of man's contradictory place in the natural order of things."[33] Indeed, the echoes of a newfound respect for the West's religious tradition are clearly present in Lasch's argument that "[s]elfhood is the painful awareness of the tension between our unlimited aspirations and our limited understanding, between our original intimations of immortality and our fallen state, between oneness and separation."[34]

However, in Lasch's account selfhood is not threatened so much by these social movements as it is by the therapeutic ideology promoted by mass industrial culture. In frustrating individual initiative and accountability, this ideology teaches individuals not to trust their own judgment, indeed to see the self as an object, while paradoxically seeing external objects as extensions or projections of the self. Though "self-liberation" is the ostensible goal of therapeutic ideology, the liberation of the self from a stable public or common world has revealed more clearly than ever that the self only takes shape in the presence of external constraints; or at least that absent such constraints the imagination is exposed "more directly than before to the tyranny of inner compulsions and anxieties."[35]

The defenders of mass, consumer culture claim that whatever is lost in its rise is more than made up for by the spread of comforts and wealth throughout all classes, especially the lower, notes Lasch. In other words, the wide array of choices once available only to the rich are available to all in a consumer culture, and so to deplore consumerism is to unwittingly reveal one's aristocratic snobbery. Lasch rebuts this argument by noting that the choices open to the weakened, dependent selves that pervade consumer culture are trivial, having to do with "lifestyles" rather than matters of moral import. The only choices a consumer society will accept are those that are nonbinding and hence relatively meaningless. "A society of consumers defines choice not as the freedom to choose one course of action over another but as the freedom to choose everything at once. 'Freedom of choice' means 'keeping your options open.' . . . [S]uch is the open-ended, experimental conception of the good life upheld by the propaganda of commodities, which surrounds the consumer with images of unlimited possibility."[36] Industrialism and genuine democracy, therefore, are anything but mutually reinforcing.

After *The Minimal Self,* Lasch drifted away from Freud, Marx, and their Frankfurt School interpreters. His break with the cultural Left also became more thorough and more obvious. In the 1960s and 1970s he had been a frequent contributor to organs of Left opinion like the *Nation* and the *New York Review of Books,* publishing in those periodicals twelve and forty-five articles, respectively. But his last article for the *Nation* appeared in 1980, and after 1984 he wrote only one article (on Reagan) for the *New York Review.* The postmodern Left irritated him, and the feeling was mutual.

In the late 1980s, Lasch began to explore systematically his instinct that the best way to transcend the Left-Right impasse in American life was through the reinvigoration of the populist tradition. This was the thesis of *The True and Only Heaven,* which begins by noting that both the contemporary Left and Right had contempt for the idea of "limits" of any kind, since the idea that there could be any immovable constraints on human endeavor threatened the underlying progressivist ideology to which both subscribed. Even conservatives, he observes (citing Paul Gottfried and Thomas Fleming's history of the conservative movement) had all but abandoned whatever residual "skepticism about progress" they may once have harbored.[37] The rhetoric of their most recent political hero, Ronald Reagan, was infused with the rhetoric of shallow optimism. Reagan was a true believer in Progress. He spoke of "traditional values," but the values he wished to promote had very little to do with tradition. They summed up the code of the cowboy, the man in flight from his ancestors, from his immediate family, and from everything that tied him down and limited his freedom of movement. Reagan played on the desire for order, continuity, responsibility, and discipline, but his program contained nothing that would satisfy that desire. On the contrary, his program aimed to promote economic growth and unregulated business enterprise, the very forces that have undermined tradition. A movement calling itself conservative might have been expected to associate itself with the demand for limits not only on economic growth but on the conquest of space, the technological conquest of the environment, and the ungodly ambition to acquire godlike powers over nature. Reaganites, however, condemned the demand for limits as another counsel of doom.[38]

Still, the idea of progress retained appeal because it envisioned a future of unlimited economic growth, a vision for which the experience of the previous two or three centuries admittedly provided ample support. (Lasch assumed, without arguing the matter, that this expectation was no longer rationally tenable.) But it also retained appeal because it had been finally detached from utopianism. The most viable progressive ideology—the only one to emerge intact from the rise and fall of the modern era's revolutionary and totalitarian regimes—was the one created by the new science of political economy in the eighteenth century. It was not to "those second-rate thinkers more conventionally associated with the idea of progress—Fontenelle, Condorcet, Godwin, Comte, Spencer" but rather to the moralists associated with this new science—Bernard Mandeville, David Hume, Adam Smith, and others—"that we should look for the inner meaning of progressive ideology."[39] For Smith and colleagues promised not utopia but the indefinite expansion of prosperity, a lower but seemingly more achievable goal.

However, even this more modest project required the dramatic alteration of traditional moral valuations. For one thing, unlike the classical, Christian, and republican traditions, "the modern conception of progress depends on a positive assessment of the proliferation of wants."[40] Austerity and self-denial have no place in the modern, progressive conception of the good life. For "thrift and self-denial" mean nothing less, ultimately, than "economic stagnation."[41] Desire and appetite, on the other hand, must now carry a positive valence. Formerly condemned as potentially insatiable and therefore subject to a panoply of private, public, and religious constraints, for there to be progress desire and appetite had now to be continually stimulated. Furthermore, this progressive ideology, by proposing a world continually improving and without end, necessarily entails the institutionalization of a sense of impermanence, the sense "that nothing is certain except the imminent obsolescence of all our certainties."[42]

Lasch's book attempts to highlight the most important critics of this new idea of progress while showing that the most effective criticism can be traced to the populist tradition and its preference for a rooted life centered on family, neighborhood, and church. In this sense, *The True and Only Heaven* may be regarded as Lasch's attempt to provide a pedigree for a more radical, more democratic—and more consistent—brand of cultural conservatism.

There is nothing farfetched about this interpretation. By the time *True and Only Heaven* was published in 1991, Lasch clearly thought of himself as a cultural conservative. Indeed, in a revealing 1990 *First Things* article titled "Conservatism against Itself," he referred to the populist tradition he hoped to rejuvenate as the natural home of cultural conservatives, so long as they truly wished to be associated with "a respect for limits, localism, a work ethic as opposed to a consumerist ethic, a rejection of unlimited economic growth, and a certain skepticism about the ideology of progress."[43] By the same token, however, Lasch had little interest in movement conservatism and what he saw as its illogical embrace of consumer capitalism. As early as 1987, in a *New Oxford Review* symposium on "humane socialism and traditional conservatism," he had called on cultural conservatives "to take cultural conservatism back from the capitalists," a call he repeated elsewhere.[44]

Lasch denied, furthermore, that conservatism necessarily implied a defense of social hierarchy and existing distributions of power. Economically, he was a leveler, convinced that cultural conservatism was "quite compatible . . . with a commitment to radical democracy."[45] This may be one reason why he had little use for traditionalist thinkers, including the Southern Agrarians. In *The New Radicalism,* in one of his few published mentions of conservatives of the first half of the twentieth century, Lasch argues that the Southern Agrarians and their "kindred spirits" Irving Babbitt and T. S. Eliot had essentially adopted the line that artists should retreat from the political arena and focus on the cultural arena, that they should not attempt "to influence the struggle for power." The Agrarians, for instance, in *I'll Take My Stand,* besides attacking industrialism and capital-P Progress, had also "implicitly" attacked "politics itself," in Lasch's judgment, "since it was unlikely that political action founded on such a program had much chance of success in the twentieth century." In fact, for Lasch, only "some of the agrarians" had even "argued rather half-heartedly" for an agrarian political program; they "seem to have been saying that writers and artists should 'take their stand' on an issue which was cultural, not political."[46]

Lasch's gloss on the Agrarians—published, one must remember, in 1965—is not only tendentious but also somewhat contradictory. On the one hand, they had put forth an unrealistic political program; on the other, they were not really interested in politics at all but in culture. More interesting, however, is that Lasch's own proposals put forth later in his life have much in common with those of the Agrarians. He advocated, for instance, a return to a "producerist" rather than a consumer economy. Heavily influenced by Ivan Illich, Wendell Berry, and other ecological writers, he accepted as a foundational premise that the rapid exhaustion of natural resources was at hand; and of course the critique of progress, so central to agrarian thought, was the central theme of *The True and Only Heaven.* Tellingly, that book contains no discussion of the Agrarians whatsoever, an especially curious omission given that Lasch included some of their writings in one of his graduate seminars.

Finally, Lasch also kept the postwar conservative movement at arm's length because of its hard-line anti-communism. Something of an anti-anti-communist, Lasch not only rejected the notion that the Cold War demanded a final choice between one of two cultures; he also contended that even were American society "the most brilliant and virtuous in recorded history and Soviet Russia the most perfect tyranny," one could "still choose accommodation over 'victory' or even 'containment.'"[47] Plausible enough; but like so many on the Left, Lasch still underrated, at least in the 1960s, the horror of Soviet society, holding, for example, that the USSR was not inflexibly totalitarian, that Stalin was the real problem, and that "the world of the twentieth century—the Soviet Union in particular—has not turned out to be quite so grim as it looked in the late forties and early fifties."[48] One cringes to read such judgments today, but at the same time Lasch was surely right when, in a discussion of Sidney Hook, he noted that "when the adversary was 'total evil,' the 'imperfections' of democracy naturally faded from sight," and that Hook's "'critical' support of American culture was hard to distinguish from unconditional acceptance," a process we see repeated among Hook's successors today, with Islamism conveniently substituted for communism.[49]

When, in a 1991 interview, Lasch was asked where he saw signs of "hope" or "moral vision," he responded that while there was "not much" present in organized religion, "one finds flashes of it in the Catholic tradition.... One might even say that the Pope has some of the best insights into social questions"—a rather surprising answer for a former Marxist imbued with radically secularist ideals from childhood.[50] But Lasch's self-identification with the project of cultural conservatism in the final decade or so of his life had been accompanied by an increasing, if still tentative, attraction to the Christian intellectual tradition. His social thought consequently began to incorporate a consideration of religion and theological insights in highly suggestive ways. For example, turning Freud on his head, Lasch used psychoanalysis to argue that the man or woman of genuine faith actually possessed a higher degree of psychological maturity than did the religiously indifferent. And, putting a twist on Voegelin, he published a series of articles in the early '90s arguing that gnosticism, the perennial heresy, was not manifested so much in utopian totalitarianism as it was in the assumptions and implicit goals of liberal modernity.[51]

Much more might be written about the theological affinities present in Lasch's later cultural criticism. Readers of *The True and Only Heaven* will note their existence in his treatment of the virtue of hope, in his championing of religious thinkers such as Jonathan Edwards and Orestes Brownson and activists such as Martin Luther King Jr., and in his critique of abortion rights. The spiritual depth and sincerity of Lasch's writing is impossible to miss.

For all that, Lasch never claimed publicly to be a believer. Privately, however, things may have been different. After Lasch's death, one friend recalled that Lasch had once been asked by a participant at an evangelical conference, "Are you or are you not a believer?" Lasch was said to have replied, "Oh, not really." His wife, however, having heard the question, quickly interjected, "Oh, yes he is!"[52] And so, perhaps, he was.

NOTES

1. This chapter was originally published with the same title in *Modern Age* 47/4 (Fall 2005): 330–43. It appears here with permission of the author.
2. Two Lasch books have appeared posthumously. Elisabeth Lasch-Quinn edited a collection titled *Women and the Common Life: Love, Marriage, and Feminism* (New York: Norton, 1997), a collection Lasch had himself been working on for years but was unable to finish. The other book is *Plain Style: A Guide to Written English* (Philadelphia: University of Pennsylvania Press, 2002). Lasch wrote this book for departmental use at the University of Rochester as a guide for his haplessly undereducated graduate students.
3. Christopher Lasch, *The Revolt of the Elites and the Betrayal of Democracy* (New York: Norton, 1995), 5–6.
4. *Revolt of the Elites*, 246.
5. T. J. Jackson Lears, *No Place of Grace: Antimodernism and the Transformation of American Culture, 1880–1920* (Chicago: University of Chicago Press, 1994), xx.
6. See, e.g., Patrick J. Deneen, "Christopher Lasch and the Limits of Hope," *First Things* (December 2004), available at https://www.firstthings.com/article/2004/12/christopher-lasch-and-the-limits-of-hope. Also see Eric Miller, *Hope in a Scattering Time: A Life of Christopher Lasch* (Grand Rapids, MI: Wm B. Eerdmans Publishing Company, 2010).
7. This is the phrase with which Lasch ended his contribution to an October 1991 *New Oxford Review* symposium on "Transcending Ideological Conformity: Beyond 'Political Correctness,' Left or Right," 20–22. For Lasch's argument that the contemporary ideological division between Left and Right is obsolete, see his to *The True and Only Heaven: Progress and Its Critics* (New York: Norton, 1991g).
8. For this and other chronological and biographical information, I am indebted to the chronology posted at www.library.rochester.edu/rbk/LASCH.stm by the Rush Rhees Library at the University of Rochester, where Lasch's papers are housed.
9. This quotation is from Casey Blake and Christopher Phelps, "History as Social Criticism: Conversations with Christopher Lasch," *Journal of American History* 80/4 (March 1994): 1310–32. This informative interview—the best ever conducted with Lasch—is another source of many of the biographical details reported here.
10. For an appreciative but critical account of the importance of Williams from a contemporary thinker, one who proceeds from a perspective not unlike Lasch's, see Andrew J. Bacevich, *American Empire: The Realities and Consequences of U.S. Diplomacy* (Cambridge, MA: Harvard University Press, 2002), 23–31. Historian John Lukacs, with whom Lasch shared a podium on at least one occasion, was much less enamored of Williams, to say the least: see his "William Appleman Williams," included in *Remembered Past: John Lukacs on History, Historians, and Historical Knowledge—A Reader* (Wilmington, DE: ISI Books, 2005), 196–200. Another writer that apparently led Lasch to Marx was Dwight Macdonald (and, to complete the circle, Macdonald was a good friend of Lukacs's).
11. Before 1970, Genovese and Lasch were friends, even co-authoring an article on the modern university in the *New York Review of Books* in 1969. But for primarily personal reasons, at least in Lasch's mind, the relationship soon soured. In the Blake-Phelps interview, Lasch claims, "By the time I arrived in the fall of 1970, . . . [Genovese] had already alienated most of his colleagues, and the department was hopelessly divided." Lasch's own difficulties with Genovese "began immediately." It wasn't long before Genovese and Lasch were no

longer speaking, and Genovese was becoming increasingly isolated in the department. The situation is described as quite ugly (Interview with Mark Malvasi, March 2003). However, in the Blake-Phelps interview, Lasch says that by the late 1970s he and Genovese had "arrived at a kind of precarious truce. Even though I often found myself at odds with him, I continued to admire his work. We agreed, moreover, in our opposition to the kind of cultural radicalism that was becoming more and more prevalent on the Left. Our differences were personal more than political."

12. For a bibliography of Lasch's writings, see Robert Cummings, "The Writings of Christopher Lasch: A Bibliography-in-Progress," at www.lib.rochester.edu/rbk/LaschBib.HTM.

13. In the book's foreword, Lasch writes that he does not deal with conservative arguments "because I am convinced that most Americans who thought about these matters at all were unable, in the end, to accept such a position" (xii). This posture of dismissiveness toward the conservative tradition would finally dissipate in the 1980s. Christopher Lasch, *The American Liberals and the Russian Revolution* (New York: Columbia University Press, 1962).

14. Christopher Lasch, *New Radicalism in America, 1889–1963: The Intellectual as a Social Type* (New York: Knopf, 1965), ix.

15. Ibid., xi.

16. Both quotes in this paragraph are from Ibid., 147.

17. Ibid., 111.

18. Christopher Lasch, *The Agony of the American Left* (New York: Knopf, 1969); and *The World of Nations: Reflections on American History, Politics, and Culture* (New York: Knopf, 1973).

19. Lasch, *World of Nations*, xii.

20. Christopher Lasch, *Haven in a Heartless World: The Family Besieged* (New York: Basic Books, 1979).

21. Both quotes in this paragraph are from Christopher Lasch, *The Culture of Narcissism: American Life in an Age of Diminishing Expectations* (New York: Norton, 1979), xiii.

22. Lasch took these terms from Philip Rieff. See Rieff's "Reflections on Psychological Man in America," first published in 1960 and collected in *The Feeling Intellect*, Jonathan B. Imber, ed. (Chicago: University of Chicago Press, 1990), 3–10.

23. Lasch, *Culture of Narcissism*, 32.

24. Ibid., 141.

25. Ibid., 53.

26. Ibid., 232.

27. Ibid., 235.

28. See the interview with Lasch titled "His Critical Mind 'Ranges Freely'" in the Rochester, New York, *Democrat and Chronicle* (July 14, 1991d): 1B, 6B, 7B.

29. Christopher Lasch, *The Minimal Self: Psychic Survival in Troubled Times* (New York: Norton, 1984), 19.

30. Ibid., 27.

31. Ibid., 177.

32. Ibid., 240.

33. Ibid., 257.

34. Ibid., 20.

35. Ibid., 32–33.

36. Ibid., 38.

37. Lasch, *True and Only Heaven*, 22.

38. Ibid., 39.

39. Ibid., 54.

40. Ibid., 45.

41. Ibid., 53.

42. Ibid., 48.

43. Christopher Lasch, "Conservatism against Itself," *First Things* (April 1990b), available at https://www.firstthings.com/article/1990/04/conservatism-against-itself.

44. Christopher Lasch, untitled contribution to symposium, *New Oxford Review* (October 1987), 25–26. See also Christopher Lasch, "What's Wrong with the Right," *Tikkun* 1/1 (1986b): 23–29; and "Hillary Clinton, Child Saver," *Harper's* (October 1992): 74–82.

45. This quotation is taken from Lasch's contribution to a *New Oxford Review* symposium titled "Transcending Ideological Conformity: Beyond 'Political Correctness,' Left or Right" (October 1991f), 21.

46. Lasch, *New Radicalism in America*, 297.

47. Ibid., 332.

48. Ibid., 330.

49. Ibid., 306, 307.

50. Christopher Lasch, "On the Moral Vision of Democracy: A Conversation with Christopher Lasch," *Civic Arts Review* 4 (Fall 1991e), available at http://www.car.owu.edu/archives/html.

51. These arguments are included in Lasch's remarkable "Notes on Gnosticism" series of articles, published in *New Oxford Review* in five parts: October 1986a, 14–18; December 1990a, 4–10; January–February 1991a, 10–15; March 1991b, 20–26; April 1991c, 8–13.

52. The friend is Dale Vree, who tells the story in his moving "Christopher Lasch: A Memoir," *New Oxford Review* (April 1994): 2–5.

BIBLIOGRAPHY

Bacevich, Andrew J. 2002. *American Empire: The Realities and Consequences of U.S. Diplomacy*. Cambridge, MA: Harvard University Press.

Blake, Casey, and Christopher Phelps. 1994. "History as Social Criticism: Conversations with Christopher Lasch." *Journal of American History* 80/4: 1310–32.

Cummings, Robert. "The Writings of Christopher Lasch: A Bibliography-in-Progress." Available at www.lib.rochester.edu/rbk/LaschBib.HTM.

Deneen, Patrick J. 2004. "Christopher Lasch and the Limits of Hope." *First Things* (December). Available at https://www.firstthings.com/article/2004/12/christopher-lasch-and-the-limits-of-hope.

Jackson, T. J. 1994. *No Place of Grace: Antimodernism and the Transformation of American Culture, 1880–1920*. Chicago: University of Chicago Press.

Lasch, Christopher. n.d. "Christopher Lasch Papers." Rush Rhee Library. Available at www.library.rochester.edu/rbk/LASCH.stm.

———. 1962. *The American Liberals and the Russian Revolution*. New York: Columbia University Press.

———. 1965. *The New Radicalism in America, 1889–1963: The Intellectual as a Social Type*. New York: Knopf.

———. 1969. *The Agony of the American Left*. New York: Knopf.

———. 1973. *The World of Nations: Reflections on American History, Politics, and Culture*. New York: Knopf.

———. *Haven in a Heartless World: The Family Besieged*. 1977. New York: Basic Books.

———. 1979. *The Culture of Narcissism: American Life in an Age of Diminishing Expectations*. New York: Norton.

———. 1984. *The Minimal Self: Psychic Survival in Troubled Times*. New York: Norton.

———. 1986a. "Notes on Gnosticism." *New Oxford Review* (October): 14–18.

———. 1986b. "What's Wrong with the Right." *Tikkun* 1/1: 23–29.

———. 1987. No Title. *New Oxford Review* (October): 25–26.

———. 1990a. "Notes on Gnosticism." *New Oxford Review* (December): 4–10.

———. 1990b. "Conservatism against Itself." *First Things* (April). Available at https://www.firstthings.com/article/1990/04/conservatism-against-itself.

———. 1991a. "Notes on Gnosticism." *New Oxford Review* (January–February): 10–15.

———.1991b. "Notes on Gnosticism." *New Oxford Review* (March): 20–26.

———. 1991c. "Notes on Gnosticism." *New Oxford Review* (April): 8–13.

———. 1991d. "His Critical Mind 'Ranges Freely.'" In *Democrat and Chronicle* (July 14): 1B, 6B, 7B.
———. 1991e. "On the Moral Vision of Democracy: A Conversation with Christopher Lasch." *Civic Arts Review* 4 (Fall). Available at http://www.car.owu.edu/archives/html.
———. 1991f. "Transcending Ideological Conformity: Beyond 'Political Correctness,' Left or Right." *New Oxford Review*, October: 20–22.
———. 1991g. *The True and Only Heaven: Progress and Its Critics*. New York: Norton.
———. 1992. "Hillary Clinton, Child Saver." *Harper's* (October): 74–82.
———. 1995. *The Revolt of the Elites and the Betrayal of Democracy*. New York: Norton.
———. 1997. *Women and the Common Life: Love, Marriage, and Feminism*. Elisabeth Lasch-Quinn, ed. New York: Norton.
———. 2002. *Plain Style: A Guide to Written English*. Philadelphia: University of Pennsylvania Press.
Lukacs, John. 2005. "William Appleman Williams." In *Remembered Past: John Lukacs on History, Historians, and Historical Knowledge—A Reader*. Wilmington, DE: ISI Books. 196–200.
Miller, Eric. 2010. *Hope in a Scattering Time: A Life of Christopher Lasch*. Grand Rapids, MI: Wm B. Eerdmans Publishing Company.
Rieff, Philip. 1960. "Reflections on Psychological Man in America." In *The Feeling Intellect*, Jonathan B. Imber, ed. Chicago: University of Chicago Press. 3–10.
Vree, Dale. 1994. "Christopher Lasch: A Memoir." *New Oxford Review* (April): 2–5.

Chapter Eight

The Failure of Marxism through the Frankfurt School and Jürgen Habermas

Pedro Blas González

AN OVERVIEW OF MARXISM

In *Das Wesen des Christentums* (*The Essence of Christianity*), Ludwig Feuerbach's 1841 scathing criticism of Christianity, the German anthropologist pontificates on the nature of divinity by attributing divine qualities to man.[1] Feuerbach and the philosophical materialists that he inspired contend that man can be perfected once his environment is modified. This idea ushered in an overblown estimation of reason, especially as reason relates to science and the state. According to materialists, reason develops in a progressive evolutionary tract that eventually emancipates man from less rational and oppressive people and institutions.[2]

Feuerbach and Marx assert that religious transcendence is allegedly a fabrication of human intellect.[3] Instead, man must place his hope in social-political categories. Marxist utopians declare that it is man's task to change the world, even if the ends justify the means. The latter involves a perpetual reeducation of man into this utopian vision.

The empirically verifiable failure of Marxism during the twentieth century can be traced to its origin in Marx's *Communist Manifesto*.[4] Marx assures us that from the beginning of history human relations have been solely about class struggle. Marx affirms that after "the dissolution of primitive tribal society, holding land in common ownership has been a history of class struggles, contests between exploiting and exploited, ruling and oppressed classes."[5] As will be explained below, this is an anthropologically vacuous assertion.[6]

The aim and purpose of this chapter is to examine Marxism, the Frankfurt School, and Jürgen Habermas's thought. It is not my intent to offer an in-depth analysis of Habermas's thought: only a description of how a thinker who is influenced by Marxist ideas has in his later work arrived at the conclusion that Marxist thought has exhausted itself as critical theory. Western intellectual history, beginning in the twentieth century and continuing into the twenty-first, is rife with examples of such an ideological turn of mind. Habermas's case is particularly interesting for several reasons.

MARXISM'S PERPETUAL ASSAULT ON HUMAN REALITY

Marx took advantage of timely scientific and cultural conditions that allowed for the relativization of truth. Man's idea of truth was thought absolute and objective by ancient philosophers and God-centered in the Middle Ages.[7] During the Enlightenment, Auguste Comte offered a vision of human history that, like Marx's, was equally motivated by messianic zeal. Marx applied Comte's three laws of history to his materialist dialectical account: 1) the theological age; 2) the metaphysical age; and 3) the positive age which ushered the opportunity to eradicate theological, God-centered truth.[8] Marx's philosophy launched philosophical reflection into a historical stage that manipulates truth for political gain, what Karl Jaspers calls in *Philosophy of Existence* "the sophistically arbitrary use of pseudo truth."[9] Marxism's deformation of human reality into historical stages and anti-metaphysical stance destroys belief in a creator of the universe, which permits humans to create a social and political utopia. This line of reasoning is what Jürgen Habermas inherited through his association with the Frankfurt School.

According to Marx, religions serve belief in God and its attendant values to Western man.[10] For example, in capitalism, the bourgeois create God to justify their exploitation of the proletariat.[11] According to Marxism, the creation of God is a necessary opiate of the people that capitalism creates in order to relieve the alienation of the working class.[12] Alienation, proletariat, worker, and class warfare are catch-all words that serve as the foundation of the ever-shifting dialectic of power that Marxism employs, and on which the Frankfurt School expands. Marxists assert that eventually workers will liberate themselves from the veil that nourishes the illusion of God.[13] Only then will workers take control of their lives. This will mean the end of capitalist alienation and the beginning of genuine happiness for the masses.

Marxist ideology is a fundamental cause of the systematic spread of atheism through cultural channels that begins in the second half of the twentieth century.[14] In the beginning of the twentieth century, Western man witnessed an explosion in what is today referred to as the "culture industry" (Adorno's term).[15] In the twentieth century, Adorno and Gramsci attempted to remake society by undermining emerging industries, technologies, and new forms of work. The advent of critical theory and cultural studies is the brainchild of neo-Marxists. In these disciplines, Marxist social engineers saw a powerful vehicle to display their perpetual slander of bourgeoisie, capitalist society, and ultimately human reality. Over time under Marxist influence the media and cultural institutions served not as purveyors of what human reality is, but rather as a forum to forge the Marxist vision of what reality ought to be. According to Marxism, when capitalism is eventually dissolved, only then will there exist universal suffrage.[16]

Marxism is not a descriptive worldview but rather a prescriptive manner to foment global social and political unrest and change. The French philosopher, Jean-Francois Revel aptly explains this in *The Totalitarian Temptation*:

> It is also agreed that this new order is the only framework in which solutions can be implemented to problems that, because of the interdependence of the groups that make up humanity, can no longer be resolved on a national basis. Socialism, therefore, can neither be conceived nor brought into being except on a global scale.[17]

At the heart of Marxism in the twentieth century, we encounter the work of social-engineers like Antonio Gramsci (1891–1937), Theodor Adorno (1903–1969), Max Horkheimer (1895–1973), Herbert Marcuse (1898–1979), and many other self-styled cultural theorists.[18] They insist that in order to eradicate capitalism, it is necessary to influence the masses through their culture. This includes religious belief and family life. This also means that music, art, philosophy, sex, sports, agriculture, technology, health—education at every level—and the way that people communicate with each other must become the target of Marxism. The latter holds special interest for Jürgen Habermas.[19]

THE LEGACY OF THE FRANKFURT SCHOOL ON WESTERN CULTURE

The legacy of Marxism raises the question of the validity of pseudo philosophy and activist sociology in light of empirical data, which Marxism ignores.[20] This is a fundamental question that informs the thought of twentieth century Marxists, regardless of their academic discipline. As such, we must ask, what is the value of an intellectual orientation that does not take empirical conditions of human reality into consideration? This is the essential question that must be asked about Jürgen Habermas's work.

The creation of the Frankfurt School, dating back to its infancy as the Institute for Social Research in 1923, is a significant turning point in Marxism in the twentieth century.[21] At the dawn of the twentieth century Marxism introduced unprecedented systematic revolution, social unrest, and the technique of terror and violence in the Western world. The latter are not incidental characteristics of Marxism, rather central components of Marxism's dialectic of power that seeks intellectual legitimization. The secular messianism of the Frankfurt School declared war on God, truth, and other values that were now repackaged and vilified as being the tools of capitalism.[22] While having useful ideas like culture, the Frankfurt School made it fashionably expedient to disregard truth, data, information, and any verifiable aspects of human reality that did not conform and promote Marxists causes and ideology.

Historically, the Frankfurt School serves as the intellectual pillar of today's cultural war. In order for Marxism to stretch its talons as a social-political theory of human reality, it needed to take command of the popular psyche. This meant the creation of popular, social, and political myths that would encompass the whole of human life, as Stephen R. C. Hicks describes:

> Modern debates were over truth and reality, reason and experience, liberty and equality, justice and peace, beauty and progress. In the postmodern framework, those concepts always appear in quotation marks. Our most strident voices tell us that "Truth" is a myth. "Reason" is a white male Eurocentric construct. "Equality" is a mask for oppressions. "Peace" and "Progress" are met with cynical and weary reminders of power—or explicit *ad hominem* attacks.[23]

Michael Polanyi also writes of Marxism:

> Marxism embodies the boundless moral aspirations of modern man in a theory which protects his ideals from skeptical doubt by denying the reality of moral motives in public life. The power of Marxism lies in uniting the two contradictory forces of the modern mind into a single political doctrine.[24]

Jean Francois Revel, one of the giant philosophers of twentieth-century social and political thought, argues that Marxism's ranks are filled by those who possess a totalitarian impulse. Revel's reflection on Marxism is as lucid and penetrating as Camus's *The Rebel*, Milosz's *The Captive Mind*, Solzhenitsyn's *Warning to the West*, Aron's *The Opium of the Intellectuals* and François Furet's masterful account of the totalitarian mind-set in *The Passing of an Illusion: The Idea of Communism in the Twentieth Century*.[25] Revel explains:

> The distinctive characteristic of communism, its very reason for being, is to eliminate the possibility of any challenge to its rule, thus to deny to the people, and indeed to the ruling minority itself, any opportunity to change their minds, once the regime is in power.[26]

Marxism requires a militant and corrosive form of atheism to erode man's existential inquietude. According to Marxism, human suffering must not remain a private affair. Suffering and misery must be exploited for angry social-political opportunism. This is one reason why atheism is today a potent worldview that enjoys intoxicating modish appeal.[27]

THE FAILURE OF MARXIST SECULARIZATION AND HABERMAS'S RETURN TO METAPHYSICS

It is important to reiterate that when Marxists attempt to philosophize—a reflective, metaphysical and existential activity that is anathema to Marxist ideology—they can only do so in a political fashion. This is because Marxism ignores that the core of philosophical reflection, as disinterested inquiry, is metaphysics. Philosophy is a constructive effort to make sense of human reality, regardless of the often unsavory truths that man discovers.[28] Philosophy is toil that comes about as the result of observation of the world around perspicuity, intuition, common-sense intelligence, and us. Philosophy is not the result of theory-building bravado. For this reason, the heart of philosophical reflection—metaphysics—refuses politicization.

For Habermas, the traditional concept of man grappling with the world and human reality is offered as a "monological consciousness."[29] This implies that man's interaction with human reality exists in the form of a monologue. This is one way that Habermas criticizes philosophical idealism. He argues that through the interactions of people (subjects), who agree to value-claims by what Habermas calls "communicative acts," does man attain truth. This idea suggests that truth exists, if at all, through a collective mechanism where individuals determine its value. This is what underlies Habermas's critique of metaphysics, which attacks idealism. Yet what truth can two individuals who have never confronted themselves as objects of their own reflection, that is, as subjects, aspire to communicate to each other?

Habermas attempts to avoid some of the aforementioned difficulties by asserting that while metaphysics and its attendant language must be discarded, contemporary philosophy can retain a postmetaphysical thinking by stressing the value of reason.[30] Yet reason is not a social construct that originates in a collective, or what Habermas refers to as communicative acts. Regarding the latter problem, one must ask, how do individuals, which by definition must exist prior to all forms of collectivization, encounter the objective value of the world, which includes the subject as one of its central components? Another and more important question is whether man's engagement with other people is not fundamentally first an encounter with the world at large? That is, is an individual's dealing with other people not ultimately the same kind of relational preoccupation that individuals have with the world and the cosmos? If this is the case, then man's orientation is first and foremost metaphysical.

The bulk of Habermas's thought rallies around the idea of negating the importance of metaphysics to human existence.[31] This means that throughout his earlier writing religion cannot take part in the public sphere because it cannot be accepted on reason. For this reason, religion can never be universal. This belief leaves Habermas searching for a secular system of thought on which to pin his hope of a universal society. His answer to this is what he calls "principles of secular universal ethic of responsibility."[32] These beliefs are in keeping with Habermas's formation in Marxism and abides to his being influenced by the Frankfurt School.

Habermas's social political theory adheres to Marxism. This is one reason that his turn late in life to some form of metaphysics, whether through religion or the importance of transcendence in human existence, is pivotal. Habermas focuses on three areas of human interest: physical, biological, and the social sciences. One conspicuous aspect of Marxism in Habermas's early thought is his vague reflection on the philosophical/anthropological question, what is man? Habermas suggests that reason unites these three areas of interest.[33]

Yet this is rarely the case in history. After the onset of the age of science in the Enlightenment, the model of reason that won the day was overly-analytical.[34] I would argue this type of reason is pathologically rooted in philosophical materialism and positivism.[35] Part of the failure of Marxism is its lack of concern for man as an existential entity. Instead, Marxism employs a calculative and rational concept of man.

HABERMAS AND BENEDICT XVI

Communicative rationality is Habermas's corrective to the alleged entrenchment of the self in idealism. Habermas writes, "Metaphysics labors in vain on certain key problems that seem to result from the rebellion of a disenfranchised plurality against a unity that is compulsory and, to that extent, illusory."[36] However, because the subjective effectiveness of communicative rationality is to be determined by materialist, Habermas's utopian form of communication is a form of Marxism that ultimately becomes a vehicle for Marxist monologue. This is demonstrated by history, for if Marxism views all human relations as informed by warring-class struggle, the best that Habermas's communicative rationality can achieve is coercion of one participant by another. To demand that communicative rationality be embraced by everyone de jure misses the point of the de facto metaphysical differences in human essence. Thus, even though, in *Communication and the Evolution of Society* Habermas purports to create "empirical philosophy of history with a practical (political) intent," the failure of critical theory is that it disregards the empirical and dismal historical events that Marxism first unleashed in the twentieth century.[37]

Habermas could have easily broken with the empirically proven failure of Marxism and the critical theory of the Frankfurt School. Of course, this is precisely the point of critical theory, which as Marxist dialectic, must protect itself from empirical data that contradicts it. Already at the time of the creation and subsequent fruitful years of the Frankfurt School, many thinkers had already exposed the empirical conditions that Marxist critical theory promoted. Many thinkers, including people like Solzhenitsyn, Aron, Milosz, Koestler, and Muggeridge saw through the split between critical theory and the real-world conditions Marxism condones.[38] For thinkers who reject Marxism, the fundamental question has always been: What is the value of thought that obfuscates reality and promotes appearance?

Habermas recognizes this in *The Dialectics of Secularization*, an insightful dialogue with Pope Benedict XVI, where Habermas admits to the mistake of rejecting metaphysics and religious sentiment. What Habermas proposes is that the language of religious metaphysics and the institutions this supports be made accessible to a secular society. He writes in *The Dialectics of Secularization*:

> The neutrality of the state authority on questions of world views guarantees the same ethical freedom to every citizen. This is incompatible with the political universalization of a secularist world view. When secularized citizens act in their role as citizens of the state, they must not deny in principle that religious images of the world have the potential to express truth. Nor must they refuse their believing fellow citizens the right to make contributions in a religious language to public debates. Indeed, a liberal political culture can expect that the secularized citizens play their part in the endeavors to translate relevant contributions from the religious language, into a language that is accessible to the public as a whole.[39]

The latter is essentially a roundabout way of returning to the language and questions posed by metaphysics. Habermas suggests that the glue that serves as the unity of societies, whether religious or secular, is the prepolitical moral foundation of man and a free state. That is the main factor that makes it necessary that man augment his metaphysical language once again in a postmetaphysical epoch. Hence, Pope Benedict cites both, the excessive language of science and Marxism as coconspirators in the balkanization of human relations:

> The question of what the good is (especially in the given context of our world) and of why one must do the good even when this entails harm to one's own self—this fundamental question goes generally unanswered. It seems to me obvious that science as such cannot give birth to such an ethos. In other words,

a renewed ethical consciousness does not come about as the product of academic debates.[40]

The Frankfurt School, including Habermas, neglect the broad view of metaphysics and man's role in human reality.[41] When these scholars invoke reason, they mean pure reason. Thus, in their formulation of a prescriptive ideal social and political organization, pure reason overrides all other forms of human reflection. Because thinkers of the Frankfurt School were intent on creating a vision of social and political reality through critical theory, theirs was a worldview that stifled serious reflection on the nature of the human person. Consequently, the Frankfurt School annihilated reflection on what is possible and attainable by man and the social and political limitations of human reality.

In the contemporary world, atheism has joined forces with philosophical materialism. The latter form of radical empiricism employs science and technology to create a narrative about man. The suggestion is that while God has failed man, science, technology, and the state will assuage man's existential inquietude. Not surprisingly, radical empiricism leads to skepticism because it removes man's capacity to know objective reality from the equation. Ironically, while destroying genuine reflection on the nature of subjectivity—the interiority that man intuits as personhood—radical skepticism emboldens primitive subjectivism. In the last two hundred years Marxism has failed to disprove the claim that philosophical materialism paralyses human aspiration and atrophies free will.[42] Jürgen Habermas's thought appears to be a latecomer to this historical reality.

NOTES

1. Ludwig Feuerbach, *Das Wesen des Christentums* (New York: Continuum, 1990), 9. Feuerbach writes, "No being can fail to approve itself, its own nature; no being is to itself something imperfect. On the contrary, each being is in itself and for itself something perfect and has its God, its 'Highest Being,' in itself."

2. Martin Jay, *The Dialectical Imagination: A History of the Frankfurt School and the Institute of Social Research, 1923–1950* (Berkeley: University of California Press, 1996), 55.

3. Feuerbach, *Das Wesen des Christentums*, 12.

4. Karl Marx and Frederick Engels, *Manifesto of the Communist Party* (Peking: Foreign Languages Press, 1977), 32. Marx's assertion that "the history of all hitherto existing society is the history of class struggles" is a perversion of human contingency; also see Mark Kramer, ed., *The Black Book of Communism: Crimes, Terror, Repression* (Cambridge: Harvard University Press, 1999); Jean-Francois Revel, *Last Exist to Utopia: The Survival of Socialism in a Post-Soviet Era* (New York: Encounter Books, 2000).

5. John Somerville and Ronald E. Santoni, eds., *Social and Political Philosophy: Readings from Plato to Gandhi* (New York: Doubleday & Company, Inc., 1963): 343; also see Pedro Blas González, "The Economics of Being: The Struggle for Existence in Prehistory," *Cultural International Journal of Philosophy of Culture and Axiology* 11/1 (2014): 23–39.

6. For example, see Jacquetta Hawkes, *The Atlas of Early Man* (New York: St. Martin's Press, 1976), 33.

7. For the ancient Greek philosophers, Alethea signified that truth was revealing-unrevealing. This meant that truth demanded effort from man in order to become patent.
8. Frederick Copleston, SJ, *A History of Philosophy, Book Two* (New York: Image Books, 1985), 417.
9. Karl Jaspers, *Philosophy of Existence* (Philadelphia: University of Pennsylvania, 1971), 35.
10. Robert C. Tucker, ed. *The Marx-Engels Reader* (New York: W. W. Norton & Company, 1978), 143. In *Theses on Feuerbach*, Marx criticizes Feuerbach for his failure to "grasp the significance of 'revolutionary,' of practical-critical, activity."
11. Ibid., 72.
12. Ibid., 144.
13. Roger Scruton, *Thinkers of the New Left* (London: Claridge Press, 1985), 1. Scruton explains: "In the long run such shifts of opinion matter, and they have mattered disastrously. It is again necessary, I believe, to demonstrate the extent of the fraud that has been perpetuated in the name of the 'theoretical correctness' and the 'moral superiority' of socialism."
14. Ibid., 120. Marx writes: "Just as atheism, being the annulment of God, is the advent of theoretic humanism."
15. Max Horkheimer and Theodor Adorno, *Dialectic of Enlightenment: Philosophical Fragments* (Stanford: Stanford University Press, 2002); and Antonio Gramsci, *The Prison Notebooks* (London: Lawrence and Whishart, 1978).
16. Tucker, *The Marx-Engels Reader*, 599.
17. Jean-Francois Revel, *The Totalitarian Temptation* (Garden City, NY: Doubleday & Company, Inc., 1977), 20.
18. Jay, *The Dialectical Imagination*, 173.
19. Ibid., 298
20. Kramer, ed. *The Black Book of Communism*; Revel, *Last Exit to Utopia*.
21. Tom Bottomore, *The Frankfurt School and Its Critics* (London: Routledge, 2002), 46.
22. Scruton, *Thinkers of the New Left*, 210.
23. Stephen R. C. Hicks, *Explaining Postmodernism: Skepticism and Socialism from Rousseau to Foucault* (Roscoe, IL: Ockham's Razor Publishing, 2011), 20. Hicks adds: "Postmodern debates thus display a paradoxical nature. Across the board, we hear, on the one hand, abstract themes of relativism and egalitarianism. Those themes come in both epistemological and ethical forms. Objectivity is a myth; there is no Truth, no Right Way to read nature or a text."
24. Michael Polanyi, *The Tacit Dimension* (Chicago: University of Chicago Press, 2009), 59. Polanyi writes of Marxism: "Marxism embodies the boundless moral aspirations of modern man in a theory which protects his ideals from skeptical doubt by denying the reality of moral motives in public life. The power of Marxism lies in uniting the two contradictory forces of the modern mind into a single political doctrine."
25. François Furet, *Lies, Passions & Illusions: The Democratic Imagination in the Twentieth Century* (Chicago: University of Chicago Press, 2012).
26. Revel, *The Totalitarian Temptation*, 27.
27. Vincent Miceli, *The Gods of Atheism* (New Rochelle, NY: Arlington House, 1971).
28. Karl Jaspers, *Way to Wisdom* (New Haven: Yale University Press, 1954), 17. Jaspers locates the greatest strength of philosophy in wonder. He cites Plato and Aristotle.
29. Jürgen Habermas, *Moral Consciousness and Communicative Action* (Cambridge: MIT Press, 1999), 116.
30. Jürgen Habermas, *Postmetaphysical Thinking: Philosophical Essays* (Cambridge: MIT Press, 1996), 30.
31. Jürgen Habermas, *The Philosophical Discourse of Modernity* (Cambridge: MIT Press, 2000), 131.
32. Jurgen Habermas and Joseph Ratzinger, *The Dialectics of Secularization: On Reason and Religion* (San Francisco: Ignatius Press, 2005). Universal ethic of responsibility is a central feature of Habermas's debate with Pope Benedict XVI.

33. Jürgen Habermas, *Communication and the Evolution of Society* (Boston: Beacon Press,1979), 72. It is hard to recognize the human person in Habermas's mechanistic description of the ego.
34. Jay, *The Dialectical Imagination*, 256.
35. Jürgen Habermas, *Theory and Practice*, (Boston: Beacon Press, 1973), 111. Habermas explains, "Marx only has to confront the expectations of the liberal, Natural-Law construction of bourgeois society with the developmental tendencies of this society itself in order to confront the bourgeois revolution polemically with its own concept."
36. Habermas, *Postmetaphysical Thinking: Philosophical Essays*, 120.
37. Alexander Solzhenitsyn, *From under the Rubble* (Boston: Little, Brown and Company, 1974), 81. Solzhenitsyn writes, "The Marxist theory of class struggle has become not a means of defending the workers' interests but an ideology to justify terror and hegemony over them."
38. See Marxism as intellectualized terror in Malcolm Muggeridge's *Time and Eternity: Uncollected Writing* (New York: Orbis Books, 2011), 34.
39. Habermas and Ratzinger, *The Dialectics of Secularization*, 51.
40. Ibid., 56.
41. See Bottomore's assessment of the failures of critical theory and Habermas's work in *The Frankfurt School and Its Critics*, 72.
42. Scruton, *Thinkers of the New Left*, 125. Scruton writes: "It is only socialism that has set up, in the place of the government of men, that faceless 'administration of things' which is to be judged by the 'technical rules' of social engineering. And, if there is, in the modern world, a 'deficit of legitimacy,' it is greatest where socialism has most made its mark."

BIBLIOGRAPHY

Albert, Michael. 1974. *What Is to Be Undone: A Modern Revolutionary Discussion of Classical Left Ideologies.* Boston, MA: Horizons Book, 1974.
Berstein, Richard J., ed. 1998. *Habermas y la modernidad.* Madrid: Ediciones Cátedra, S. A.
Bottomore, Tom. 2002. *The Frankfurt School and Its Critics.* London: Routledge.
Copleston, Frederick, SJ. 1985. *A History of Philosophy, Book Two.* New York: Image Books.
Crossman, Richard. 1965. *The God That Failed.* New York: Bantam Books.
Djilas, Milovan. 1957. *The New Class: An Analysis of the Communist System.* New York: Frederick A. Praeger, Publisher.
Fukuyama, Francis. 1992. *The End of History and the Last Man.* New York: The Free Press.
Feuerbach, Ludwig. 1990. *Das Wesen des Christentums.* New York: Continuum.
Furet, François. 2012. *Lies, Passions & Illusions: The Democratic Imagination in the Twentieth Century.* Chicago: University of Chicago Press.
Gasset, José Ortegea. 1968. *The Dehumanization of Art and Other Essays on Art, Culture, and Literature.* Princeton: Princeton University Press.
González, Pedro Blas. 2014. "The Economics of Being: The Struggle for Existence in Prehistory." *Cultural International Journal of Philosophy of Culture and Axiology* 11/1: 23–39.
Gramsci, Antonio. 1978. *The Prison Notebooks.* London: Lawrence and Whishart.
Habermas, Jürgen. 1972. *Knowledge and Human Interests.* Boston: Beacon Press.
———. 1973. *Theory and Practice.* Boston: Beacon Press.
———. 1979. *Communication and the Evolution of Society.* Boston: Beacon Press.
———. 1989. *The Structural Transformation of the Public Sphere: An Inquiry Into a Category of Bourgeois Society.* Cambridge, MA: MIT Press.
———. 1993. *Postmetaphysical Thinking: Philosophical Essays.* Cambridge, MA: MIT Press.
———. 1999. *Moral Consciousness and Communicative Action.* Cambridge, MA: MIT Press.
———. 2000. *The Philosophical Discourse of Modernity.* Cambridge, MA: MIT Press.
Habermas, Jürgen, and Joseph Ratzinger. 2005. *The Dialectics of Secularization: On Reason and Religion.* San Francisco: Ignatius Press.
Hawkes, Jacquetta. 1976. *The Atlas of Early Man.* New York: St. Martin's Press.
Heilbroner, Robert L. 1980. *Marxism for and Against.* New York: W. W. Norton & Company.

Hicks, Stephen R. C. 2011. *Explaining Postmodernism: Skepticism and Socialism from Rousseau to Foucault*. Roscoe, IL: Ockham's Razor Publishing.
Horkheimer, Max, and Theodor Adorno. 2002. *Dialectic of Enlightenment Philosophical Fragments*. Stanford: Stanford University Press.
Jacobs, Harold. 1970. *Weatherman*. San Francisco: Ramparts Press, Inc.
Jaspers, Karl. 1954. *Way to Wisdom*. New Haven: Yale University Press.
———. 1971. *Philosophy of Existence*. Philadelphia: University of Pennsylvania Press.
Jay, Martin. 1996. *The Dialectical Imagination: A History of the Frankfurt School and the Institute of Social Research, 1923-1950*. Berkeley: University of California Press.
Kramer, Mark ed. 1999. *The Black Book of Communism: Crimes, Terror, Repression*. Cambridge: Harvard University Press.
Marx, Karl, and Frederick Engels. 1977. *Manifesto of the Communist Party*. Peking: Foreign Languages Press.
Miceli, Vincent. 1971. *The Gods of Atheism*. New Rochelle, NY: Arlington House.
Muggeridge, Malcolm. 2011. *Time and Eternity: Uncollected Writing*. New York: Orbis Books.
Polanyi, Michael. 2009. *The Tacit Dimension*. University of Chicago Press: Chicago.
Revel, Jean-Francois. 1977. *The Totalitarian Temptation*. Garden City, NY: Doubleday & Company, Inc.
———. 2000. *Last Exit to Utopia: The Survival of Socialism in a Post-Soviet Era* New York: Encounter Books.
Scruton, Roger. 1985. *Thinkers of the New Left*. London: Claridge Press.
Solzhenitsyn, Alexander. 1974. *From under the Rubble*. Boston: Little, Brown and Company.
Somerville, John, and Ronald E. Santoni, eds. 1963. *Social and Political Philosophy: Readings from Plato to Gandhi*. New York: Doubleday & Company, Inc.
Tucker, Robert C., ed. 1978. *The Marx-Engels Reader*. New York: W. W. Norton & Company.

Chapter Nine

Analytical Marxism and the Meaning of Historicism

Reflections on Kai Nielsen and G. A. Cohen

Grant Havers

In retrospect, analytical Marxism seemed like a good idea at the time. This new Marxism, which emerged in the late 1970s, promised to be "analytical," strengthening the most salvageable parts of traditional Marxism while jettisoning metaphysical language and premises that had undermined the impact of the theory. As the analytical Marxist Andrew Levine explains, "mainstream philosophers in the English-speaking world preferred to engage in tasks that appear pedestrian from the Olympian vantage point continental philosophers assumed—discerning conceptual structures, making distinctions (where appropriate), collapsing distinctions (where they are inappropriately drawn), and marshaling clear and sound arguments."[1] In sharp contrast to the Marxist theorizing of Althusser, who enjoyed considerable popularity in Europe around this time, the analytical Marxists were determined to provide a solid empirical basis to the theory of historical materialism. The Canadian philosopher G. A. Cohen (1941–2009) was the first analytical Marxist to provide a substantive version of this revamped Marxism in his seminal work *Karl Marx's Theory of History: A Defence* (1979).[2] The sheer rigor of Cohen's study inspired the hope that obituaries for Marxism were premature. Cohen's analytical approach also encouraged other Marxists in the English-speaking philosophical tradition to defend historical materialism with a renewed sense of optimism and resolve. The American Marxist philosopher Kai Nielsen (1926–) clearly sympathizes with Cohen's scholarship.[3] Although Cohen is the more famous of the two, Nielsen also deserves considerable credit for subjecting Marxism to "analytical scrutiny" at a time when there was considerable debate over the meaning or validity of this ideology.[4]

In the decades following the inception of analytical Marxism, there has been serious doubt regarding its viability. A few critics have argued that this movement is not truly Marxist, given its use of non-Marxist ideas such as game theory and methodological individualism.[5] Ambitious works of analytical Marxists, such as Jon Elster's *Making Sense of Marx* (1985),[6] further reinforced the impression that this new type of Marxism would save the theory only by killing its most central premises. Elster, who rejected Marxist staples such as the labor theory of value, a teleological belief in "laws of history," and an overreliance on functionalism, seemed to leave an empty shell of Marxism.[7] Despite the best intentions of analytical Marxists, even sympathetic devotees of this movement such as Levine admit that their entire project had helped to kill what they wanted to save: "One might therefore say that, without realizing it, the analytical Marxists saved Marxism by destroying it; that they breathed new life into the Marxist project, even as they came eventually—and regretfully—to the conclusion that they were its gravediggers."[8]

Is there any remnant of analytical Marxism that is worth preserving? This question is hard to answer, given the prevailing consensus that Marxism in all its varieties is historically obsolete (although a few writers insist that it has made a comeback since the economic crisis of 2008).[9] My contention is that analytical Marxism "breathed new life" into *historicism*, one of the most maligned philosophies of modernity. In basic terms, historicism teaches that human beings cannot transcend history. As Nielsen writes in *Naturalism Without Foundations* (1996), "We can hardly jump out of our cultural and historical skins."[10] We owe this insight to Hegel, who taught that "no one can overleap history" (*NWF*, 28). Philosophers must be historicists as well. "To be a historicist is to believe that the warrant for interesting and at least potentially controversial knowledge claims is always historical-epoch dependent" (*NWF*, 28). Taking aim at the ahistorical universalism of the Enlightenment, Cohen writes: "Marxist universalism suffers from the abstractedness of the Enlightenment universalism criticized by Hegel. The Enlightenment was wrong because the universal can exist only in a determinate embodiment: there is no way of being human which is not *a* way of being human" (*KMTH*, 354; author's italics). In short, historicism teaches that there is no idea or action that is inseparable from history. To assert that one can transcend history is tantamount to claiming that human beings can escape their own humanity.

Although these brief definitions may suggest that historicism is more of an exercise in the history of ideas rather than a philosophical viewpoint, I shall contend that Nielsen and Cohen defend historicism on valid philosophical grounds that support the legitimacy or validity of this perspective. In the process of rethinking Marxism, both of these philosophers have provided a version of historicism that is open to preserving traditional practices (e.g., nationalism, Christianity) that orthodox Marxism once dismissed as reactionary. Although neither Nielsen nor Cohen abandoned his leftist politics in a categorical manner, both of these philosophers later in life embraced positions that fit more comfortably into the opposite side of the political spectrum. In the case of Nielsen, a new openness to the importance of the nation-state emerged. In the case of Cohen, a deep appreciation of the Christian tradition's influence on morality became evident.

My choice of historicism as a valuable by-product of analytical Marxism may strike some readers as odd for two reasons. First, this movement originally emerged as a *rejection* of the historicism that underpinned Marxism on the European continent. When analytical Marxists thought of historicism at all, they tended to associate it with the unscientific teleological metaphysics of history that Engels associated with Marx when he eulogized his famous collaborator as a "man of science" who discovered laws of history that were analogous to laws of nature.[11] Consequently, analytical Marxists were determined to purge Marxism of this historicist heritage that had imposed a problematic metaphysical determinism onto Marxism.[12] Second, historicism has had a rough time of it in the twentieth century, even apart from its association with Marxism. It has faced severe scrutiny from distinguished philosophers such as Leo Strauss, who accuses historicism of promoting a teleological concept of history that subordinates human freedom to the fatalistic power of history while it dogmatically affirms the relativistic denial of truth or certainty. I shall show that Nielsen and Cohen are determined to avoid a historicism that embraces both fatalism and relativism. In the process of repudiating the rigid materialist teleology of classical Marxism, the analytical version also eschews the dogmatic Marxian preoccupation with class interest in favor of appreciating nonmaterial loyalties (national pride, religion) that at times sound conservative.

OVERLEAPING TELEOLOGY (BUT NOT HISTORY)

According to Cohen, what separates analytical Marxism from every other version of Marxism is the former's repudiation of the belief that history is a "dialectical" process. "Belief in dialectic as a *rival* to analysis thrives only in an atmosphere of unclear thought" (*KMTH*, xxiii; author's italics). This dialectical thinking, which Cohen elsewhere associates with Hegel, should be rejected precisely because it reduces human freedom or agency to God's providence.[13] (Whether his interpretation of Hegel is accurate is another question, since Hegel understands history as the greatest expression of human freedom.)[14] As a defender of "methodological individualism," Cohen affirms the agency of human individuals in the creation of history. "Insofar as analytical Marxists are analytical in this narrower sense, they reject the point of view in which social formations and classes are depicted as entities obeying laws of behavior that are not a function of the behaviours of their constituent individuals" (*KMTH*, xxiii).

Nielsen is equally opposed to defending a grand theory of history that, in anti-empirical fashion, proposes that there are laws or "ends" that history must obey. Instead, he insists that analytical Marxism must reject this "teleological orientation or talk of meaning" in favor of a theory that operates in "an empirically disciplined manner."[15] Cohen in a similar vein rejects the "obstetric doctrine" of traditional Marxism which insisted that history operates in a manner analogous to an "organic" process of birth, growth, and decay. In his view, it is "false" and even dangerous to assume, as orthodox Marxists like Rosa Luxemburg did, that socialism would inevitably (or organically) emerge out of a decayed capitalism, as a babe emerges from its mother's womb.[16]

As Nielsen explains, analytical Marxism seeks to

> avoid such grand a priori and teleological roads; instead they [analytical Marxists] construct accounts of historical materialism that are empirically testable, which give us a causal account of epochal social change, have clearly articulated concepts of class, and show us both that and why we have class and strata in our societies and how and why capitalist societies, no matter how human their faces come to be with social democracy, will remain class societies. These accounts are nonteleological and consist of testable theories.[17]

In brief, Cohen and Nielsen embrace a historicism that is stripped of metaphysical baggage which emphasizes laws or goals of history, subjecting human beings to forces beyond their control. There is such a thing as human freedom: human beings can (and must) change the world. Yet they also insist that human beings cannot transcend history altogether. Obviously, some large questions arise here. If we are stuck in history, how can we be free? Moreover, given the constant movement of history, how can we know that anything (even historicism) is universally true or certain? Are analytical Marxists any more successful than their orthodox predecessors in combating these tu quoque objections, which essentially expose the self-contradictory nature of historicism?[18]

STRAUSS ON HISTORICISM

Leo Strauss certainly would not think that it is possible or desirable to salvage historicism. It is hard to imagine more different philosophers than Strauss and analytical Marxists. True to his historicism, Nielsen defends John

Dewey's hope that "philosophy should transform itself by setting aside the perennial problems of philosophers—problems (so-called problems) like the problem of the external world or of other minds—and concern itself with the live context-dependent, epoch-dependent problems of human beings: centrally political, social problems; religious problems; and live moral problems that beset human beings" (*NWF*, 32). Strauss, in sharp contrast, avers that the great questions of philosophy are as relevant as ever. "Far from legitimizing the historicist inference, history seems rather to prove that all human thought, and certainly all philosophic thought, is concerned with the same fundamental themes or the same fundamental problems, and therefore that there exists an unchanging framework which persists in all changes of human knowledge of both facts and principles."[19]

This vast disagreement may in part explain why analytical philosophers have generally not taken Strauss very seriously. Nielsen probably represented the majority opinion of the analytical world when he once dismissed Strauss and his student Allan Bloom as unphilosophical because of their failure to meet the "necessary condition" of subjecting their ideas to "cross-examination," as Plato did.[20] He also chides Strauss and Hegel alike for constructing "grand philosophical narratives" that compare poorly to the rigor of analytical Marxism.[21] (It is worth noting, however, that Cohen once devoted critical attention to Strauss's early study of Hobbes.)[22] These attitudes notwithstanding, I believe that Strauss's critique of historicism deserves serious philosophical attention, not least because other major philosophers of the Anglosphere such as Karl Popper and Isaiah Berlin have leveled similar charges against historicism.[23]

In attacking historicism, Strauss is not rejecting the study of history per se. Historicism is not identical to an appreciation of history. In Strauss's view, it is a dangerous doctrine that threatens to abolish political philosophy or critical thought altogether. Strauss does not object to studies of the history of thought, properly understood. The danger stemming from historicism is that it reinvents the history of thought according to the fashion or bias of the moment. "The task of the historian of thought is to understand the thinkers of the past exactly as they understood themselves, or to revitalize their thought according to their own interpretation. If we abandon this goal, we abandon the only practicable criterion of 'objectivity' in the history of thought."[24] Yet historicists show no interest in the original intention of these thinkers, since they typically assume that they can understand these thinkers better than the thinkers understood themselves. Historicists (especially progressivist ones) can make this claim because of their assumption that these thinkers lacked a proper understanding of their historical context. "The historicist thesis amounts then to this, that there is an inevitable contradiction between the intention of philosophy and its fate, between the nonhistorical intention of the philosophic answers and their fate always to remain 'historically conditioned.'"[25]

Based on this critique, Strauss faults historicism for two related reasons. First, it denies that human beings can escape from the historical influences of their age. Strauss's use of the term "fate" is central to his overall critique of historicism. In *Natural Right and History* (1953), he accuses historicists of denying that human beings have the freedom to change or even philosophically understand the times in which they live:

> All human thought depends on fate, on something that thought cannot master and whose workings it cannot anticipate. Yet the support of the horizon produced by fate is ultimately the choice of the individual, since this fate has to be accepted by the individual. We are free in the sense that we are free either to choose in anguish the world view and the standards imposed on us by fate or else to lose ourselves in illusory security or in despair.[26]

Under historicism, then, we are only free to be unfree, unable to understand or resist the currents of history.

Second, historicism denies that there are universal truths that transcend history. For this reason, Strauss has no difficulty in pointing out that historicism is self-contradictory. If historicism is applied to itself, then it is a doctrine that is relative to its own historical period. Consequently, historicism cannot be true in any universal or absolute sense, given the fact that it denies there is such a doctrine in the first place. "No view of the whole, and in particular no view of the whole of human life, can claim to be final or universally valid. Every doctrine, however seemingly final, will be superseded sooner or later by another doctrine."[27] Although historicists (notably Hegel) may claim that their moment in history is an "absolute moment" or one that allows them the objectivity to understand history in a final sense,[28] they too must admit that their ideas are subject to the fatal destiny of endless change in history. If all standards of justice are relative to a historical era, then human beings lose the "critical distance" necessary to distinguish a civilized society from a cannibalistic one.[29] In short, historicism leaves us with "mutable" standards of truth or justice, without any sense of what is permanently or universally valid and true.[30]

Given the teleological and deterministic baggage of orthodox Marxism, it is no wonder that even critics of Strauss admit that Marxism "may be the historical theory that comes closest to Strauss's description of the historicist fallacy" or its self-contradictory nature.[31] Sympathetic readers of Marx have admitted that there is a Marxian version of fatalism that underscores the theory of historical materialism.[32] (It does not help matters that prominent Marxists have at times embraced the crudest determinism. Adorno once observed that Kierkegaard became an existentialist because he "sustained major losses in the market fluctuations of 1848"!)[33] For this reason, Nielsen and

Cohen have attempted to defend Marx against the charges of relativism or crude historicism.[34] For my purposes, however, it is important to show that the Nielsen-Cohen version of historicism (which does not require adherence to every aspect of analytical Marxism) can withstand Strauss's associations of historicism with fatalism and relativism. How, exactly, does their version of historicism avoid these aporias?

AVOIDING FATALISM OR DETERMINISM

Neither Nielsen nor Cohen supports the orthodox Marxian expectation that history is inevitably on the side of their political program. Still, Cohen freely admits that Marx relies on a saving tale that promises the end to all conflict in history:

> This rhythm of primitive whole, fragmentation, and reunification asserts itself widely in Western thought. It beats not only in Hegel and, as we shall see, in Marx, but in much religious doctrine, in the Christian triad of innocence, fall, and redemption, in Aristophanes' account of love in Plato's *Symposium*, in some psycho-analytic narrations of the genesis of the person, and—seminally for German philosophy of history—throughout Schiller's *Letters on the Aesthetic Education of Mankind*. (*KMTH*, 21)

Cohen and Nielsen absolutely repudiate this eschatology that inspired the false prophesy that socialism would triumph in history. Whereas "strong" (or orthodox) historical materialism is riddled with this happy determinism, the "weak" historical materialism, which they defend, is not. "Weak historical materialism does not tell us what *must* happen; it only shows us what reasonably and empirically *could* happen."[35] To say the least, history did not cooperate with classical Marxian expectations that a revolution is just around the corner. As Cohen soberly notes, "Capitalism does not produce its own grave-diggers."[36]

To make matters worse for orthodox Marxism, the two "supposedly irrepressible historical trends" that would guarantee the "future material equality" of a communist society did not materialize. These trends include the rise of an organized working class as the majority class in a capitalist society as well as the development of productive (economic) forces that would create material abundance for all.[37] "History shredded each of these predictions," in Cohen's view. Advances in automation actually reduced the size of the working class to nonmajority status. Additionally, the full development of productive forces has run up against natural limits imposed by planet Earth, whose "resources turn out to be not lavish enough for continuous growth in technical knowledge to generate unceasing expansion of use-value."[38] It is worth noting that Cohen did not abandon his socialist politics in the face of this evidence, but only abandoned any dependence "on ambitious theses about the whole of human history" (*KMTH*, 341).[39]

Although it is tempting to conclude that the sheer weight of historical evidence forces analytical Marxists to abandon the most fatalistic predictions of classical Marxism, there are more philosophical reasons that they can draw upon as well. Nielsen, for example, categorically rejects any theoretical attempt (Marxist or otherwise) to explain human behavior according to a rigidly deterministic teleology based on classical physics. Although Nielsen describes himself as a "naturalist" who believes in only one (physical) reality, this version of materialism is not a reductive one (*NWF*, 25, 35, 44). In response to Alasdair MacIntyre's conflation of naturalism with scientism, Nielsen explains:

> What should be apparent from the very articulation of my fallibilistic, pragmatic, nonscientistic, contextualized, historicized naturalism is that I am neither asserting nor presupposing any of these things that MacIntyre says are constitutive of naturalism. . . . I do not think that there is such a thing as a final theory and with that I do not think natural science, or anything else, is to be understood (to quote MacIntyre again) "as in progress towards a complete account not only of the laws governing nature, but also of the phenomena of nature."[40] (*NWF*, 47)

Crude historicists who claim that we must be on the right side of history or "jump on the wave of the future" are also easy prey for Strauss's critique of historicism as philosophically untenable.[41] Yet Nielsen is not guilty of this simplistic historicism. As a philosopher, he would agree with Strauss that the validity of an idea does not depend on its historical context or influence.[42] For example, Nielsen rejects the thesis that the decline of religion's influence in the West automatically undermines the validity of belief.[43] In short, Strauss and Nielsen share some common ground on the defects of unreflective historicism.

AVOIDING RELATIVISM

Does the Nielsen-Cohen version of historicism avoid relativism as well? The key idea that is most relevant here in Nielsen's "historicized naturalism" (or historicism) is *fallibilism*, which essentially teaches that "no principles or beliefs or convictions, not even the most firmly held, are, in principle at least, free from the possibility of being modified or even set aside, though some moral truisms may always in fact be unquestionably accepted" (*NWF*, 15). Although fallibilism shares with crude historicism a suspicion of "timeless" or "ahistorical" truths, the former is thoroughly empirical in rejecting "final theories" of any kind (*NWF*, 26). At the same time, it opposes relativism, or the denial of any standards that could measure the validity of claims:

> Historicism goes well with fallibilism. But it is not saying that everything is relative or subjective or that no view can be any better than any other view or more adequately grounded. It is surely not saying that anything goes. It is saying just the opposite, namely, that knowledge is often cumulative, but still is always incomplete and always, where issues of substance are concerned, less than certain. But this is not to say that all is relative or subjective or that all views are equally adequate or equally valid (whatever that means) or anything of the kind. (*NWF*, 29)

As Nielsen further points out, fallibilism and historicism need each other. Fallibilism makes use of the historicist premise that knowledge is "cumulative" in history, that in fact one period of history may be in a better position to understand the prejudices of a past era than those who lived in that era (*NWF*, 28). With a nod to Hegel's famous Owl of Minerva flying at dusk, human beings generally understand historical change in retrospect. None of this should imply that historicism in this sense justifies uncritical passivity toward change. If anything, Nielsen and Cohen stress the importance of constant critique of what stands for conventional wisdom in a given era. Nielsen and Cohen are particularly aware of the common accusation that the Marxist critique of morality must lead to moral relativism precisely because it reduces ethical credos to their origin or role in a given historical context (or, as Marx and Engels famously put it: "The ruling ideas of each age have ever been the ideas of its ruling class").[44]

In response to the accusation that Marxism is necessarily relativistic on matters of morality, Nielsen counters that analytical Marxists distinguish between the *sociology* of morals and the *epistemology* of morals.[45] In the case of sociology, Marxists question the ideological and mystifying role that moral language and concepts play in an established socioeconomic structure. What the ruling class deems "right" and "wrong" should be subjected to scrutiny, based on the assumption that it identifies morality with its own class interest. Yet the epistemology of morals is a different kettle of fish, targeting on meta-ethical grounds the belief that we can have knowledge of ethics. If Marxists embraced this epistemology, their critique of capitalist injustice would founder on endless questions about what counts as "justice." Yet Marx never bothered himself with debates over the meaning of right and wrong, given his bedrock conviction that exploitation under capitalism is unjust. In short, the critique of the ideological misuse of morality does not logically lead to the conclusion that morality itself is conceptually up for grabs.

Still, is Nielsen manifesting the sort of crude historicism that, according to Strauss, fails to "teach us whether the change [in history] was sound or whether the rejected view deserved to be rejected"?[46] I believe that the answer must be negative here, if we accurately understand what Nielsen has in mind. Truth still exists, even if our idea of truth is intelligible only in historical terms. It is simply a fact that modern science continues to advance our understanding of nature in ways that ultimately affect how other disciplines (e.g., the humanities, social sciences) think about the world. It is not relativistic of Nielsen to deny such a thing as "comprehensive knowledge of our own mistakes." In fallibilistic terms, it is prudent and reasonable to admit that what we know at a given moment in history is *probably* true until such a time when new evidence challenges these knowledge claims.

The fact that Nielsen values modern science does not make him a defender of the scientistic view that science can explain *all* human behavior, as we have seen. However, it clearly illustrates Nielsen's view that what we consider to be knowledge (universal or contextual) should respect the integrity of modern science. If Nielsen is right, philosophers in the modern age must avoid the "allegedly unwobbling pivots" that, he believes, characterize Strauss's grand history of philosophy (*NWF*, 19). Nevertheless, if Strauss is right, historicism leaves us trapped in our historical context without escape. Put differently, historicism fundamentally kills philosophy or thought, leading to nihilism.[47] Because they are caught in their historical context, philosophers cannot even hope to transcend or critically scrutinize their times. Political philosophy's traditional quest for the best or most just regime must then come to an end.[48]

Does historicism necessarily leave us in this lurch? Historicism, as Nielsen presents it, never denies the need to be critical of one's assumptions (or the conventional wisdom of one's times). In fact, it insists on this practice. What historicism categorically denies is a transhistorical standard that is so certain that it is completely invulnerable to critique. (Even Strauss admits at times that the idea of "an eternal and unchangeable order within which History takes place and which is not in any way affected by History . . . is not self-evident.")[49] Nielsen writes: "But that we cannot overleap culture and history is no justification or excuse for *remaining uncritically* with our initial convictions, convictions that we cannot avoid *starting* with" (*NWF*, 17; author's italics). Strauss would likely agree that we need this starting point, or what he calls the "pre-philosophical."[50] Still, how exactly does Nielsen's historicism lead us beyond parochial beginnings based on our tradition, upbringing, or society?

Nielsen's approach is, once again, fallibilistic. In his discussion of John Rawls's idea of "wide reflective equilibrium" (WRE), he describes this process as one that comes to "modify or even excise some considered judgments" while "seeking a wider and more coherent web of beliefs and practices" (*NWF*, 17). The best that we can hope for is a fallibilistic modification of beliefs that may no longer correspond with our knowledge. WRE is more reasonable than appealing to an eternal order of "moral realism," which

Nielsen would consider "mythical" anyway (*NWF*, 17). WRE, however, is never complete nor is it just an exercise in coherence (*NWF*, 59, 68–69). The method or practice of WRE requires not only coherence among our moral convictions, principles, and background theories arising from our society but also an empirically based account of human nature and society (*NWF*, 189). Contrary to Strauss, there is no such thing as an "unassisted human mind" that escapes the influence of these contextual assumptions absolutely.[51] Nevertheless, we can and must use our reasoning to justify our beliefs while recognizing that they may face the possibility of revision. Nielsen and Cohen have applied this fallibilistic reasoning to Marxism itself so as to avoid the pitfalls arising from the old deterministic Marxism.

Is there anything that we can know with certainty about human nature, according to this fallibilistic historicism? The closest that Cohen and Nielsen perhaps get to embracing a metaphysics of humanity is the assumption that human beings create history (although, as Marx famously cautioned, "they do not make it just as they please . . . but under circumstances directly found, given and transmitted from the past").[52] Human beings are history-making animals (*KMTH*, 23–25). Yet this is not an appeal to an "ahistorical" essence. (How can it be, if we have no choice but to act in history?) Rather, this is a paradoxical metaphysics which teaches that we human beings have no choice but to create history even though we still have the freedom (however limited) to create history. This open-ended historicism enables Cohen and Nielsen to reevaluate traditional Marxist views on nonclass loyalties.

RETHINKING RELIGION

The revamped historicism that Nielsen and Cohen articulate is not only more pragmatic on matters of historical inevitability and universalism than its orthodox predecessors. It also offers a more comprehensive understanding of history, recognizing the importance and even beneficial nature of nationalism and religion. In repudiating teleological metaphysics, analytical Marxists have also found it necessary, as good fallibilists, to modify the economic determinism that has characterized historical materialism. This is no easy task, given the fact that Marx constantly emphasized the primacy of economic or class identity at the expense of other modes of identity such as religion or patriotism. (Even Engels admitted that he and Marx "are ourselves partly to blame for the fact that the younger people lay more stress on the economic side than is due to it.")[53] In *The Communist Manifesto*, he and Engels confidently predicted that capitalism would sweep away the prejudice of religion by forcing on proletarians the awareness that only materialism can explain reality. "All that is solid melts into air, all that is holy is profaned, and man is at last compelled to face with sober senses, his real conditions of life, and his relations with his kind."⁵⁴ They also confidently predicted that "National differences and antagonisms were vanishing" in the face of capitalist globalization, which would unwittingly inspire proletariats of all lands to form a united front against the bourgeoisie.⁵⁵ This dismissal of nationalist sentiment was so deeply felt among Marxists that they completely failed to anticipate the upsurge of patriotic feelings among the European working classes on the eve of World War I. As Cohen notes in his defense of historical materialism, Lenin concluded that a single nation-state (e.g., Russia) could not establish socialism successfully; it would need the support of revolutionary movements from around the world (*KMTH*, 394).

The fact that religion and nationalism show no signs of extinction in the present age have forced analytical Marxists such as Nielsen and Cohen to rethink classical Marxism further while maintaining a robust historicism. According to Cohen, analytical Marxists should aim for a "restricted" historical materialism that does not seek to reduce all phenomena in history to an economic or class causality (one that is different from the "inclusive" historical materialism that is crudely reductionist) (*KMTH*, 364–88). In the process, Cohen and Nielsen have taken on positions that are to *the right* of the socialist politics that they embraced in an earlier time of life.

Cohen, in one of his last essays, "Rescuing Conservatism: A Defense of Existing Value," rethinks the progressivist-Marxist dismissal of conservatism. What inspired him to take this heterodox turn was the survival of his place of employment, All Souls College at Oxford, in the face of pressures to accept corporate funding, which endangered the identity and autonomy of this college. Cohen draws from two unlikely sources of inspiration for guidance: Hegel's philosophy and the Gospel account of Jesus's arrest at the Garden of Gethsemane (although he does not develop the implications of this intellectual debt). Both communicate the same conservative message, "that of accepting the given, of valuing the valuable, and of valuing the valued, the subject is at peace with the object."⁵⁶ Cohen goes on to remark that "All Souls is a valuable social creation, partly *because* of what makes it different from otherwise similar social creations. As a valuable social creation, it merits preservation, and a radical enough transformation would induce both deformation of our identity and, with that, a loss of (some of) the distinctive value that the college embodies." Moreover, "it is the legitimate desire of its members (All Souls College) to preserve their particular corporate identity."⁵⁷ Cohen sounds even more conservative when he inveighs against the progressivist assumption that it is legitimate to replace one valuable thing with a more valuable (or beneficial) thing. Loyalty to a valuable tradition may count for more than preference for a new innovation:

> The conservative impulse is to conserve what is valuable, that is, the particular things that are valuable. I claim that we devalue the valuable things we have if

we keep them as long as nothing even slightly more valuable comes along. Valuable things command a certain loyalty. If an existing thing has intrinsic value, then we have reason to regret its destruction as such, a reason that we would not have if we cared only about the value that thing carries or instantiates.[58]

In defending conservatism, Cohen is not abandoning socialism, since he retains the Marxian view that, given capitalism's role as a solvent of tradition, a socialist revolution is "necessary to preserve the fruits of civilization against the ravages of capitalism."[59]

Which other traditions have "value," worthy of preservation, even though their value is not measurable according to egotistical calculation? In his provocatively titled *If You're an Egalitarian, How Come You're So Rich?* (2000), Cohen provides an un-Marxist answer. He contends that the Christian belief in equality is necessary as a foundation for a humane liberalism or socialism. In his view, the Marxian reliance on the sheer force of class struggle is no more successful in convincing human beings to treat others as equals than the Rawlsian reliance on rules to enforce justice. "For Christians, both the Marxist and the Rawlsian conceptions are misguided, since equality requires not mere history and the abundance to which it leads, or mere politics, but a moral revolution, a revolution in the human soul."[60] The liberal preference for these rules is no substitute for the actual practice of egalitarian justice. Taking aim at Rawls in particular, Cohen writes:

> My critique of Rawls reflects and supports a view that justice in personal choice is necessary for a society to qualify as just. . . . Jesus would have spurned the liberal idea that the state can take care of justice for us, provided only that we obey the rules it lays down, and regardless of what we choose to do within those rules. And I believe that Jesus would have been right to spurn that idea.[61]

To be sure, Cohen is not the first Marxist to appreciate the historical (or even necessary) influence of Christianity on modern or secular ideas of equality. Engels also recognized that Christianity was the "first possible world religion" because it addressed "all peoples without distinction."[62] Still, Cohen's sympathy with Christianity would not convince everyone that this faith is still necessary as a vital source of egalitarian sentiment. Why does egalitarianism require the leavening influence of Christian universalism?

Cohen's debt to Hegel, to whom he alluded in his essay on conservatism, now becomes clearer. We have already seen Cohen praise Hegel for exposing the ahistorical abstractions of Enlightenment universalism. Cohen goes on to credit Hegel with being the first philosopher to scrutinize the abstract nature of Enlightenment philosophy, particularly the latter's inattention to the historical differences between peoples (*KMTH*, 4). He also recognizes

Hegel as the first philosopher to reconcile what is particular (the nation-state) with what is universal (freedom). The historic particularity of nations is compatible with the universal "world spirit." Yet this reconciliation, according to Hegel, is not possible until the Christian era. The idea of universal freedom (and equality) was unknown even to Greek democracy. Hegel writes:

> No land was so rich as Greece, alike in the number of its constitutions, and in the frequent changes from one to another of these in a single state; but the Greeks were still unacquainted with the abstract right of our modern states, that isolates the individual, allows of his acting as such, and yet, as an invisible spirit, holds all its parts together. . . . The freedom of citizens in this signification is the dispensing with universality, the principle of isolation; but it is a necessary moment unknown to ancient states.[63]

Long before Cohen embraced Christianity as a necessary precondition to equality, he still appreciated Hegel's attempt at explaining how "Coherent national characters exist as phases of realization of the spirit of the world" (*KMTH*, 6). The answer is: Christianity.

> Hegel believed that Protestantism spoke the truth about man and the universe. But his religious faith was matched by a faith in reason which said that every truth which Christianity expresses in a wrap of myth or image may be stated without imagery by philosophy. This meant that there was a need for a philosophical formulation of the idea of Providence, of God's will manifesting itself in history. (*KMTH*, 6)

Although it is doubtful that Cohen thinks in the Protestant terms that Hegel did, he ultimately concedes Hegel's main thesis, that secular or modern ideas on equality are also intelligible (and historically rooted in) the "imagery" of Christianity.

To recall Cohen's critique of Rawls, only Christianity could effect a "moral revolution" that would foster true egalitarian justice. Once again, Hegel is the first philosopher to understand this revolution in historical terms. The paradox is that this moral universalism is specific to one historical faith tradition. Hegel writes:

> First, under Christianity Slavery is impossible; for man is man—in the abstract essence of his nature—is contemplated in God; each unit of mankind is an object of the grace of God and of the Divine purpose: "God will have *all* men to be saved." Utterly excluding all speciality, therefore, man, in and for himself—in his simple quality of man—has infinite value; and this infinite value abolishes, *ipso facto*, all particularity attaching to birth or country.[64]

Perhaps needless to say, Cohen's reasoning sets him apart from other analytical Marxists (e.g., Nielsen) who do not want to revive Christianity in any sense. The fact that Christianity exerts an important influence in history does not convince them that this faith is still necessary as an ethical force. As Nielsen observes, such a claim is an example of the genetic fallacy.[65] Even though Christianity was the first egalitarian faith, it does not follow that human beings in the twenty-first century should cherish this faith. After all, as Nielsen has often pointed out, the Christian church has also impeded the cause of social reform throughout history.[66] Nevertheless, the modern debt to Christianity is not so easy to dismiss.

RETHINKING THE NATION-STATE

In reconsidering the value of nationalism or the nation-state, Nielsen shows how far he has distanced himself from classical Marxism, which disdained this parochial attachment to ethnicity. Levine has even remarked that "no one who knew him (Nielsen) years ago would have expected his thinking to take this turn."[67] One early antecedent of this unexpected turn is Nielsen's acknowledgment, in a 1987 essay on identity, that Enlightenment universalism does not cancel out the claims of the counter-Enlightenment, which emphasizes the historical particularity of persons.[68] Still, only relatively late in his philosophical journey has Nielsen defended the idea of a nation-state that is "cosmopolitan" in its approach to justice. Two large historicist questions arise from his attempt to reconcile a universal moral responsibility to other human beings with the legitimacy of the nation-state to puts its own citizens first. What are the historical preconditions that make this desired reconciliation possible? Additionally, with a nod to Cohen, can we moderns think in cosmopolitan or egalitarian terms without the leavening influence of Christianity?

In order to get some purchase on what is at issue here, I shall examine Nielsen's definition of what counts as a "cosmopolitan" nation-state. He writes:

> We would become more internationalist and less ethnocentric and, with the free and extended circulation of peoples, our cultural life would be enriched. While most of us no doubt would continue to think of ourselves as members of groups which make us distinct peoples where typically we would cherish our distinctness, the very globalization process would make it easier, and with a more secure sense of reality, to also think of ourselves as a worldwide community of peoples and to cherish that thought.[69]

Nielsen's reflections raise several questions, but one in particular is relevant to my thesis. How, exactly, do we "become more internationalist and less ethnocentric"? Or, how exactly do we ultimately "think of ourselves as a worldwide community of peoples" and "cherish that thought"? As a Marxist, Nielsen does not believe that capitalism can achieve this feat, although, as Marx and Engels averred in *The Communist Manifesto*, the earliest stage of capitalism made globalization possible. With globalization comes the possibility (or inevitability for Marx) that humanity can understand itself as one community at long last in history (an idea that Cohen has dismissed, as we have seen). So far, this great unity has not transpired. Can Christianity do any better? Nielsen's answer would be a negative one. Still, does he provide a credible alternative?

Nielsen sees no necessary conflict between a state's primary commitment to its citizens and the same state's consideration of everyone else's interests that might be affected (as in the case of secession). He cites with approval Isaiah Berlin's essay on Herder as a source of good reasons for defending this type of state:

> Isaiah Berlin has made vivid for us Johann Gottfried Herder's eighteenth-century resistance to Enlightenment rationalism. People will suffer and will not flourish where they do not have a secure social identity. Among our very deep needs is the need to belong to a group, to be, that is, a member of some community. But this means, Herder argues, an attachment to local identities and not *just* to humanity in general.[70]

If I interpret his intent correctly here, Nielsen is committed to a "liberal nationalism" that protects its citizens and adheres to human rights. Moreover, liberal democracies are far more suited than dictatorships to the task of negotiating differences between ethnic groups: Scotland is far more successful than Chechnya.[71] In short, he rejects the inevitability of a tragic choice between the interests of one's citizens and duties to humanity as a whole.

There is, however, a striking omission in his account. What Nielsen does not discuss here is what exactly makes this type of cosmopolitan state possible. For Herder, there was no mystery as to why some nation-states are better than others in avoiding xenophobia or bigotry while protecting their citizenry. Christianity is the necessary source of this moral universalism, which somehow coexists with national pride. Like Herder (and Hegel), Nielsen believes that universalism and particularity need not clash with each other or cancel each other out, even though they often do. Yet Herder thought that the only religion that saved humanity from the most parochial versions of particularity is Christianity. He writes in "Another Philosophy of History for the Education of Mankind" (1774):

> It is undeniable that this same religion, created in so peculiar a manner, was *by the intentions of its founder* meant to be (I shall not pronounce on whether this is what it became in the practices of the various ages) the *actual religion of all*

> *mankind*, an *impulse towards love*, and *a bond between all the nations* to make of them an *army of brothers*—this was its *purpose* from *beginning to end*. . . . All preceding religions, even those of the best times and peoples, were, after all, only *narrowly national*, full of *images and masquerades*, full of *ceremonies* and *national practices* to which the essential duties were only ever *attached and appended*—in short, religions of *one people, one corner of the earth, one lawgiver, one age*! This one, on the other hand, was evidently just the opposite in everything: the *most honorable moral philosophy*, the *purest theory* of *truths* and *duties, independent* of all legislation and petty local constitutions. In short, if you will, the *deism with the greatest love for man*.[72]

It is not hard to imagine Nielsen's response here. Besides appealing to the genetic fallacy cited above, Nielsen has argued that the moral equality which appears in the Christian tradition has not exactly persuaded most self-identified Christians in history to treat their fellow human beings as equals:

> There have been, and indeed still are, courageous Christians such as Dietrich Bonhoeffer, Father Berrigan, and today in South Africa, Beyers Naudé, who have struggled against the oppressive existing social order, but massively and not surprisingly the Christian churches have been on the side of the dominant ruling interests and have functioned to reconcile people, against their own interests, to such a class rule. They have repeatedly offered them illusory hopes in such a way as to stem revolt and, wherever possible, to batten down the struggle for human liberation.[73]

Although Nielsen's response has merit, it is vulnerable to the counterargument that Christian morality is one of several preconditions that are essential to the creation of a humane society. The fact that the defenders of apartheid misused Christian beliefs to justify a profoundly immoral social order does not demonstrate that Christianity is unnecessary to social progress. It simply proves that other factors (e.g., the level of economic development or affluence) must also be at play in order to build a just regime. Apartheid in South Africa lasted as long as it did because it took advantage of millions of vulnerable people living in a developing nation that provided little if any education to its poorest subjects. Even Nielsen concedes at times that the liberalism of Rawls is suited to advanced nations that lack "extensive intolerances."[74]

Like Nielsen, Herder recognizes the mixed record of the church, or the gap between the "intentions of its founder" and "what it became in the practices of the various ages." Moreover, Herder may be vulnerable to an accusation that Nielsen has hurled at other Christian philosophers, namely that he has overemphasized Christian love at the expense of other important doctrines and in the process constructed a "Godless Christianity."[75] Nevertheless, this interpretation does not alter the fact that a Christian morality was necessary to provide the moral universalism to which liberal democracies at least pay lip-service today. A truly broad and fallibilistic historicism would have to accept the insight (common to both Herder and Hegel) that Christianity, as Cohen argued, is still necessary as a force that inspires belief in moral equality.

We have come full circle. Although Nielsen and Cohen set out to articulate an historicism that is independent of Hegelian metaphysics, their debt to Hegel is considerable. Notwithstanding their fallibilistic view that knowledge is cumulative or modifiable in history, the Nielsen-Cohen version of historicism heavily leans (albeit indirectly at times) on one of Hegel's most recurrent ideas: that a universal morality of freedom and equality would not have emerged without Christianity. Moreover, Christianity is still necessary for this purpose. *Pace* Strauss, this dependence on Hegel does not fall into the aporias of fatalism or relativism. Nor does it require an embrace of Marxism. Rather, this conservative historicism reminds us of the necessity to save what is most valuable within the history of humanity. We cannot escape history precisely because we are responsible for creating and preserving history with thought and resolve. This is one saving tale that is worth preserving.

NOTES

1. Andrew Levine, *A Future for Marxism? Althusser, the Analytical Turn, and the Revival of Socialist Theory* (London: Pluto Press, 2003), 126.

2. G. A. Cohen, *Karl Marx's Theory of History: A Defence* (Princeton: Princeton University Press, 2000). This work was originally published by Oxford University Press in 1979. The 2000 edition contains a new introduction and additional chapters. This work is henceforth cited as *KMTH* in the text.

3. Kai Nielsen, "Analytical Marxism: A Form of Critical Theory," *Erkenntnis* 39/1 (July 1993): 3.

4. Andrew Levine, "Whatever Happened to Marxism?" in *Reason and Emancipation: Essays on the Philosophy of Kai Nielsen*, Michel Seymour and Matthias Fritsch, eds. (Amherst, NY: Humanity Books, 2007), 185.

5. Michael A. Lebowitz, "Is 'Analytical Marxism' Marxism?" *Science and Society* 52/2 (Summer 1988): 191–214. See also Richard Norman, "What Is Living and What Is Dead in Marxism?" in *Analyzing Marxism*, Robert Ware and Kai Nielsen, eds. (Calgary: University of Calgary Press, 1989), 59–80.

6. Jon Elster, *Making Sense of Marx* (Cambridge: Cambridge University Press, 1985).

7. Kai Nielsen, "What Is Alive and What Is Dead in Marx and Marxism a la Elster," *Laval théologique et philosophique* 49/2 (Juin 1993): 278.

8. Levine, *A Future for Marxism*, 123.

9. Terry Eagleton, *Why Marx Was Right* (New Haven: Yale University Press, 2011).

10. Kai Nielsen, *Naturalism Without Foundations* (Amherst, NY: Prometheus Books, 1996), 17. This work is henceforth cited as *NWF* in the text.

11. Friedrich Engels, "Speech at the Graveside of Karl Marx," in *The Marx-Engels Reader*, 2nd edition, Robert C. Tucker, ed. (New York: W. W. Norton and Co., 1978), 682.

12. Levine, *A Future for Marxism*, 125, 130, 134–35.

13. G. A. Cohen, *If You're an Egalitarian, How Come You're So Rich?* (Harvard: Harvard University Press, 2001), 45–47.

14. See Brayton Polka, "Hegel and the Myth of the Fall," in *Rethinking Philosophy in Light of the Bible: From Kant to Schopenhauer* (Lanham, MD: Lexington Books, 2014), 21–52; H. S. Harris, "Would Hegel Be a 'Hegelian' Today?" *Cosmos and History: The Journal of Natural and Social Philosophy* 3/2–3 (2007): 5–15.

15. Nielsen, "Analytical Marxism: A Form of Critical Theory," 10.

16. Cohen, *If You're an Egalitarian*, 76.

17. Nielsen, "Reply to Richard Rorty," in *Reason and Emancipation*, 140

18. See G. A. Cohen, "The Workers and the Word: Why Marx Had the Right to Think He Was Right," in G. A. Cohen, *Lectures on the History of Moral and Political Philosophy*, Jonathan Wolff, ed. (Princeton: Princeton University Press, 2014b), 268–83. In this essay, Cohen attempts to refute the tu quoque argument that targets the Marxian idea of truth as relative to class origins by contending that Marxism itself is subject to the same genesis.

19. Leo Strauss, *Natural Right and History* (Chicago: University of Chicago Press, 1953), 23–24. See also pages 15, 31–32, and 38. See also Strauss, "Political Philosophy and History," in *What Is Political Philosophy? And Other Studies* (Chicago: University of Chicago Press, 1988), 57, 59–60, 69.

20. Kai Nielsen, "Reconsidering the Platonic Conception of Philosophy," *International Studies in Philosophy* 26/2 (1994): 52.

21. Nielsen, "Reply to Richard Rorty," in *Reason and Emancipation*, 140. Nielsen is probably referring to Strauss's grand thesis that philosophers throughout history have been forced to engage in secret writing in order to avoid persecution.

22. G. A. Cohen, "Hobbes," in *Lectures on the History of Moral and Political Philosophy*, 78, 80–83, 112. Cohen briefly discusses Strauss's 1936 study, *The Political Philosophy of Hobbes: Its Basis and Its Genesis*, Elsa M. Sinclair, trans. (Chicago: University of Chicago Press, 1996).

23. Karl Popper, *The Poverty of Historicism* (New York: Routledge, 2002). This book was originally published in 1957. 51. See also Isaiah Berlin, "Historical Inevitability," in Isaiah Berlin, *The Proper Study of Mankind: An Anthology of Essays* (New York: Farrar, Straus, and Giroux, 1998b), 119–90. This essay first appeared in 1954.

24. Strauss, "Political Philosophy and History," 67.

25. Ibid., 70.

26. Strauss, *Natural Right and History*, 27. See also pages 19 and 28.

27. Ibid., 21. See also "Political Philosophy and History," 72–73, 77.

28. Ibid., 29.

29. Ibid., 3.

30. Ibid., 29.

31. Paul Edward Gottfried, *Leo Strauss and the Conservative Movement in America: A Critical Appraisal* (Cambridge: Cambridge University Press, 2012), 45. Gottfried and I offer conservative critiques of Strauss's anti-historicism. See my *Leo Strauss and Anglo-American Democracy: A Conservative Critique* (DeKalb, IL: Northern Illinois University Press, 2013).

32. Georges Sorel, "Necessity and Fatalism in Marxism," in *From Georges Sorel: Essays in Socialism and Philosophy*, edited with a new introduction by John L. Stanley, translated by John and Charlotte Stanley (New Brunswick, NJ: Transaction Books, 1987), 111–29.

33. Theodor Adorno, *Construction of the Aesthetic*, translated and edited by Robert Hullot-Kentor (Minneapolis, MN: University of Minnesota Press, 1989), 48.

34. See Kai Nielsen, "If Historical Materialism Is True Does Morality Totter?" *Philosophy of the Social Sciences* 15 (1985): 389–407. See also Cohen, "The Workers and the Word."

35. Kai Nielsen, "Reply to Andrew Levine and David Schweikart on Marx and Marxism," in *Reason and Emancipation*, 204 (author's italics).

36. Cohen, *If You're an Egalitarian*, 112.

37. Ibid., 104.

38. Ibid., 104–5. See also pages 112–15.

39. See also Cohen's last book, *Why Not Socialism?* (Princeton: Princeton University Press, 2009). Nielsen passionately defended his deceased friend Cohen, at a conference devoted to his works, against the "absurdly false" accusation that he had abandoned Marxism and socialism

towards the end of his life. See Nielsen, "Rescuing Political Theory from Fact-Insensitivity," *Socialist Studies* 8/1 (Winter 2012b): 239 n1.

40. Nielsen is responding to MacIntyre's essay "Hume, Testimony to Miracles, the Order of Nature, and Jansenism," in *Faith, Scepticism, and Personal Identity: A Festschrift for Terence Penelhum*, J. J. MacIntosh and H. A. Meynell, eds. (Calgary: University of Calgary Press, 1994), 83–99.

41. Strauss, *Natural Right and History*, 17. See also "Political Philosophy and History," 61.

42. Ibid., 13. See also "Political Philosophy and History," 62, 64, 74, 76.

43. Kai Nielsen, "Rationality, Intelligibility, and Alasdair MacIntyre's Talk of God," in Kai Nielsen, *God, Scepticism, and Modernity* (Ottawa: University of Ottawa Press, 1989b), 78–93.

44. Karl Marx and Friedrich Engels, "Manifesto of the Communist Party," in *The Marx-Engels Reader*, 2nd edition, Robert C. Tucker, ed. (New York: W. W. Norton and Co., 1978), 489. See also Nielsen, "If Historical Materialism Is True, Does Morality Totter?"; and Cohen, "Freedom, Justice, and Capitalism," *New Left Review* 126 (March–April, 1981): 12.

45. Kai Nielsen, "The Crisis of Socialism and Analytical Marxism," in *Globalization and Justice* (Amherst, NY: Humanity Books, 2003a), 71–72.

46. Strauss, *Natural Right and History*, 19.

47. Ibid., 18, 24, 26, 32 . See also "Political Philosophy and History," 57, 59–60, 69.

48. Ibid., 15, 21. See also "Political Philosophy and History," 70–71.

49. Leo Strauss, *On Tyranny: Including the Strauss-Kojève Correspondence*, revised and expanded edition, Victor Gourevitch and Michael S. Roth, eds. (Chicago, IL: University of Chicago Press, 2000), 212.

50. Leo Strauss, *The City and Man* (Chicago: University of Chicago Press, 1964), 242. Strauss and Nielsen would, of course, disagree on what should properly count as *useful* prephilosophical belief. Unlike Nielsen, Strauss contends that religious myth is indispensable in the political realm, a position which I support as well. Nielsen and I have debated the desirability and necessity of myth in our unpublished exchange, "On Morality and Religious Belief: Grant Havers vs. Kai Nielsen." (2016), available at https://www.kainielsen.org/unpublishedworks.html.

51. Strauss employs this term in the context of explaining the basis of political philosophy. See his "What Is Political Philosophy?" in *What Is Political Philosophy?* 13.

52. Marx, "The Eighteenth Brumaire of Louis Bonaparte," in *The Marx-Engels Reader*, 595.

53. Friedrich Engels, "Engels to Bloch," in Karl Marx and Friedrich Engels, *On Religion* (Mineola, NY: Dover Publications, 2008b), 276–77. This correspondence is dated September 21–22, 1890.

54. Marx and Engels, "Manifesto of the Communist Party," 476.

55. Ibid., 488.

56. G. A. Cohen, "Rescuing Conservatism: A Defense of Existing Value," in G. A. Cohen, *Finding Oneself in the Other*, edited by Michael Otsuka (Princeton: Princeton University Press, 2013), 143 (author's italics).

57. Ibid., 147.

58. Ibid., 153.

59. Ibid., 173.

60. Cohen, *If You're an Egalitarian*, 2.

61. Ibid., 6. See also pages 120 and 128.

62. Engels, "Bruno Bauer and Early Christianity," in Marx and Engels, *On Religion*, 203.

63. G. W. F. Hegel, *Lectures on the History of Philosophy*, vol. 2: *Plato and the Platonists*, E. S. Haldane and Frances S. Simson, trans. (Lincoln, NE: University of Nebraska Press, 1995), 209.

64. G. W. F. Hegel, *The Philosophy of History*, translated by J. Sibree (Amherst, NY: Prometheus Books, 1991), 334 (author's italics).

65. Kai Nielsen, *Ethics Without God*, revised edition (Amherst, NY: Prometheus Books, 1990), 18. See also page 123.

66. Ibid., 125.

67. Levine, "Whatever Happened to Marxism?" 188.

68. Kai Nielsen, "Cultural Identity and Self-Definition," *Human Studies* 10/3–4 (1987): 383–90.
69. Nielsen, "Introduction," in *Globalization and Justice*, 33.
70. Kai Nielsen, "Liberal Nationalism, Liberal Democracies, and Secession," in *Pessimism of the Intellect, Optimism of the Will: The Political Philosophy of Kai Nielsen*, David Rondel and Alex Sager, eds. (Calgary: University of Calgary Press, 2012a), 310 (author's italics). See also Isaiah Berlin, "Herder and the Enlightenment," in Berlin, *The Proper Study of Mankind*, 359–435.
71. Ibid., 321.
72. Johann Gottfried Herder, "Another Philosophy of History for the Education of Mankind," in *Another Philosophy of History and Selected Political Writings*, translated with introduction and notes by Ioannis D. Evrigenis and Daniel Pellerin (Indianapolis, IN: Hackett, 2004), 36 (author's italics). Berlin, in "Herder and the Enlightenment," notes that Herder "never abandoned" his position on the universal nature of Christianity (372).
73. Kai Nielsen, "Politics and Theology: Do We Need a Political Theology?" in Kai Nielsen, *God and the Grounding of Morality* (Ottawa: University of Ottawa Press, 1991a), 185.
74. Kai Nielsen, "Rawls and the Socratic Ideal," *Analyse and Kritik* 13 (1991b): 82.
75. Kai Nielsen, "Christian Empiricism," in *God, Scepticism, and Modernity*, 176–88. See also Sonia Sikka, *Herder on Humanity and Cultural Difference* (Cambridge: Cambridge University Press, 2011), 220.

BIBLIOGRAPHY

Adorno, Theodor. 1989. *Construction of the Aesthetic*, Robert Hullot-Kentor, trans. and ed. Minneapolis, MN: University of Minnesota Press.
Berlin, Isaiah. 1998a. "Herder and the Enlightenment." In Isaiah Berlin, *The Proper Study of Mankind: An Anthology of Essays*. New York: Farrar, Straus, and Giroux: 359–435.
———. 1998b. "Historical Inevitability." In Isaiah Berlin, *The Proper Study of Mankind: An Anthology of Essays*. New York: Farrar, Straus, and Giroux:119–90.
Cohen, G. A. 1981. "Freedom, Justice, and Capitalism." *New Left Review* 126 (March–April): 3–16.
———. 2000. *Karl Marx's Theory of History: A Defence*. Princeton: Princeton University Press.
———. 2001. *If You're an Egalitarian, How Come You're so Rich?* Harvard: Harvard University Press.
———. 2009. *Why Not Socialism?* Princeton: Princeton University Press.
———. 2013. "Rescuing Conservatism: A Defense of Existing Value." In *Finding Oneself in the Other*, Michael Otsuka, ed. Princeton: Princeton University Press. 143–74.
———. 2014a. "Hobbes." In *Lectures on the History of Moral and Political Philosophy*, Jonathan Wolff, ed. Princeton: Princeton University Press. 65–102.
———. 2014b. "The Workers and the Word: Why Marx Had the Right to Think He Was Right." In *Lectures on the History of Moral and Political Philosophy*, Jonathan Wolff, ed. Princeton: Princeton University Press. 268–83.
Eagleton, Terry. 2011. *Why Marx Was Right*. New Haven: Yale University Press.
Elster, Jon. 1985. *Making Sense of Marx*. Cambridge: Cambridge University Press.
Engels, Friedrich. 1978. "Speech at the Graveside of Karl Marx." In *The Marx-Engels Reader*, 2nd ed., Robert C. Tucker, ed. New York: W. W. Norton and Co. 681–82.
———. 2008a. "Bruno Bauer and Early Christianity." In Karl Marx and Friedrich Engels, *On Religion*. Mineola, NY: Dover Publications. 194–204.
———. 2008b. "Engels to Bloch." In Karl Marx and Friedrich Engels, *On Religion*. Mineola, NY: Dover Publications. 273–77.
Gottfried, Paul Edward. 2012. *Leo Strauss and the Conservative Movement in America: A Critical Appraisal*. Cambridge: Cambridge University Press.
Harris, H. S. 2007. "Would Hegel Be a 'Hegelian' Today?" *Cosmos and History: The Journal of Natural and Social Philosophy* 3/2-3: 5–15.

Havers, Grant N. 2013. *Leo Strauss and Anglo-American Democracy: A Conservative Critique*. DeKalb, IL: Northern Illinois University Press.

Havers, Grant, and Kai Nielsen. 2016. "On Morality and Religious Belief: Grant Havers vs. Kai Nielsen." Available at https://www.kainielsen.org/unpublished-works.html.

Hegel, G. W. F. 1991. *The Philosophy of History*, J. Sibree, trans. Amherst, NY: Prometheus Books.

———. 1995. *Lectures on the History of Philosophy*, vol. 2: *Plato and the Platonists*, E. S. Haldane and Frances S. Simson, trans. Lincoln: University of Nebraska Press.

Herder, Johann Gottfried. 2004. "Another Philosophy of History for the Education of Mankind." In *Another Philosophy of History and Selected Political Writings*, Ioannis D. Evrigenis and Daniel Pellerin, trans. Indianapolis, IN: Hackett.

Lebowitz, Michael A. 1988. "Is 'Analytical Marxism' Marxism?" *Science and Society* 52/2 (Summer): 191–214.

Levine, Andrew. 2003. *A Future for Marxism? Althusser, the Analytical Turn, and the Revival of Socialist Theory*. London: Pluto Press.

———. 2007. "Whatever Happened to Marxism?" In *Reason and Emancipation: Essays on the Philosophy of Kai Nielsen*, Michel Seymour and Matthias Fritsch, ed. Amherst, NY: Humanity Books: 183–91.

MacIntyre, Alasdair. 1994. "Hume, Testimony to Miracles, the Order of Nature, and Jansenism." In *Faith, Scepticism, and Personal Identity: A Festschrift for Terence Penelhum*, J. J. MacIntosh and H. A. Meynell, eds. Calgary: University of Calgary Press: 83–99.

Marx, Karl. 1978. "Manifesto of the Communist Party." In *The Marx-Engels Reader*, Robert C. Tucker, ed. New York: W. W. Norton and Co.: 469–500.

Marx, Karl, and Friedrich Engels. 1978. "The Eighteenth Brumaire of Louis Bonaparte." In *The Marx-Engels Reader*, Robert C. Tucker, ed. New York: W. W. Norton and Co. 594–617.

Nielsen, Kai. 1985. "If Historical Materialism Is True Does Morality Totter?" *Philosophy of the Social Sciences* 15: 389–407.

———. 1987. "Cultural Identity and Self-Definition." *Human Studies* 10/3-4: 383–90.

———. 1989a. "Christian Empiricism." In *God, Scepticism, and Modernity*. Ottawa: University of Ottawa Press: 172–89.

———. 1989b. "Rationality, Intelligibility, and Alasdair MacIntyre's Talk of God." In *God, Scepticism, and Modernity*. Ottawa: University of Ottawa Press. 78–93.

———. 1990. *Ethics Without God*, revised edition. Amherst, NY: Prometheus Books.

———. 1991a. "Politics and Theology: Do We Need a Political Theology?" In *God and the Grounding of Morality*. Ottawa: University of Ottawa Press: 177–207.

———. 1991b. "Rawls and the Socratic Ideal." *Analyse und Kritik* 13 (1991): 67–93.

———. 1993a. "What Is Alive and What Is Dead in Marx and Marxism a la Elster." *Laval théologique et philosophique* 49/2 (June): 277–93.

———. 1993b. "Analytical Marxism: A Form of Critical Theory." *Erkenntnis* 39/1 (July): 1–21.

———. 1994. "Reconsidering the Platonic Conception of Philosophy." *International Studies in Philosophy* 26/2: 51–71.

———. 1996. *Naturalism Without Foundations*. Amherst, NY: Prometheus Books.

———. 2003a. "The Crisis of Socialism and Analytical Marxism." In *Globalization and Justice*. Amherst, NY: Humanity Books. 41–80.

———. 2003b. "Introduction." In *Globalization and Justice*. Amherst, NY: Humanity Books. 11–40.

———. 2007a. "Reply to Andrew Levine and David Schweikart on Marx and Marxism." In *Reason and Emancipation: Essays on the Philosophy of Kai Nielsen*, Michel Seymour and Matthias Fritsch, ed. Amherst, NY: Humanity Books: 201–13.

———. 2007b. "Reply to Richard Rorty." In *Reason and Emancipation: Essays on the Philosophy of Kai Nielsen*, Michel Seymour and Matthias Fritsch, ed. Amherst, NY: Humanity Books: 131–42.

———. 2012a. "Liberal Nationalism, Liberal Democracies, and Secession." In *Pessimism of the Intellect, Optimism of the Will: The Political Philosophy of Kai Nielsen*, David Rondel and Alex Sager, ed. Calgary: University of Calgary Press. 301–48.

———. 2012b. "Rescuing Political Theory from Fact-Insensitivity." *Socialist Studies* 8/1 (Winter): 216–45.

Norman, Richard. 1989. "What Is Living and What Is Dead in Marxism?" In *Analyzing Marxism: New Essays on Analytical Marxism*, Robert Ware and Kai Nielsen, eds. Calgary: University of Calgary Press. 59–80.

Polka, Brayton. 2014. "Hegel and the Myth of the Fall." In *Rethinking Philosophy in Light of the Bible: From Kant to Schopenhauer*. Lanham, MD: Lexington Books. 21–52.

Popper, Karl. 2002. *The Poverty of Historicism*. New York: Routledge.

Sikka, Sonia. 2011. *Herder on Humanity and Cultural Difference*. Cambridge: Cambridge University Press.

Sorel, Georges. 1987. "Necessity and Fatalism in Marxism." In *From Georges Sorel: Essays in Socialism and Philosophy*, John and Charlotte Stanley, trans. New Brunswick, NJ: Transaction Books. 111–29.

Strauss, Leo. 1953. *Natural Right and History*. Chicago: University of Chicago Press.

———. 1964. *The City and Man*. Chicago: University of Chicago Press.

———. 1988. "Political Philosophy and History." In *What Is Political Philosophy? And Other Studies*. Chicago: University of Chicago Press. 56–77.

———. 1996. *The Political Philosophy of Hobbes: Its Basis and Its Genesis*, Elsa M. Sinclair, trans. Chicago: University of Chicago Press.

———. 2000. *On Tyranny: Including the Strauss-Kojève Correspondence*, revised and expanded edition, Victor Gourevitch and Michael S. Roth, ed. Chicago: University of Chicago Press.

Index

Abrams, Elliot, 43
Addams, Jane, 124
Adler, Mortimer, 101, 104, 105, 108, 109; *Dialectic*, 105
Adorno, T. W., 126, 140, 141, 156
Afghanistan, x, 43, 44, 47, 48
Agrarians, 133; *I'll Take My Stand*, 133
Albertus, Magnus Lyceum, 112
Alinsky, Saul, 17
Althusius, Johannes, 21
Althusser, Louis, 151
alt-right, 9
American Enterprise Institute, 42
American Political Science Review, 26
Americans for Democratic Action, 36
Angus, Ian, 67; *The Undiscovered Country*, 67
Aquinas, Thomas, xii, 85, 86, 93, 101–103, 104, 105, 107–108, 109, 110–111, 112, 113, 114, 115
Aristotle, xii, 71, 72, 85, 87, 88, 93, 95, 101–102, 111, 112–113, 114, 115; *Metaphysics*, 112–113; *Physics*, 112, 114
Armour, Leslie and Elizabeth Trott, 67; *The Faces of Reason*, 67
Aron, Raymond, 142, 145; *The Opium of the Intellectuals*, 142
Ashley, Benedict, xii, xv, xvi, 101–115; background, 101, 102–110; Aquinas, xii, 101–103, 104, 105, 107–108, 109, 110–111, 112, 113, 114, 115; Aristotle, 101–102, 111, 112–113, 114, 115; Dominican, 106, 110, 112; *Live Fight Know Delight*, 108; Marxism, xii, 101–103, 104, 105, 106, 107, 108, 109, 110, 112; philosophy, 110–115; *Summa Contra Marxistes*, 101, 109; Trotskyites, xii, 101, 106; *The Way toward Wisdom* and *Theologies of the Body*, 110
Athanasius, St., 16

Babbitt, Irving, 133
Balkans, 45
Baltics, viii, 2
Beer, Jeremy, xiii, 121, 183
Beiner, Ronald, 74; "Hermeneutical Generosity and Social Criticism", 74
Bell, Daniel, x, 36, 37, 38, 129; *The End of Ideology*, 37
Benedict XVI Pope, xiv, 144–146
Berger, Peter, 9
Berlin, Isaiah, 155, 166
Berrigan, Daniel, 167
Berry, Wendall, 133
Blond, Philip, 71; *Red Tory*, 71
Bloom, Allan, 47, 104, 155; *The Closing of the American Mind*, 104
Bolton, John, 49
Bonhoeffer, Dietrich, 167
Boudin, Louis B., 21

Bourne, Randolph, 124
Bozell, L. Brent Jr., 18
Brooks, Cleanth, 17
Brooks, David, 47
Brownson, Orestes, 122
Bryn Mawr College, 122
Buck Hill Falls, Pennsylvania, 25
Buckley, William, 1, 9, 18, 37; *God and Man at Yale*, 18; *McCarthy and His Enemies*, 18
Burke, Edmund, 68
Burnham, James, viii, ix–xii, xv, 1–11, 18; background, 2–3; conservatism, 8–11; communism and Marxism, viii, xv, 1, 3, 7, 8, 9–10; Congress for Cultural Freedom, 2, 8; *Containment or Liberation*, 1, 10; *The Machiavellians*, 1, 6, 7, 11; *The Managerial Revolution*, 3, 4–6, 10; *Science and Style: A Reply to Comrade Trotsky*, 3; Socialist Worker Party, 2, 3, 4; Spanish Civil War, 8; *The Struggle for the World*, 1; *Suicide of the West*, 1, 7, 9; Trotskyite, 2; United States, 4–6, 9–10
Burns, James MacGregor, 18
Bush, George W., x, 35, 46–48, 49

Caddell, Patrick, 129, 130
Callinicos, Alex, 82
Cambridge University, 81
Camus, Albert, 142; *The Rebel*, 142
Canada, xi, 67–77; CBC Massey Lectures, 72, 78; Liberty Party, 69; Montreal, 123; New Democratic Party, 68, 75; Progressive Conservative Party, xi, 69
Carter, James, 43, 129–130
Central Intelligence Agency (CIA), ix, 2, 18
Chambers, Whitter, viii, xi, xii
Chicago, 2
Chicago Sun, 122
Chicago Sun-Times, 122
China, 46, 49, 84
Churchill, Winston, vii; "Consistency in Politics", vii
Clinton, William, 45
Cohen, G. A., xv, xvi, 151–168; analytical Marxism, xv, 151–154, 156–165, 168; historicism and relativism, xv, 152–153, 154–156, 158–161; *Karl Marx's Theory of History*, 151; *If You're an Egalitarian How Come You're So Rich?*, 163; nation-state and nationalism, 162, 165–168; religion, xv, 161–165; "Rescuing Conservatism", 162–163
Coleridge, Samuel Taylor, 69
Collingwood, R. G., 18
Columbia University, 123
Commentary, 9, 38, 46
communism. *See* Marxism
Comte, Auguste, 132, 140
Condorcet, Nicolas de Caritat marquis de, 132
Coolidge, Calvin, 38
Cooper, Danny, 48
Cooperative Commonwealth Federation, 68
Craipeau, Yvan, 4

Dahl, Robert, 24
Daily Iowan, 124
D'Arcy, Martin, 2
Dart, Ron, xi, 67, 183; "Charles Taylor and the Hegelian Eden Tree", 73
Dartmouth University, 16
Deely, John, 104
Dewey, John, 104, 154
Diefenbaker, John, 68, 69; *Lament for a Nation: The Defeat of Canadian Nationalism*, 68, 69
Diggins, John, viii, 10, 11; *Up from Communism*, viii, 10
Douglas, Tommy, 68, 69
Doull, James, 67, 68
Draper, Theodore, 41
Drolet, Jean-François, 48, 49
Drury, Shadia, 71

East, John P., 16
Eaton, 93
Eliot, T. S., 133
Ellul, Jacques, 122
Elster, Jon, 152; *Making Sense of Marx*, 152
Encounter, 2
Engels, Friedrich, 153, 159, 161, 163, 165

Enlightenment, xii, xiv, 83, 84, 140, 144, 152, 163, 165

Faul, Denis, 91–95
Federal Bureau of Investigation (FBI), 106
Feith, Douglas, 48
Feuerbach, Ludwig, 139; *The Essence of Christianity*, 139
First Things, 45
Fischer, Louis, 2
Fontenelle, Bernard Le Bovier de, 132
Foreign Policy Initiative, 49
Francis, Samuel T., 3, 9, 11
Franco, Francisco, 8, 109
Frankfurt School, xiii–xiv, 122, 124, 126, 131, 140, 141–143, 145, 146
French Revolution, 84
Freud, Sigmund, and Freudianism, xiii, 104, 126, 130
Fukuyama, Francis, xiii, 45, 47
Furet, François, 142; *The Passing of an Illusion: The Idea of Communism in the Twentieth Century*, 142

Gadamer, Hans-Georg, 73, 75
Geach, Peter, 88
Genovese, Eugene, 123
George, Henry, 122
Germany, 87; Nazi, viii, 4–5, 6, 81; Nazi-Soviet Pact, 2, 3
Gide, Andre, 2
Gidler, George, 44
Gilson, Etienne, 103, 110
Glazer, Nathan, x, 36, 39; *Beyond the Melting Pot*, 39
Global Governance Watch, 49
Goldwater, Barry, 37, 70
Godwin, William, 132
González, Pedro Blas, xiv, 139, 183
Gottfried, Paul, viii, xiii, 1, 184
Gramsci, Antonio, 140, 141
Grant, George, xi, xv, 67–74, 76–77; background, 67, 68; conservatism, xi, 67, 68–73; *English Speaking Justice*, 72; "An Ethic of Community", 68; Marxism, 69; New Left, 70; *Philosophy in Mass Age*, 68; *Technology and Empire*, 73; *Technology and Justice*, 73; *Time as History*, 72

Gray, John, 73; *Enlightenment's Wake*, 73
Great Britain, 81–82, 84, 87, 91, 93; British Empire, 5, 93; Communist Party, 81; Scotland, 166; Socialist Worker Party, 82, 83, 90; University and College Union, 90
Greece: Athens, 25; democracy, 163–164
Green, T. H., 93
Grossman, Vasily, 91, 92, 93, 94–95

Habermas, Jürgen, xiv, xvi, 140–146; *Communication and the Evolution of Society*, 144; *The Dialectics of Secularization*, 145; Frankfurt School, xiv, 140, 141–143, 145, 146; Enlightenment, xiv, 140, 144; Marxism, xiv, 140–141, 144–145; philosophy, 143–146; Pope Benedict XVI, xiv, 144–146; religion, xiv
Haiti, 45
Halper, Stefan and Jonathan Clarke, 48
Hart, Jeffrey, 16
Harvard University, 123
Havers, Grant, xv, 151, 183
Hayek, Friedrich von, 37
Hegel, Frederick, xi, 67–68, 69, 72, 73–74, 76, 85, 107, 152, 153, 155, 159, 162, 163–164, 166, 168
Heidegger, Martin, 72, 87
Herder, Johann Gottfried, 166, 167; "Another Philosophy of History for the Education of Mankind", 166
Hicks, Stephen R. C., 142
Hiss, Alger, 106
Hobart College, 19
Hobbes, Thomas, 21, 68, 155
Hofstadter, Richard, 123
Hook, Sidney, 2, 134
Hooker, Richard, 69
Hoover, Hebert, 38
Hoover, Institute, 42
Horkheimer, Max, 126, 141; *The Authoritarian Personality*, 126
Horowitz, Gad, 70
Howe, Irving, 36
Hume, David, 68, 132
Humphrey, Hubert, 10, 36
Hussein, Saddam, 46
Hutchins, Robert Maynard, 104, 105, 106

Hyneman, Charles S., 19

Illich, Ivan, 133
Institute for Educational Affairs, 42
Iran, 43–46, 48, 49
Iraq, x, 35, 46–48
Islam, 46
Israel, x, 8, 35, 42, 43; Arab-Israeli War, 43
Italy, 93; Rome, 111

Jackson, Henry "Scoop", 10, 41
Jackson, Jesse, 129
Jaffa, Harry, 10, 15
James, C. L. R., 91, 92, 94–95
Jaspers, Karl, 140; *Philosophy of Existence*, 140
Jesus, 162
Johnson, Lyndon B., 10, 16, 35, 38
Johnson, Samuel, 69

Kagan, Robert, 45
Kaltwasser, Cristóbal, 17
Kane, William Humbert, 111, 112
Kansas, 101
Kant, Immanuel, xii, 82, 84, 87
Kelly, Daniel, 8
Kendall, Katherine, 23
Kendall, Willmoore, viii, ix–xi, xv, 15–29; "American Decision and the 'Prayer Decisions'", 24, 27; background, 18–19; "The Case of the People vs. John Stuart Mill", 26–27; communism, ix, 15; conservatism, 15–17; *John Locke and the Doctrine of Majority Rule*, 21–24, 28; "The Majority Principle of the Scientific Elite", 20–21; "On the Preservation of Democracy for America", 20, 21; "The Open Society and Its Fallacies", 24; Rousseau, Jean-Jacques, ix, xv, 15, 17, 20, 21, 28; Trotskyites, ix, 19; "The Two Majorities", 24–25; United States, 15, 20, 21, 22, 24–25, 27–29
Kennan, George, 123
Kennedy, John, 38, 69
Kerwin, Jerome, 109
Khalilzad, Zalmay, 47
Kierkegaard, Søren, 156

Kirk, Russell, 25, 37
Kirkpatrick, Jeane, 38, 42, 43, 45
Kissinger, Henry, 42–43
Knight, Kelvin, xii, 82, 184; with Paul Blackledge *Virtue and Politics*, 71
Koestler, Arthur, 2, 145
Kristol, Irving, x, xiii, xvi, 36, 38, 41, 44, 45, 122; "Confessions of a True Self-Confessed Neoconservative", 38
Kristol, William, 45

Lasch, Christopher, xiii, xv, xvi, 121–135; Agrarians, 133; *The American Liberals and the Russian Revolution*, 124; *The Agony of the American Left*, 125; background, 122–124; *The Culture of Narcissism*, 126, 127–130; Frankfurt School, xiii, 122, 124, 126, 131; Freudianism, xiii, 126, 130; *Haven in a Heartless World*, 126–127; Marxism, xiii, 123, 124, 125, 127, 131, 134; *The Minimal Self*, 126, 130–131; New Left, xiii, 122; *The New Radicalism in America 1889–1963*, 124–125; *The Revolt of the Elites and the Betrayal of Democracy*, 121, 124; *The True and Only Heaven*, 121, 125, 131–133, 134; *The World of Nations*, 125
Lasch, Elisabeth, 121
Lasch, Nell Commager, 123
Lasch, Robert, 122, 123
Lasch, Zora, 122, 123
Lawrence, D. H., 92
Layton, Jack, 68
Lears, T. J. Jackson, 122
Lenin, Vladimir, 161
Leuchtenburg, William, 123
Levine, Andrew, 151, 165
Lind, Michael, 47
Lindberg, Tod, 38
Lippman, Walter, 18, 123
Lipset, Seymour Martin, 36
Locke, John, 21–23, 68; *The Second Treatise*, 22, 23
London Metropolitan University, 81
London School of Economics, 81
Louisiana State University, 19
Loury, Glenn, 39
Luhan, Mable Dodge, 124

Macgregor, David, 67
Machiavelli, Niccoló, viii, 6
MacIntyre, Alasdair, xii, xv, xvi, 71–72, 81–95, 158; Aquinas, xii, 85, 86, 93; Aristotle, xii, 85, 87, 88, 93, 95; *After Virtue*, 83–86, 87, 91, 93, 94; background, 81–82; capitalism, xii, 82–84, 93; Centre for Contemporary Aristotelian Studies in Ethics and Politics, 90–91; communism and Marxism, xii, 81, 82–85, 87, 88, 92, 94–95; *Dependent Rational Animals*, 86; *Edith Stein*, 86; Enlightenment, xii, 83, 84; *Ethics in the Conflicts of Modernity*, 91, 94; *God Philosophy Universities*, 86; International Society for MacIntyrean Enquiry, 90; *Intractable Disputes about the Natural Law*, 86; shared practice, 84–89; *Three Rival Versions of Moral Enquiry*, 85, 86; *Whose Justice? Which Rationality?*, 85, 86
Macpherson, C. B., 68
Madison, James, 15, 27
Mandeville, Bernard, 132
Marcuse, Hebert, 124, 126; *Eros and Civilization*, 124
Maritain, Jacques, 86
Marshall, John, 27
Marx, Karl: analytical, xv, 151–154, 156–165, 168; Ashley Benedict, xii, 101–103, 104, 105, 106, 107, 108, 109, 110, 112; Burnham, James, viii, xv, 1, 3, 7, 8, 9–10; Cohen, G. A., xv, 151–154, 156–165, 168; *Communist Manifesto*, 139, 161, 165; Grant, George, 69; Habermas, Jürgen, xiv, 140–141, 144–145; Kendall, Willmore, ix, 15; Lasch, Christopher, xiii, 123, 124, 125, 127, 131, 134; MacIntyre, Alasdair, xii, 81, 82–85, 87, 88, 92, 94–95; Marxism and communism, viii, x, xv, 15, 36, 40–43, 69, 139–143, 165; Neoconservatives, x, xv, 36, 40–43; Nielsen, Kai, xv, 151–154, 156–165, 168
Massachusetts, 27, 82; North Brookfield, 27
McCarthy, Daniel, 16

McCarthy, Joseph, 8, 17, 24, 106
McGovern, George, 17, 41
McKeon, Richard, 105
McMaster University, 71
Mexico City, 2
Meyer, Frank, 3, 9, 18
Meynell, Robert, 67; *Canadian Idealism and the Philosophy of Freedom*, 67
Michels, Robert, 6–7
Midwest Journal of Politics, 24
Mill, John Stuart, 26–27, 87; *On Liberty*, 26
Milosz, Czesław, 142, 145; *The Captive Mind*, 142
Mises, Ludwig von, 128
Morrissey, Christopher S., xii, 101, 184
Mosca, Gaetano, 6, 7
Moyers, Bill, 129
Moynihan, Daniel Patrick, 36, 38, 39, 40; *Beyond the Melting Pot*, 39; *The Negro Family: A Case for National Action*, 39
Mudde, Cas, 17
Muggeridge, Malcolm, 145
Mumford, Lewis, 122
Muravchik, Joshua, 38
Murray, Charles, 39

Nash, George H., 17
The Nation, 131
The National Interest, 44, 45
National Review, viii, ix, 1, 2, 3, 18, 23
Naudé, Beyers, 167
Nebraska, 122, 123
Neoconservative, x, xvi, 35–49; anti-Semitism and Jewish, x, xv, 36, 42; communism, x, xv, 36, 40–43; economic policy, 44, 45, 46; foreign policy, x, 40–44, 45–49; Great Society, 35, 37, 38, 40; ideology, 35; New American Century, 45; Neal Deal, x, xvi, 36, 37, 49; New Left, x, 35, 36, 37–38, 39, 40–41, 42, 45, 49; Trotskyites, x, 36; social policy, 38–40, 45, 49; Vietnam War, 37, 38, 40–42
The New Criterion, 45
The New Oxford Review, 133
The New Scholasticism, 112
New York: Geneva, 19; New York City, viii, 2, 3, 127; Pittsford, 121

The New York Review of Books, 131
New York University, 2
Nicaragua, 44
Niebuhr, Reinhold, 36, 40, 122
Nielsen, Kai, xv, xvi, 151–168; analytical Marxism, 151–154, 156–165, 168; historicism and relativism, xv, 152–153, 154–156, 158–161; *Naturalism Without Foundations*, 152; religion, xv, 161–165, 166–167; nation-state and nationalism, 162, 165–168
Nietzsche, Friedrich, 72, 85, 87, 94–95
Nixon, Richard, 16
Nogar, Raymond Jude, 112
Northern Ireland, 91, 95; Irish Republican Army, 95
North Korea, 46, 48
Northwestern University, 18, 123

Obama, Barrack, 49
O'Connor, Sandra Day, 91–92, 94–95
Ogren, Quentin "Bud", 105, 108, 109
Oklahoma, ix, 18
Oliver, Michael, 68; *Social Purpose in Canada*, 68, 69
Orwell, George, 6; *Nineteenth Eighty-Four*, 6
Owen, Christopher H., ix, 15, 184
Oxford University, ix, 2, 18, 68, 81, 93, 122, 162

Paine, Thomas, 68
Pareto, Vilfredo, 6, 7
Partisan Review, 8, 23, 122
Pearle, Richard, 43, 47
Pearson, Lester, 68, 69
Plato, 21, 71, 72, 73, 74, 155
Plotinus, 114
Podhoretz, Norman, 38, 41
Poland, viii, 2
Polanyi, Michael, 142
Policy Review, 38
Popper, Karl, 26, 155
Princeton University, 2
The Public Interest, 38–39, 42, 44
Pufendorf, Samuel von, 21

Ramparts, 8
Rawls, John, 72, 87, 160, 163, 164, 167

Reagan, Ronald, 35, 38, 43, 44, 48, 131; Strategic Defense Initiative, 44
Resnick, Philip, 77
Revel, Jean-Francois Revel, 141, 142; *The Totalitarian Temptation*, 141
Rice, Condoleezza, 48
Rieff, Philip, 122
Rizzi, Bruno, 4; *La Bureaucratisation du Monde*, 4
Rockefeller, Nelson, 1
Roosevelt, Eleandor, 36
Roosevelt, Franklin, 36, 38
Roosevelt, Theodore, 38
Rothbard, Murray, 8, 9, 15, 25
Rwanda, 45

Salt Lake City, 107
Schachtman, Max, 2
Schlesinger, Arthur, Jr., x, 36, 40
Selznick, Philip, 36
Shields, Leo, 105
Sibley, Mulford Q., 18
Sibley, Robert, 67; *Northern Spirits: John Watson George Grant and Charles Taylor*, 67
Silone, Ignazio, 2
Smith, Adam, 68, 132
Smith, J. Allen, 21
Soapbox, 106
Socrates, 25
Solzhenitsyn, Aleksandr, 142, 145; *Warning to the West*, 142
Somalia, 45, 46
Sorel, Georges, 6, 7, 11
South Africa, 167
South Bend Indiana, 109
Southern Review, 20, 21, 24
Soviet Union and Russia, viii, x, xiii, 1–2, 3, 6, 9–10, 36, 42–43, 44, 46, 84, 91, 93, 94, 134, 161; Chechnya, 166; Intermediate-Range Nuclear Force Treaty, 44; Soviet invasion of Afghanistan, 43; Strategic Arms Limitation Talk Treaties, 42–43, 47
Spain, ix, 8; Civil War, 8, 18–19; Madrid, 18
Spencer, Hebert, 132
Spinoza, Baruch, 21, 104

Stalin, Josef, and Stalinism, viii, 2, 83–84, 91, 92, 93, 94
Steele, Henry Commager, 123
Steffens, Lincoln, 124
St. John's College, 104
St. Louis Post-Dispatch, 122, 124
Stoics, 114
Strauss, Leo, xv, 15, 24, 29, 37, 47, 153, 154–156, 158, 159–160; *Natural Right and History*, 156
Swift, Jonathan, 69

Taylor, Charles, xi, 67–68, 72, 73–77, 83; "Agony of Economic Man", 68; background, 67, 68, 73; *A Catholic Modernity*, 76; *Hegel*, 74; *Hegel and Modern Society*, 74; *The Pattern of Politics*, 68; political thought, 73–77; *A Secular Age*, 76; *Sources of Self*, 75; *Varieties of Religion Today*, 76
Teamsters, 106
Thernstorm, Abigail, 39
Thernstorm, Stephen, 39
Thompson, E. P., 83
Tolkien, J. R. R., 2
Trilling, Lionel, 123
Trinidad, 91
Trotsky, Leon, and Trotskyism, viii–x, xii, 2, 4, 19, 36, 94, 101, 106
Trepanier, Lee, x, 35, 183
Trudeau, Pierre, 68
Truman, Harry, 36
Trump, Donald, ix–x, 49

United Nations, 42, 47
United States, x–xi, 1, 4–6, 81, 91–92; 9/11 and terrorist attacks, 46–48; Coalition for the Democratic Majority, 41, 43; Democratic Party, x, xvi, 1, 19, 35, 40–43; Cold War, viii, xi, xv, xvi, 36–37, 81, 123, 125, 134; Great Depression, viii–ix, xii, 15, 109; Great Society, 35, 37, 38, 40; Korean War, 18, 24; Neal Deal, x, xvi, 4, 36, 37, 49; Socialist Worker Party, 2, 3, 4, 107, 108, 109; Republican Party, x, xvi, 1, 35, 36, 43, 123; Vietnam War, xi, 37–38, 40–42, 70, 123
University of Chicago, 47, 101, 103–104, 105, 108, 109
University of Essex, 81, 82
University of Illinois, 19
University of Iowa, 123
University of Notre Dame, 109
University of Oklahoma, 18
University of Richmond, 19
University of Rochester, 123
University of Wisconsin, 123
Updike, John, 123
Utilitarianism, xii, 82, 83

Vaïsse, Justin, 48, 49
Voegelin, Eric, 24, 28, 29, 37

Wallace, George, 17, 27
Walsh, J. Raymond, 19
Wanniski, Jude, 44
The Weekly Standard, 46
Whitehead, A. N., 3
Wilde, Oscar, 92
Williams, William Appleman, 123
Wilson, James Q., 39–40
Wise, S. W., 71; *God's Peculiar Peoples*, 71; with Robert Craig Brown *Canada Views the United States*, 71
Wittgenstein, Ludwig, 87, 93
Wohlstetter, Albert, 47
Wolfowitz, Paul, 47, 48
World War I, 5, 87, 161
World War II, 1, 2, 15, 16, 19, 24, 93

Yale University, 18, 24

About the Editors and Contributors

Lee Trepanier is a professor of political science at Saginaw Valley State University and editor of Lexington Books series Politics, Literature, and Film and the academic website, *VoegelinView*. He is author and editor of over twenty books, with the latest being *The Socratic Method Today* (2018), *Tradition v. Rationalism: Voegelin, Oakeshott, Hayek, and Others* (Lexington Books, 2018), and *Why the Humanities Matter Today: In Defense of Liberal Education* (Lexington Books, 2017).

Grant Havers is professor of philosophy and political studies at Trinity Western University. He is author of *Lincoln and the Politics of Christian Love* (2009) and *Leo Strauss and Anglo-American Democracy: A Conservative Critique* (2013).

* * *

Jeremy Beer is the principal partner of American Philanthropic. He is author and editor of numerous books, the latest being *Oscar Charleston: The Life and Legend of Baseball's Greatest Forgotten Player* (2019) and *The Philanthropic Revolution: An Alternative History of American Charity* (2015).

Ron Dart is an associate professor of political science at the University of the Fraser Valley in British Columbia. He has published more than thirty-five books, the most recent being *The North American High Tory Tradition* (2016).

Pedro Blas González is a professor of philosophy at Barry University. He is author of numerous books, the latest being *Unamuno: A Lyrical Essay* (2007) and *Ortega's "The Revolt of the Masses" and the Triumph of the New Man* (2007)

Paul Edward Gottfried is the Horace Raffensperger Professor of Humanities at Elizabethtown College. He is author of numerous books, the latest being *Fascism: The Career of a Concept* (2015) and *Revisions and Dissents* (2017).

Kelvin Knight is a reader in ethics and politics, director of the Centre for Contemporary Aristotelian Studies in Ethics & Politics, and course leader of the MA in Human Rights & International Conflict at London Metropolitan University. He is editor of *The MacIntyre Reader* (1998) and author of *Aristotelian Philosophy: Ethics and Politics from Aristotle to MacIntyre* (2007).

Christopher S. Morrissey is a faculty member in the Department of Philosophy at the Seminary of Christ the King, Westminster Abbey, and a sessional instructor of philosophy at Trinity Western University. He is author of *The Way of Logic* (2018) and translator of *Hesiod: Theogony/Works and Days* (2012).

Christopher H. Owen is a professor of history at Northeastern State University. He is author of *The Sacred Flame of Love: Methodism and Society in Nineteenth-Century Georgia* (1998).

Printed by Amazon Italia Logistica S.r.l.
Torrazza Piemonte (TO), Italy